HAL DAVID:
HIS MAGIC MOMENTS

THERE IS ALWAYS SOMETHING THERE TO REMIND ME

BY

EUNICE DAVID

DORRANCE
PUBLISHING CO
EST. 1920
PITTSBURGH. PENNSYLVANIA 15238

Dorrance Publishing Co
585 Alpha Drive
Suite 103
Pittsburgh, PA 15238
Visit our website at *www.dorrancebookstore.com*

ISBN: 978-1-4809-3100-8
eISBN: 978-1-4809-3123-7

ENDORSEMENTS

"What the World Needs Now is Love Sweet Love"
I was privileged to be the first recording artist to record
these iconic lyrics written by Hal David. Eunice David
has delivered a unique and mesmerizing memoir of her life with Hal.
He is considered one of the greatest songwriters in musical history.
This book is a must read. I couldn't put it down.
Jackie DeShannon

**

A loving, strong, and tenderly told tale.
Elvis Costello

**

I am flattered to have been asked to write a few words
on what the relationship of Hal and Eunice David represented to me.
I witnessed a married couple that completely Adored, and Truly Loved one
another...The happiness I saw in their eyes, the smiles they shared,
the hand holding, the total dedication displayed for All to see.
Without a doubt I'd say they were the complete model
of a Happily Married couple and the Best of Friends.
Yep, Eunice and Hal were the "Love Story"
we all should be so lucky to mirror!!!
Dionne Warwick

Eunice and Hal, circa 2007. Photograph by Trevor Augustus Brown

I dedicate this book to my family, who, although they don't live near me in terms of miles, always let me know that they are near to me in their hearts.

This book is also dedicated to my many friends who have helped ease the sorrow of Hal's passing, and to someone very special who has helped create a whole new chapter in my life.

Very shortly after my husband Hal David died on the morning of September 1, 2012, I received a request from his estate to turn over all of his awards: his Academy Award, Grammy awards, memorabilia, photographs, and all of his music-related artifacts. It stripped the walls and table tops of the office that Hal and I shared in our home in Los Angeles. Living with those mementos had become the fabric of my life for the twenty-five years that Hal and I were married.

On Hal's passing, I received hundreds of condolence cards and letters from his peers, business associates, and a myriad of friends who lived all over the world; everyone wishing me well and telling me of their great love and respect for my husband. But one card I received struck a special chord with me, especially since it arrived on the very day the movers were packing up everything to be taken away to their new home. The card read: *What the heart has once owned and had, it shall never lose.* Those words became my mantra during the dark days when I was first struggling to learn how to live alone, and they inspired the title of this book - the title of one of Hal's songs. "There's Always Something There to Remind Me" was recorded by Lou Johnson, and it reached No. 49 on the *Billboard Hot 100* in the summer of 1964. Sandie Shaw's version in the UK spent three weeks in the No. 1 spot. R. B. Greaves' recording in 1970 topped Johnson's at 27, and an Ahmet Ertegun production of Greeve's recording reached No. 3 on the *Easy Listening* chart. It was also a reminder that although Hal's sons were stripping me of physical things that might remind me of their father, they couldn't erase my treasured memories: those were mine to keep.

This memoir sets down stories about Hal's songs, his career, his family and his life, along with some highlights of our travels and what was happening in the world during the time that Hal and I were together. The events are described as I remember them, prompted by the detailed journals I kept and supplemented by Hal's own recollections, and what was told to me by many of his collaborators and friends.

Hal never had a publicist. He never retained a PR person, and he remained in the background throughout his storied career with Burt Bacharach, but I hope that some of what is recounted here will help underscore just how important Hal's contribution as a lyricist was to the great success of all the songs that bore his name.

He said he liked my backhand. I asked him what he did.

That was my introduction to Hal David on October 28, 1987, a day that changed my life forever. A friend of mine, Babe Eagle, invited me to play mixed doubles tennis at Mountaingate Country Club, a lovely tennis and golf facility high above the 405 freeway in Los Angeles, California. I was not interested in playing tennis that day, much less in meeting anyone new. For the previous seven years I'd been seeing a wonderful man by the name of King Hirsch, who had passed away only one month before that phone call from Babe. I was still burying my head under a pillow and hardly leaving my apartment. But Babe was insistent, and I finally agreed to join her and her husband Herbert and their tennis-playing friend for the game. However, in typical Southern California style, I hedged, telling them, "Okay, I'll meet you, but I'll drive my own car," while thinking that if I didn't like the situation I would be able to make a quick getaway.

It's amazing that my relationship with Hal got beyond that tennis match. My first gaffe was in thinking that his last name was Davis. When that was straightened out, I asked him what he did for a living. As if that weren't bad enough, when he told me that he wrote songs, I asked if I might possibly know the names of any of the songs that he had written. With a perfectly straight face, he replied that there was a book that contained his lyrics, and he'd see that I got a copy of it.

All I knew about my tennis partner before that fateful afternoon was that Babe and her husband used to play tennis with him and his recently deceased wife on the rare occasions when they were in Los Angeles together. I later learned that Hal's home was in New York, but that he and his wife Anne came to the west coast periodically and, rather than staying at the Beverly Wilshire Hotel, where Hal was usually put up while working on a movie, they bought a condominium in the gated community of Mountaingate so they would have a home-like setting where they could visit with their two grown sons, both of whom were living in Los Angeles during those years.

For the whole time we played tennis and all during the dinner we went to afterwards, I had no idea who Hal David really was, but I enjoyed the easy camaraderie we had. It seemed as though I had known him forever. We got so caught up in our own conversation that we almost forgot that the couple who had introduced us was still with us. At the end of the evening, Hal asked for my phone number and said he'd like to call me.

With that, we went our separate ways, and I wondered if he really would call. He seemed like the sort of man who would follow through, but I'd heard that line before. Still, I drove home with a smile on my face, hoping that he would.

I'd recently sold a big house in Bel Air, which I'd been awarded in my divorce settlement from Bif Forester, and, after rattling around in it by myself for five years, I decided that I wanted to be more in the heart of things. I found a beautiful compact condominium on South Spalding Drive in Beverly Hills, but the building had no front desk or concierge to accept packages. So I was pleasantly surprised when my doorbell rang the next morning, and a messenger handed me the book of lyrics that Hal had promised: *What the World Needs Now and Other Love Lyrics*. Finally, I realized just whom it was I'd played tennis with. The last paragraph in his book read: *"Reliving my career, I realize how lucky I am. To do well at something you would do for nothing is every man's dream. It came true for me. I'm glad I'm a songwriter."* Having read that, I knew I'd met a happy man.

I called my youngest son, Donald Forester, to tell him about the previous night's date with a very nice man who had a very strange profession: he was the songwriter who had written "Raindrops Keep Fallin' on my Head." Donald said, "Oh, Mom, don't tell me you're dating Burt Bacharach!" Frankly, I, too, thought Burt Bacharach had written that - and so many other wonderful songs, songs that were among my all-time favorites. At the time I was not aware of how important the lyric writer is to the success of a song. That, I soon learned, was a sore point with many lyricists.

True to his word, Hal did call after sending the book, and we made arrangements to play tennis the following week. But the day we were to play dawned dark and dreary, and by afternoon, it was raining. I figured that was the end of that. Happily, though, Hal suggested that we have dinner at Ruth's Chris Steak House in Beverly Hills, which soon became one of our favorite restaurants.

As newly dating couples do, we shared a lot about our past lives. We found we had much more in common than just the recent loss of loved ones. Hal told me that he was used to living in hotels and eating out, and that he liked it that way. Since cooking was definitely not my forte I added this nugget of information to the things I was learning about Hal that were already making me feel that he could be the guy for me: his gentle manner, his interest in art, music and history, and his obvious love of life. We began a whirlwind courtship, during which we ate in as many different restaurants in town as we could, since that was what Hal liked to do and throughout the fun-filled, exciting twenty-six years we spent together, we continued to have a grand time enjoying hotels all over the world and dining in some pretty amazing restaurants.

It was clear early on that Hal was destined to become a professional wordsmith. When he wasn't playing basketball or running on the track team for Thomas Jefferson High School in Brooklyn, New York, where he grew up, he was writing poems, short stories and articles for the school paper, of which he was the editor.

Hal David (center, holding paper), with his Jefferson literary magazine staff, 1939.

When he and his two brothers were young, they learned to play the violin, though, according to Hal, not very well. They owned just the one instrument, and they each took lessons on it in turn. It was their mother, Lena, who felt they should have some musical training and be exposed to the arts. Hal had a small band which played for neighborhood bar mitzvahs, birthday parties and weddings, and in the summers they performed at a little hotel called The Brills Inn in the town of Ellenville in the famed Catskill Mountains. Fortunately for the band and for their listeners, Hal was the leader of the band, leaving his violin at home. The Brills Inn wasn't one of the better-known hotels, but it was definitely on the Borscht Circuit, that well-known enclave where musicians and comedians performed in the twenties, thirties, and even on into the seventies, and where many famous acts were honed.

Hal's brother, Mack David, who was nine years his senior, was a songwriter of considerable note. He encouraged Hal to take advantage of his writing ability by working at an advertising agency, but he did not support Hal's ambition to be a songwriter. Hal later suspected that this was because Mack wanted to be the only songwriter in the family. But some things were just meant to be, and in spite of Mack's discouragement, Hal went on to great success in his chosen field, eventually far surpassing brother Mack's achievements.

Hal attended the School of Journalism at New York University for a couple of years, and then got a summer internship at the *New York Post* as a lowly copy boy. When he applied for the job, he was told that one of the requirements was that he had to know how to type. At that time, Hal had hardly even seen a typewriter, much less used one. But his sister-in-law's family owned a car agency, and he figured they'd have a typewriter in their office. He went there and practiced all night so he would be ready to get to work the next day, though he was unsure of his newly acquired typewriting skills.

At the *Post,* Hal was assigned to work for a man by the name of Lou Meyer, whose uncle, as it happened, was George Meyer, a great songwriter who wrote, among other songs, "For Me and My Gal." At the end of Hal's internship, Lou Meyer asked him if he wanted to stay at the paper and become a newspaperman. Hal, remembering his brother's advice, accepted the position, in spite of his own inclination to pursue songwriting, at that point still thinking that perhaps his older brother knew what was best for him.

In 1942, during World War II and while still working at the newspaper, Hal was drafted into the army and sent for basic training to Ft. Ord, all the way across the country to San Jose, California. For a young man who grew up in Brooklyn and had been no further away from that borough of New York than Manhattan and the Catskills, San Jose seemed like the end of the world.

Hal was often asked where he got the inspiration for his songs. Obviously there were many people and experiences that influenced him over the years, but there is no doubt in my mind that later on when he wrote the lyrics to "Do You Know the Way to San Jose?" his stint in the army at Ft. Ord played a part in his choosing the setting of that song. After it became a huge hit, Hal eventually received the key to the city of San Jose.

Dionne Warwick recorded "San Jose" in 1968, even though she had publically said she really didn't like the song too much. But it helped to make her famous, and thanks to Burt's melody and Hal's lyrics, she won her first Grammy for Best Female Contemporary Pop Vocal Performance. So that first army posting wound up affecting quite a few lives.

When Hal and his fellow recruits finished their basic training in California, they were shipped out to Oahu, Hawaii, where, upon their arrival, they found to their dismay that Harry Bridges, an avowed Communist and then the head of the Longshoreman's Union, had called a strike, even though it was wartime. So the newly arrived young soldiers had to unload their own ship.

At the end of that first day of backbreaking physical labor (not the sort of work the young man from Brooklyn was used to), Hal headed to camp to try to find his bunk and to take a shower. Lost and turned around as usual (Hal's sense of direction was a running joke among family and friends), he came across the orderly's tent, and as he was about to step inside to ask directions, he spotted a notice which said that writers, dancers, singers and comedians were wanted for shows that the army was putting on. That really grabbed Hal's attention, and he immediately went inside to tell the fellow in charge all about his qualifications as a songwriter, greatly aggrandizing them since writing songs was still more of a dream than a reality for him. The sergeant, whose name Hal was never able to remember but to whom he was always grateful, wrote out special orders for him and told him that at the next morning's roll call he would be given instructions to go to Honolulu, where auditions were being held.

When Hal arrived at the University of Hawaii for the audition, he was dismayed to see a line that stretched all the way around the block. But he hung in, and when he finally reached the table where soldiers were gathering information about the applicants, he put on a show of his own, describing his various as yet totally untested talents as a songwriter in an enthusiastic way that made them take notice of him. He later sheepishly admitted that he had again greatly embellished his credentials. He was told to wait until the end of the day, when the Major of the outfit would interview him.

That officer turned out to be the talented British-born Shakespearean actor Maurice Evans, who had become an American citizen and thus had been drafted into the army when the war broke out. Evans was impressed enough by Hal's inflated description of his talents take him on, telling him to report back to his unit and pack his duffel bag. In the morning Hal would receive papers assigning him to Major Evans on a thirty-day detached leave from his original outfit. Hal had no idea what that meant, but it sounded exciting so he asked no questions.

The next morning, he was driven into Honolulu and shown to his quarters, which were in newly erected barracks on the grounds of the University of Hawaii. The shows were performed in the University's auditorium, Farrington Hall. Hal realized that he was now in the Central Pacific Entertainment Section of the Armed Services, his assignment there being to write shows to be performed for servicemen and women throughout the Pacific area of combat. That thirty-day detached leave turned into close to three years of service in that outfit, and he loved every minute of it.

He received his first writing assignment from George Schaefer who once out of the army, would go on to become a prolific producer and director but at that time was just out of Yale Drama School. The show he was directing needed a song for its opening number. Hal was taken to meet Roger Adams (the son of Odette Myrtil, a well-known American singer and actress who was born in Paris in 1898 and died in 1978). Roger asked Hal to write lyrics to go with some music he'd already written. Hal quickly sat down and penned a song called "Shape Ahoy." Everyone liked the title so much that they named the whole show *Shape Ahoy*, and Hal then wrote his very first hit, "Send a Salami to Your Boy in The Army," the chorus of which went as follows:

Send a salami to your boy in the army
It's the patriotic thing
That everyone should do
Send a salami to your boy in the army
Don't just send him things to wear
Send him something he can chew

Once again, Hal's life experience influenced his lyric: his father, Gedalie, and mother, Lena, owned a delicatessen/restaurant on the corner of Pennsylvania and Pitkin Avenues back in Brooklyn, where Hal had sliced his fair share of salami. The sign over the salami section there read "once tried, never denied," which Hal no doubt viewed as his family's coat of arms.

Only a kid from Brooklyn, a budding songwriter like Hal David, would have dared to rhyme "salami with "army."

Years later, Estelle Reiner, comedian Carl Reiner's wife, wanted to sing that song in her cabaret act, but Hal could never find the lyrics to all the verses, he just remembered the chorus. He eventually thought to ask Ilene Graff (a talented singer/actress whose father, Jerry Graff, had been in the army with Hal) if she knew where he might find a copy of the song. She told us that she had a box full of her father's "stuff" in her garage, and that she would look through it to see if the song was in it. Sure enough, Ilene found an old-fashioned 4-track cassette that had been made of the whole score of the show Shape Ahoy. We quickly had the cassette converted to a DVD, and Hal finally got the full lyrics of his song but sadly, by then it was too late for Estelle to perform it in her act. We searched all over for another show Hal wrote while in the army called Jumpin' Jupiter, which was recorded by RCA, but we could never find a recording of it.

Hal's army outfit was somewhat loosely run, with soldiers straggling out for reveille in their kimonos and scarcely following army regulations. This was fine until the brass turned up for inspection one day. The men were ordered to get their rifles and to stand at attention. Half of the fellows hadn't seen their rifles since they'd arrived in Hawaii, and the rifles that were found hadn't been oiled, and were rusty, and clearly unused. As punishment, the whole unit was sent on a long, forced overnight march, but not Hal. His friend who was in the band which was going to be playing for a special function in the Officer's Mess that night, handed Hal a bass fiddle, showed him a few rudiments of how to strum it, and by becoming a one-time-only member of the band, Hal got out of going on that arduous hike.

During those years in the army Hal was happy: he was doing what he had dreamed of doing since he was a teenager writing songs and learning invaluable lessons in lyric-writing while working with a variety of composers and learning to write under pressure. He was also meeting a remarkable roster of stars who, when passing through Hawaii to entertain the troops, always stopped off to pay their respects to Major Evans. And he was surrounded by a gifted group of performers/actors/writers, such as the multi-talented writer and performer Carl Reiner, television personality and talk show host Alan Ludden (who later married Betty White), actor Werner Klemperer, comedic actor Howie Morris, producer Steve Krantz (who married successful novelist Judith Krantz) and Charles Lowe, (who managed Carol Channing's career for decades until their acrimonious divorce).

The army hired local women to appear in their shows, and Hal would still smile long after the war was over whenever he described those singers and dancers. One night, long after we were married, we attended a party in Beverly Hills at the home of Donna and Lalo Schifrin. Lalo is a wonderful composer, pianist, and conductor, as well as a good friend. Minna Duncan, one of the young dancers who had been in the shows happened to be at the party, and she recognized Hal. They chatted about those good old days all night long: with Hal grinning as though he were a Cheshire cat all during their conversation.

Years later, when interviewed for a video called *Expressing a Feeling* that the United States Information Agency made about Hal's career, Carl Reiner was quoted as saying: "We knew that Hal was very talented. This little guy was turning up wonderfully rhyming things. When I moved to Hollywood fifteen years later, I lived next door to Mack David. Hal, Mack's kid brother outran us all. He became one of the biggest lyricists in the country."

Hal's army years came to an abrupt end in 1945 when he suffered a bad asthma attack and the army doctors in Hawaii decided that he needed to return to the States. He was air-lifted on an army plane heading from Honolulu to New York, but they had to stop in California because during the war there were restrictions about flying at night. Hal's army writing partner, Roger Adams arranged for him to stay overnight at his mother's home, and once there, Hal vowed that he would someday return to live in Southern California. The views from the Hollywood Hills house where Odette Myrtil lived looked like heaven to him compared to the middle-to-lower income class area in Brooklyn which, in the 1930's when he was growing up, was inhabited mostly by Italian, Jewish, German, and Russian immigrants. Rough though it was, Hal always felt safe in his neighborhood because Murder, Inc. had their headquarters nearby and many members of the organized crime group, known as the Jewish Mafia, and originally headed by Louis "Lepke" Buchalter, frequented the David family's delicatessen. Hal figured they would protect their own, and those around them. Others, who also often ate at the deli, included teachers from nearby schools which the David children attended. It was the teachers, not the mobsters, who made Hal uncomfortable, since he feared that if he misbehaved at school (which he frequently did) the teachers would be sure to let his father know.

Back in New York and out of the hospital, Hal recuperated quickly, and was discharged from the Army. His experience in Hawaii strengthened his decision to leave journalism behind in favor of becoming a songwriter. Toward that goal, he immediately started knocking on doors in the legendary Brill Building (the Tin Pan Alley of the twentieth century), which is still located at 1619 Broadway in the heart of the theater district of Manhattan.

He met with almost immediate success, soon working with a variety of composers and getting songs published and played on the air, although his first published work, "Horizontal," written with Louis Ricca and recorded by jazz singer Bunty Pendleton on the now-retired RCA Victor label, was banned because, in those years, the title was deemed too sexy. In 1953, he wrote "Bell Bottom Blues" with Leon Carr (not to be confused with Eric Clapton's 1971 song with the same title).

Hal remembered playing the song for criminal defense attorney/songwriter Elliot Shapiro and for Dick Volter, the general manager of the publishing company. They both loved the song and encouraged him to play it for Louis Bernstein of Shapiro/Bernstein Publishing. Bernstein didn't get the song at all; he kept asking if it was about a girl liking a pair of pants. But Shapiro and Volter, along with Al Gallico, an influential independent publisher who also liked the song, convinced Bernstein to publish it at Shapiro/Bernstein in 1953. Teresa Brewer's version of "Bell Bottom Blues" became Hal's first number one song.

The hits kept coming. "My Heart's an Open Book," which Hal wrote with Lee Pockriss, became Carl Dobkins, Jr.'s biggest hit when it sold over a million copies in 1959. "Broken Hearted Melody," written in 1958 with Sherman Edwards, was a major hit for Sarah Vaughan the following year. Another Sherman Edwards melody became "Johnny Get Angry," recorded by Joanie Sommers in 1962. It was given a feminist reinterpretation by k.d. laing. Hal also collaborated with Red Evans and Arthur Altman in writing "American Beauty Rose," which Mitch Miller gave to Frank Sinatra to record in a 1961 album. Hal was especially pleased that Sinatra recorded one of his songs so early in his career.

"Sea of Heartbreak," written with Paul Hampton, an actor, singer, lyricist and writer, was first recorded by Don Gibson in 1961 and subsequently by many other artists, including Paul Hampton himself, the Everly Brothers, and Johnny Cash, and much later, in 2009, Johnny's daughter Rosanne Cash recorded "Heartbreak" as a duet with Bruce Springsteen. Johnny had made a list of 100 songs he thought his daughter should record, and "Heartbreak" was high up on that list. It became the number one song on Rosanne's album titled The List, and was her first top ten album in twenty-two years.

A restaurant that Hal frequented in those early days was Hector's, on Broadway between Forty-Ninth and Fiftieth. Hector's was the least expensive of all the restaurants near the Brill Building. So when Hal and his friends were on a tight budget, they used to go there and order some inexpensive food to eat for lunch. The restaurant always had dishes of coleslaw that the fellows could just help themselves to; they would pay for their inexpensive meal, then take four or five or even six dishes of coleslaw to fill up on, until Hector caught on and put an end to their freeloading.

In those early years Hal also worked with Vincent Lopez, Frankie Masters, and Frankie Carle - all young fellow-writers who used to hang out at the Brill Building and, when they could afford it, eat downstairs in the Turf Restaurant. There the guys would kibbutz and tell each other tall stories about their successes or commiserate about their lack thereof. Once in a while, if they were really flush, they'd pop into Jack Dempsey's, but Dempsey's was pretty expensive, so they didn't go there very often.

One day Hal met a fellow by the name of Don Rodney, who played guitar in Guy Lombardo's band. Don worked nights and slept late in the morning, so they didn't have a lot of time to collaborate. But they started working on a song that Hal titled "The Four Winds and the Seven Seas." Before it was finished, Don took it with him and, between sets that evening, he played it for Guy Lombardo. Guy liked it, and Don telephoned Hal to tell him. Then between another set, Don played it for Carmen Lombardo, Guy's brother, who was also in the band. Hal got another call about that. The calls went on until about two in the morning as Don played the song for different musicians in the band and even for some other people who were just hanging around, as song pluggers and publishers did in those days.

Finally, at about three in the morning, Hal got the call he'd been hoping for all along telling him to come to the Brill Building because Guy Lombardo wanted to publish the song through his publishing company, Bregman, Vacco

& Kahn, and he would record it on Decca Records, which was his label in those years.

The next day, Hal rushed to the Brill Building, signed on the dotted line, and got a $100 advance on the song. Naturally, he was overjoyed, but he was in such a daze that he didn't even realize until he was almost out the door that unlike all the others, he hadn't yet heard the whole melody. He had given Don the completed lyric, but Don hadn't finished the song until he went to work that night.

On the basis of that $100 advance and his girlfriend's salary of $35 a week as a schoolteacher, Hal and Anne Rauschman, whom Hal had started courting once he was out of the army, decided to get married, and set up housekeeping in a garage apartment in Queens, New York.

"The Four Winds and the Seven Seas" went on to become a huge hit in 1949, with the definitive recording sung by Vic Damone. In those years many singers recorded the same song, so "Four Winds" was also recorded by Bing Crosby, Rosemary Clooney, Johnny Desmond, Mel Tormé, Guy Lombardo, and Sammy Kaye, as well as Carmen Caballero.

Bandleader Sammy Kaye liked the song so much that he asked one of the fellows who used to turn up at the hotels where the bands played to ask Hal to come to the Astor Roof, where Kaye and his band were playing. When Hal got there Kaye said, "Hey, kid, you know, I like the way you write. How'd you like to work for me?" He told Hal that he would publish his songs, and Hal could also write some special material for him. Of course, Hal's answer was "of course." Hal didn't write Sammy's tag line "Swing and Sway with Sammy Kaye," but he did write numerous gags for Sammy, as well as special lyrics for him to sing on his radio show.

But soon Hal found that he felt boxed in working for someone; he wanted to be on his own, to freelance. There was just one problem about leaving Kaye's employ: he was broke. With all the chutzpah he could muster, Hal told Sammy that he wanted to leave, and asked if he could borrow a thousand dollars. Incredibly, Sammy agreed to the loan and had his lawyer draw up an agreement. Sammy's lawyer was Lee Eastman - later to become the Beatles' lawyer and Paul McCartney's father-in-law. Hal was so taken with Eastman's ability that he hired him as his own lawyer, and Eastman remained so throughout Hal's long career. Hal also remained friends with Sammy Kaye all throughout Kaye's life.

Eddie Wolpin, a music publisher at Famous Music in the Brill Building, was enthusiastic about what he had seen of Hal's work and came up with an idea that turned out to be life-changing for both parties involved. He thought that Burt Bacharach and Hal should try writing together, so in 1956 he arranged a meeting. Burt had been the musical director for Marlene Dietrich and had worked as a conductor and arranger for other performers as well, and Hal was certainly open to meeting with him. They immediately hit it off and soon started working together, meeting daily at the Famous Music office in the Brill Building. Hal would come in with some titles and ideas for lyrics and Burt would come in with some snippets of a tune. Hal compared it to "show and tell." Whatever grabbed one of them the most would be the song they'd begin to write that day. They frequently went home with an unfinished song, rounded it out, and came in the next day with that song finished, and ideas for another one already perking.

At that time both Burt and Hal were still collaborating with other people; they had not yet formed their famous partnership. Burt frequently composed with lyricist Bob Hilliard and Hal often worked with composer Sherman Edwards, among others; each having some success with those collaborators.

Later on, Burt and Hal shared a tiny office in the Brill Building which had no windows, just an old upright piano for Burt and a beat-up scarred table for Hal.

Hal was a heavy smoker in those days, and he wondered how Burt, who didn't smoke, could stand the pungent smell of those stale cigarettes as they gradually piled up in a tin ashtray that was the only adornment in the room.

When they were first assigned to that office, they'd frequently see a stranger come in, lift up the cover of the piano and surreptitiously put something inside, and then saunter out. That happened day after day without Burt or Hal thinking to check on what was being deposited in the piano. When they finally took a look, they discovered that the fellow had been using their office as a drop-off spot, stashing betting slips in the piano. He was a bookie. He must have thought that neither Burt nor Hal could afford to place a bet, since he never asked them if they wanted to.

The first success of the Bacharach/David team came with "The Story of My Life," recorded by Marty Robbins in 1957. Mitch Miller, a big fan of Hal and Burt's who had been successful in placing many of their early hits, gave it to Marty. It reached #15 on the charts in December of that year, quickly followed by a Perry Como recording of another song of theirs,

"Magic Moments," which vaulted up to #4 in the UK. "The Story of My Life," recorded by Michael Holliday, got to #1, but was then replaced by Perry Como's "Magic Moments," which spent eight weeks at the top, the first time any songwriters had consecutive #1 hits on the UK charts. Hal was ecstatic at having had two hits in a row so early in his collaboration with Burt. He was fond of saying that there was nothing wrong in a songwriter's life that a hit wouldn't cure. But he would quickly add that the flops he wrote after those early triumphs brought him back to earth because there was nothing like a flop to cure a swollen head, a good lesson, learned early on.

Not only did "Story" become a hit on the pop charts, it rose to the top of the country song charts as well. Hal hadn't even realized he'd written a country song in "Story"; he didn't hear many country songs played on the radio in Brooklyn in those days.

Many years later, Hal again struck gold with the country song "To All the Girls I've Loved Before," which he wrote with Albert Hammond, with Albert himself originally recording it. That version didn't do too much. But Albert called Hal one day to say that he thought the song might work for a young singer who was a sensation in Europe, but was not yet known in the United States. Albert asked that Hal send the song over so that Julio Iglesias could listen to it. One day, Willie Nelson walked into Albert's office, and happened to see the lead-sheet sitting on a desk. Willie said he'd always wanted to sing a Hal David song, and when he was told that it was meant for Julio, he said that he loved to sing duets, and with that, a mega-hit was born. Prior to that it had been recorded by Tom Jones, but was not released. Then it was recorded by Engelbert Humperdinck, but it wasn't released. And Bobby Vinton recorded it, and didn't release it. Hal thought that song was a goner until Julio and Willie got ahold of it.

Willie was recording the song in Texas while Julio was working in California. They realized that they needed an extra verse for the song, so they called Hal, who was in New York, to ask him to write it right away. Hal was President of ASCAP at the time, and on the day he got the call, he was getting ready to conduct a Board meeting. But the request for the extra verse was very much on his mind even while he was trying to concentrate on his Board agenda. Hal started the meeting and pretended he was listening to what was being said. But all the while he was writing down lines for the verse. When he finished writing, he got up as though to go to the men's room, but instead, quickly called in the lines, which were immediately recorded the next day. He then sauntered back into the Board Room as if nothing unusual had happened, and continued the meeting.

"To All the Girls I've Loved Before" was first performed in 1984 at the Country Music Awards show in Nashville, and took off like lightening from that moment on, and propelled Hal into the Nashville Hall of Fame. It was a breakthrough for Iglesias in the English language market: his biggest hit in the U.S.A. and Canada, and it became Nelson's biggest European hit. Nelson and Iglesias were named "Duo of the Year" by the Country Music Association and the song was named "Single of the Year" by the Academy of Country Music.

In 2002 a San Francisco rock band called Stroke 9 tried to release an altered version of "To All the Girls," with very raunchy lyrics replacing Hal's. When Hal heard about it, he invoked a long-unused, almost forgotten regulation allowing ASCAP to send a letter to all radio stations in the United States forbidding them from playing the changed version. The group complained via the *San Francisco Chronicle* that Hal was an old fogey and had missed their humor. But Hal felt that using lyrics like *"to all the girls I've loved before, who left me passed out on the floor..."* was not funny!

On January 26, 1989, a new grandchild was born, this time to Hal's youngest son Craig and Alicia David, who were living in Los Angeles at the time. We were out of town, but rushed back as soon as we could to welcome the new addition to our extended family.

The song "Wives and Lovers" was originally an exploitation song for a movie of the same name, meaning it was never intended to be used in the movie, just to advertise the title of the 1963 picture. For "Wives and Lovers" Burt wrote a jazz/waltz melody which was fresh and inspiring to Hal. He wrote the lyrics for it faster than he usually did because he was getting ready to leave town. When he and Burt were ready to play the song for the Paramount people, it turned out that Burt had come up with a few more measures of music which he felt improved the melody. So Hal needed to write two more lines in a hurry, because by then he was leaving in a couple of hours. The two additional lines that Hal wrote are:

"Hey! Little girl, better wear something pretty
Something you'd wear to go to the city."

Hal once said that in spite of the fact that the lines came to him so quickly and under pressure, he felt it was one of the best couplets he'd ever written.

However, my personal favorite is still the rhyme of "pneumonia" and "phone you" from the song "I'll Never Fall in Love Again."

Burt and Hal met Dionne Warwick in 1961 when she was a background singer working with her sister Dee-Dee and her aunt Cissy Houston (Whitney's mother). They invited her to their office where, as Hal put it, "this little girl in sneakers and blue jeans walked in and blew us away." Dionne had grown up singing gospel songs in church before graduating from Hartt School of Music.

They started using her on their demonstration records, but when she found out she wouldn't be singing the songs for publication, she complained and insisted on being the featured singer on the records. In fact, according to Dionne, the song "Don't Make Me Over" came out of something Hal heard her say as she stormed out of their office, yelling over her shoulder: "Don't make me over, man!" Hal said he didn't really remember that specific incident, but Dionne told the story so convincingly that he was ready to accept it as being the way the song came about.

Burt and Hal realized she was right; she certainly had the talent for it. They decided to take her to Florence Greenberg, the young housewife from New Jersey who had started Scepter Records. Florence agreed to produce the songs which Bacharach/David wrote for Dionne. (This was memorialized in the Broadway show *Baby It's You*, written by Floyd Mutrux and Colin Escott, which appeared at the Broadhurst Theatre in 2011). What fun it was to see someone portraying Hal on a Broadway stage!)

That new song, "Don't Make Me Over" marked the 1962 recording debut of Dionne Warwick. In 2000 that original recording of "Don't Make Me Over" was inducted into the Grammy Hall of Fame and Dionne recorded a revamped and updated version of it on her album *Dionne Sings Dionne II*, almost thirty-eight years after recording the original version. Singers from all over the world have recorded "Don't Make Me Over," including Petula Clark, Neil Diamond, Connie Francis and Thelma Houston.

Between 1962 and 1998, Warwick ended up charting fifty-six singles written by the team, including twenty-two Top 40, twelve Top 20, and nine Top 10 hits on the American Billboard Hot 100 charts!

During a lecture that Hal gave with music historian Alan Warner in 2002 titled "Music Business 101," to which ASCAP writers were invited, he emphasized that he and Burt were always respectful of one another's talents. He believed that was a primary factor in sustaining their long relationship. Of Dionne, Hal said that she could do anything both musically and lyrically. He said that he could actually hear Dionne singing a song in his ear as he was writing it. He knew just what words would sound good when she sang them.

Incidentally, the team of Bacharach/David used another talented demo singer in those early years, a fellow by the name of Jerry Landis. He later became a world-famous popular singer/songwriter under his real name: Paul Simon. Paul Hampton, who later wrote the music for the song "Sea of Heartbreak," was the demo singer on "24 Hours from Tulsa" which became a big hit for Gene Pitney, enabling him to become an international star.

In London in the early 1960's when Dionne Warwick was preparing to perform her first big concert at the Savoy Hotel, Hal and Burt were there to lend support and give her any advice she might need for that momentous occasion.

One day after rehearsals, as they were entering the Dorchester Hotel where they were staying, they ran into Charles K. (Charlie) Feldman (a major film agent/manager/producer once married to Jean Howard, a gorgeous Ziegfeld Girl), and his fiancée, Clotilde Bardot. Clotilde knew who Burt and Hal were, and suggested to Charlie that he should hire them for his new film, telling him that they were "hip." It was true that Hal and Burt were red hot at that time, turning out one pop hit after another. But they hadn't yet broken into writing for films.

Hal and Burt made an appointment to meet Charlie for coffee the next morning, and practically on the spot, Charlie offered them the opportunity to write the title song "What's New Pussycat?" for a Woody Allen movie he was producing starring Peter Sellers, Peter O'Toole, Romy Schneider, Capucine, Paula Prentiss and Ursula Andress, to be directed by Clive Donner.

(An aside about the production of that movie: The film was originally supposed to star Warren Beatty, the title being Beatty's way of answering his phone. When Woody Allen was hired to write the script, he began to downplay Beatty's character and expand his own role. That led to conflict and eventually Warren left the project. The two men never worked together again.)

Charlie's offer turned out to be a real break for the team of Bacharach/David, but a break that almost didn't happen, since they were due back in the States for a project on which they were already running late. They felt that if they stayed in London and worked on spec for Charlie Feldman's movie, they would lose the job that they knew they had, working for MGM on a movie called *Made in Paris*. But Charlie had already turned down one song that had been written for his movie by someone else, and he didn't want any more delays. He needed a new song immediately. So he cajoled them into staying in London, pointing out that his was a big picture with big stars and a big budget.

Hal and Burt didn't have an agent at that time, so Charlie introduced them to film producer John Heyman, and John and Charlie saw to it that the kids got a really good deal for their work on "What's New Pussycat?".

They wrote the song while staying at the Dorchester Hotel in April. Hal later said that while the world always considered Irving Berlin's "Easter Parade" as the definitive Easter song; in his mind, it was always "What's New Pussycat?" because he and Burt wrote it on a beautiful Easter Sunday morning in London.

Their song was nominated for an Academy Award in 1965 for Best Title Song, and was made famous by the singing and gyrations of the Welsh singer, Tom Jones. Two other songs that Hal and Burt wrote for that movie were, "Here I Am," which was performed by Dionne Warwick, and "My Little Red Book," which was sung by Manfred Mann.

In addition to Tom Jones' classic interpretation of "What's New Pussycat?" versions were also recorded by Bobby Darin, Tony Bennett, Alvin and the Chipmunks, Anita Kerr, The Wailers and The Four Seasons. Barbra Streisand sang several lines of the song in her *Color Me Barbra* album. There was even a Czech singer by the name of Pavel Novak who recorded the song under the title "Zofie" in 1966.

Since Hal had worked with Morty Nevins on four songs for the 1951 film comedy, *Two Gals and a Guy*, which starred Janis Page and Robert Alda, "Pussycat" was not Hal's first foray into writing for movies but it was certainly his most important one at that point. That fortuitous meeting with Charlie Feldman would lead Bacharach/David into becoming award-winning movie songwriters for years to come. One of their early ones was the title song for the 1966 British movie *Alfie*, starring Michael Caine. When Burt and Hal collaborated on a song, they still had no set way of going about it. Sometimes Hal would write a lyric and Burt would write the melody to the words Hal gave him, and sometimes it was the other way around. Hal had a hard time getting started on these particular lyrics because he thought the name "Alfie" had no romance to it; that it sounded like a British music hall kind of name. But he managed to get past that and gave Burt what he thought was a complete set of lyrics. However, the melody Burt wrote contained a few extra notes so, once again, more words needed to be added.

What Hal originally wrote was:

"What's it all about, Alfie?
Is it just for the moment we live?
What's it all about?"
But to match the notes Burt added, Hal wrote:
"What's it all about, Alfie?
Is it just for the moment we live?
What's it all about when you sort it out, Alfie?"

The forced change was fortuitous since Hal felt that the words "when you sort it out, Alfie" added greatly to the impact of the lyrics. In fact, "Alfie" turned out to be Hal's favorite song because he felt that with the lyrics for "Alfie" he'd written everything he ever wanted to say in that particular song. Burt too said that those lyrics were just as good as they get.

However, it was one of those songs that almost didn't make it into the movie because the producer/director Lewis Gilbert didn't like it. When he was persuaded to at least play it for others who might have a different opinion, Gilbert reluctantly agreed to play it for his son, who he said, knew all about music. But Gilbert's son didn't like the song either. It soon seemed that no one liked it, so no decision about it was made, and the lack of a title song was holding up post-production on the movie. Finally, Howard W. Koch, who was then head of film production at Paramount Pictures, heard there was a problem with the song and let it be known that he wanted to hear it for himself. The story goes that he liked the song that Burt and Hal played for him so much that, in fact, he insisted that it go into the movie or, he said he wouldn't release the picture.

In the movie, the song was performed by Cher, Lewis Gilbert's choice. People always thought it was Dionne Warwick singing the song in the movie, partly because she sang all of Hal's and Burt's songs and partly because it was she who sang the big hit recording of it, which was produced by Burt and Hal. The British singer Cilla Black had a big hit with "Alfie" in the U.K.

Years later, when Hal was rehearsing for a cabaret show he was about to perform at the Hillcrest Country Club, the president of the club heard Hal tell the story about Howard Koch being responsible for "Alfie" being used in the movie and called Howard to urge him and his wife Ruth to come to the show to hear Hal talk about the song. Hal had only met Howard briefly that one time when he and Burt had played the song for him prior to the release of the movie, but Howard came to the show that night, and Hal and I and Howard and Ruth became fast friends from that time on. "Alfie" was nominated for an Academy Award in 1967 but lost out to "Born Free," coincidentally written by Hal's friend John Barry, with Don Black.

Over the years, many artists recorded "Alfie." When Barbra Streisand was preparing to record it, being the perfectionist that she is, she wanted to make sure she understood the meaning of all of the words so that she could interpret them properly. Barbra's manager tracked Hal down while we were traveling in Japan. The call came in on my cell phone saying that Barbra wanted to know what Hal meant when he wrote, "What will you lend on an old golden rule?" To be honest, Hal said that he no longer had any idea what he'd had in mind at the time he wrote that line, but he tried to put himself back to the years when he first wrote those lyrics and came up with a plausible explanation; one which must have worked because Streisand recorded a wonderful version of the song, interpreting it brilliantly.

For many years the phrase "What's it all about, Alfie?" was listed in *Bartlett's Familiar Quotations,* and knowing that his lyrics had become part of the popular lexicon made Hal very proud.

On March 23, 1965, another wonderful song was born when Jackie DeShannon went into the Bell Sound Studio in New York to record "What the World Needs Now is Love," which was subsequently recorded or performed live by over one hundred artists. Hal thought of the first couple of lines - "What the world needs now is love, sweet love, that's the only thing that there's just too little of" - almost all at once. It then took him a good three years before he could figure out what the world didn't need besides love. For example, he thought about a bigger and better airplane that could fly higher, but that didn't grab him. He thought about a submarine that could go deeper but nothing seemed right to him until he imagined enough mountains and hillsides to climb and enough oceans and rivers to cross, and knew that he'd finally found the lines to express the message he wanted to convey.

Hal learned to drive late in life, and even in his salad days, he was a lousy driver. He told me that when he used to drive on the expressway from his home in Roslyn, Long Island into the city, he was always composing in his head. He never could understand why other drivers near him were always honking their horns at him or giving him the finger. That must have occurred often during those three years when Hal was trying to figure out the lyrics to "What the World Needs Now."

"What the World Needs Now" was presented to Dionne Warwick by Hal and Burt, as were all of their songs, but she turned it down. The lyrics just didn't speak to her. Dionne recorded just about every song that the team of Bacharach/David offered her, but this was one time she missed the boat, because the song went on to become almost a national anthem.

Up until that point, Jackie DeShannon's biggest hit had been the Sonny Bono/Jack Nitzsche song, "Needles and Pins." Hal remembered that when "World" was first suggested for her there wasn't great enthusiasm for it in her camp. But Jackie herself chose it immediately, and, besides climbing to #7 on the US charts and to #1 in Canada, the song soon led Jackie to club tours and regular appearances on television.

Dionne later sang it numerous times, and she eventually recorded it for her album *Here, Where There is Love*. One of the many artists who recorded the song was Burt himself, who performed it in the Austin Powers film *Goldmember*. But it is Jackie's rendition that has lasted through the years and will, hopefully, continue to be inspiring to us all when things go wrong in the world and in our own lives.

In 1968, following the shooting of Senator Robert Kennedy, Jackie DeShannon's version of "What the World Needs Now" was played over and over on Los Angeles radio stations.

ASCAP has calculated that "What the World Needs Now" has been played on the radio more than two million times, and it was performed in over two hundred and twenty-five films and TV shows such as *Austin Powers, Forrest Gump, Sesame Street,* and the *Late Show with David Letterman.* It was introduced to a younger generation when it was featured on the popular TV show *American Idol.*

When "What The World Needs Now" was performed in a review of Bacharach/David songs called *Love, Sweet Love* on Broadway in 2003, a Murray Matthew review online at *www.TalkinBroadway.com* stated that "one of the show's finest moments is when the entire cast ensembles on stage for one of Bacharach and David's most enduring anthems, "What the World Needs Now." They're able to lift the spirits and the heart just when they're most needed by standing and singing.

The song is still constantly performed in over forty countries around the world, some of them being Australia, Malaysia, Poland, Switzerland, Denmark, Japan, Israel, England, and France.

Another iconic song came from this fertile period of collaboration between Hal and Burt: "Raindrops Keep Fallin' on My Head." Hal was asked to travel from Long Island to Beverly Hills on a July 4th weekend in 1968, where he holed up in the Beverly Wilshire Hotel, very ill. The people at Twentieth-Century-Fox wanted him to come in for a screening of their movie called Butch Cassidy and the Sundance Kid, which was then in post-production. They needed him right away, as they were about to shut down for the long holiday weekend and he had to see the scene where a song was needed before that happened. Hal pulled himself together, and managed to get to the screening room, where he was shown the memorable scene of Paul Newman unsteadily steering a bike, with a laughing Kathryn Ross, skirts flying, perched precariously on the handlebars.

Somehow or other, even though the scene was a happy one, Hal got the idea that raindrops were always falling on Butch Cassidy's head because he was such a loser. That was the way Hal always answered the question of why he didn't choose to write a lyric about the sun shining on Butch Cassidy's head, as it appeared in that scene.

Hal brought the lyric he'd written over to Burt's home in Beverly Hills, where Burt had already composed the wonderful music - and the rest, as they say, is history. But that song wasn't an easy sell either. The director of the movie, George Roy Hill, liked the song right away but then had a hard time getting someone to record it. Ray Stevens was asked to sing it, but he didn't want to guarantee that he'd put the song out as a single. Arlo Guthrie heard the song, but he wasn't enthusiastic about it either. Hal and Burt began to worry that if too many performers turned it down, Paramount would sour on it, and it wouldn't get into the movie. Since they were close to Scepter Records because of bringing Dionne Warwick to Florence Greenberg, the head of the record company, they decided to ask Scepter for B. J. Thomas, who was under contract to the company. He was brought out to California and recorded the song for the film, and put it out a single, as Hal and Burt wanted. It went on to win the coveted Oscar at the Academy Awards ceremony in 1970, as the

Best Performed song in a Featured Film, with Hal and Burt both receiving statues, and it won many more awards over the years - not bad for a song that almost didn't make it into the movie it was written for.

In 2002, friends of ours, Arlene and Alan Lazare, asked Hal to sing "Raindrops" at their daughter's wedding. It was Lauren's favorite song because when she was a baby, her nurse used to bathe her and sprinkle drops of water on her, while singing it. Hal was always a good sport about performing when a friend asked, so of course he said yes.

The night of the wedding, we arrived early, and Hal had a quick rehearsal with the bandleader while the wedding guests were enjoying cocktails. Hal was obviously not a professional singer, but he had a darn good voice, and he loved to sing his own songs. But he was always anxious to get the key right, and to be comfortable with whoever was going to accompany him, hence his need for the rehearsal.

During dinner, we were busy chatting with the others at our table, including Liza Minnelli and Sammy Davis' third wife Altovise, and barely noticed when Alan Lazare, the father of the bride, went up to the microphone. Our ears suddenly perked up when we heard Alan announce that Hal David was now going to perform. But as Hal walked up to the stage, he suddenly realized that the band was nowhere in sight! They had gone on break, and there were Hal and Alan, up on the stage, with egg on their faces. But Neil Sedaka, a wonderful composer and performer, and a high school friend of Alan's, was also a guest at the wedding, and he saved the day when he called out that he would accompany Hal. What a double whammy: Neil Sedaka and Hal David performing "Raindrops" to wild acclaim.

Hal always stayed at the Hotel Bel Air in southern California whenever a song of his was nominated for an Academy Award. That seemed to be a lucky place for him when he was nominated, even though he always stayed at the Beverly Wilshire Hotel whenever he was actually working on a movie. But the Bel Air really wasn't the best choice of hotels for Hal: he was known for his poor sense of direction. He could always find his way to Sunset Boulevard when he was leaving the hotel, but he could never seem to get back to the hotel after the awards ceremony. And it wasn't because he was blotto: he just couldn't figure out where it was, and always ended up driving in circles, and getting very frustrated. I think one of the many reasons our marriage was so successful was that I was always the designated driver.

Hal had received many awards before I met him. His film work included Oscar-nominated title songs for the movies "What's New Pussycat" and "Alfie," "The Look of Love" from Casino Royale, and the Oscar-winning "Raindrops Keep Fallin' on My Head" from Butch Cassidy and the Sundance Kid. "Don't Make Me Over" and "Walk on By" were inducted into the Grammy Hall of Fame. Along the way, Hal received the NARM Presidential Award, the coveted Johnny Mercer Award from the Songwriters Hall of Fame, and a Grammy for his Broadway show Promises, Promises. He received many more awards after we were married, and I was always thrilled to share the excitement of his receiving those awards with him during the years we were together.

In June of 2004, the Songwriters Hall of Fame declared that "What the World Needs Now is Love" would be designated the Towering Song, one of the prestigious awards annually presented at their June gala. Hearing about that, the San Francisco-based ABC News correspondent Mike Cerre, whom Hal and I had met the year before in Forte die Marme, thought that Hal would be a good candidate for the *Person of the Week* segment on the Friday night ABC news broadcast. Mike, along with a camera crew with a ton of equipment, arrived at our apartment in the Museum Tower in New York, and with Felicia Beberica, a producer for the *ABC World News Tonight* show they went to work. It was a very exciting four hours, with the cameras whirring, Mike asking questions, and Felicia suggesting angles for the camera and other technical matters. I asked Felicia how long the segment would be, seeing as how they'd been filming for four hours and weren't even through. She said, "Oh, about ninety seconds!" I couldn't believe they could cut four hours down to ninety seconds, but Felicia said she was thrilled, because they usually are only allotted sixty seconds for the segment.

Besides filming the Towering Song segment at the Songwriters Hall of Fame gala, Mike and his ABC camera crew were on hand when Hal was honored with the American Eagle Award by the National Music Council at a luncheon held at the Players Club in New York.

We took a side-trip while we were in Paris one year, and drove to Chantilly where we visited the elegant Chateau de Chantilly, built in 1528, featuring their incredible, pristine stables. The Great Stables, as they are called, were featured in the 1985 James Bond movie *A View to a Kill*. Hal didn't write anything for that movie, but he did write the lyrics to songs that were in three James Bond films. In 1967, Charlie Feldman produced the Bond spoof,

Casino Royale, which did not get great reviews, but "The Look of Love," which Hal wrote with Burt and which was sung by Dusty Springfield, was a highlight of the movie, and had a spectacular life of its own.

Dusty's version of the song was originally put out on the "B" side (or the back side) of the recording, which is often a killer for many songs. But Pat O'Day, a disc jockey in Seattle, preferred "The Look of Love" to the now forgotten song on the "A" side of the record, and he began playing it over and over again. It soon became a hit in Seattle, spreading to California, and over the radio waves to New York; a hit every step of the way. In 1968 the song was performed by the Sergio Mendes group at the Oscars, where it received a nomination for Best Song and Dusty Springfield's version reached the *U.S. Top 40* list. Sergio Mendes' hit rendition on his Mendes '66 album *Look Around* reached No. 4 on the pop charts, and years later, in 2008, "The Look of Love" was inducted into the Grammy Hall of Fame, even though it had lost out on the Academy Award to the song "Talk to the Animals" from the 1967 movie *Dr. Doolittle,* sung by Rex Harrison. But do you hear it played any more? No. But almost everyone is still familiar with "The Look of Love." You can't win them all, but "The Look of Love" should have won!

Once again, Hal wrote this hit song at the Dorchester Hotel, where he – and later he and I – so often stayed. One year while he was there, Marlene Dietrich, an old pal of his who was also staying in the hotel asked if he would take a package back to the States, and mail it from New York to her husband, Rudolf Sieber, who lived on their ranch in the San Fernando Valley in southern California. Hal said he would find room in his suitcase for it, and Marlene's maid brought him the package, which he tucked away in his luggage and forgot all about. When he flew into New York, a fellow at Customs opened Hal's suitcase, and asked what was in the package. Hal felt stumped for an answer because he thought the agent would think he was name-dropping if he said that Marlene Dietrich had given him the package. So he just got that innocent little look on his face that he was so good at, and told the fellow that he wasn't sure what was in it. The guy poked around through the linen tablecloth that it was wrapped in, without even attempting to open the package, and opined that more linen must be inside. Hal quickly agreed.

When he told Dietrich that he had sent the package off to her husband, she thanked him profusely for delivering the Russian icons she had sent home! Hal would have been quaking in his boots had he known what was really in the package, since it was forbidden to take such icons—especially Russian ones—out of the country.

Marlene used to treat Hal like she was his proverbial Jewish mother, frequently recommending a doctor he should go to or a cold remedy he should take. When Hal heard that she was ill in Paris, he tried to call her. When someone answered the phone, Hal thought he recognized her sultry voice, but the person insisted that she was the maid, and that "Miss Dietrich" could not come to the phone. Hal asked "the maid" to send his fondest wishes to Marlene, hoping that he could have a longer conversation with the star. Sadly, Marlene Dietrich died in 1992, in her apartment on the Avenue Montagne in Paris, but Hal always felt comforted in the belief that it was she he had spoken to on the phone and that he had been able to express his warm feelings to her.

In 1969, John Barry wrote a beautiful melody for the Bond movie *On Her Majesty's Secret Service*, to which Hal wrote the lyrics, taking the title "We Have All the Time in the World," from James Bond's final words, spoken ironically after his wife's death in both the novel and the film. It was sung by Louis Armstrong, who was too ill to play his trumpet. During the recording, he kept asking Hal if he was doing okay. Hal told him that he was absolutely perfect, and he meant it! Louis died in 1971, not long after the movie came out.

Hal often told me how excited he was to have worked with the great trumpeter, who he said, was a sweet, wonderful, and humble man. John Barry felt that the song was the finest piece of music he had written for a Bond movie, if only because he had had the pleasure of working with Louis Armstrong.

It had all come about when John frantically called Hal one day from Los Angeles, where he was working on the Bond movie. They needed lyrics "yesterday" to the music that John had just written. Hal was working in New York at the time, but flew to Los Angeles on a weekend, where he heard the music and saw the film. He immediately sat down in his room at the Beverly Wilshire Hotel and wrote the lyrics to "We Have All the Time in the World" much faster than his usual studied pace.

Many years later, when Hal and I arrived in New York from one of our many trips to London, the light on the answering machine in our Museum Tower apartment was flashing like mad. The first three or four messages were from John Barry, excitedly telling Hal that they had a hit! Hal hadn't worked with John in many years, so he couldn't imagine what the message meant.

But a quick phone call to Barry's home in Oyster Bay, N.Y., resolved the mystery. Apparently a commercial for Guinness beer had appeared in the U.K., using the Louis Armstrong version of "We Have All the Time in the World." It went viral, with people calling the TV station to find out where they could get a copy of the song. The song was immediately released as a single, and quickly climbed the charts to No. 3 in Britain and a survey taken in 2005 by the BBC showed that "We Have All the Time in the World" was the third most popular love song played at weddings. Hal tried to interest the Alfred Publishing Co. to rerelease the song as a single in the United States, but sadly that never happened. My personal opinion is that they missed out on a good thing - a proven commodity!

Ten years later, in 1979, Hal wrote the lyrics for *Moonraker* to another John Barry melody. That title song to the movie of the same name was the third and final performance by Shirley Bassey in a James Bond movie.

Hal always said that he didn't feel that he and Burt had any particular "style." For example, he pointed out that "What the World Needs Now is Love" and "What's New Pussycat?" are as far apart as the North Pole and the South Pole. The same thing can be said of "Alfie" and "Wives and Lovers." They are totally different. The main thing the two tried to do was to find an original approach to whatever song they wrote. When he and Burt achieved the freshness they were looking for, they agreed it was a wonderful feeling, one that Hal especially felt about "What the World Needs Now."

Hal always strove for simplicity in his lyrics. He thought that Cole Porter was very sophisticated and described Irving Berlin as being earthy; he deemed Oscar Hammerstein poetic and found Lorenz Hart witty. But he pointed out that the one thing they all had in common was that their lyrics were the epitome of simplicity, in the best sense of the word. Of his favorite lyricist, Johnny Mercer, he said, "Whether he is being poetic or humorous, he is never complicated." About his own lyrics Hal said that he liked to use everyday words and tried to paint a picture that conveyed what he felt. And about his longtime collaboration with Burt he said that they tried hard not to be contrived with their songs. He felt that a song should be so seamless that it should sound like one person wrote it, never giving away that it was a collaboration.

Hal described Burt as a man of many talents, a masterful arranger, an outstanding conductor, but first and foremost, a brilliant composer. Among songwriters there are many tune writers, but just a handful of composers. Burt is one of the few who are composers. Burt wrote all the arrangements for the songs he wrote with Hal, which often included an eleven-member string section and flugelhorns (a Bacharach signature sound).

Hal was once asked if he had ever written any music himself. At the very beginning of his career, he did write both words and music, but his success was always with lyrics. He felt that if a lyric writer wasn't musical, he would be unable to succeed as a lyricist. He pointed out that a lyric writer was not necessarily writing poetry, but rather lyrics to be sung, so a lyric writer had to hear words sung in his head in order to set up the structure.

I was always fascinated to watch Hal when he had an assignment to write a song. The first thing he would do was clear off his desk, which usually was a hodgepodge of papers, clippings, books, and accumulations of other bits and pieces of things. I always thought that was symbolic of him clearing his head for what he had to do because, interestingly enough, he never wrote lyrics at his desk. Once the desk was cleared, he would sit in his special rocking chair, legal pad and pencil in hand, and only then would he begin to work.

That chair was purchased in the early 1940's for about twenty-five dollars, and it has since been recovered, refinished, and even re-sprung. It followed Hal from house to house and from apartment to apartment - even from state to state. It was the chair in which Hal sat to think, to read, and even to take the occasional nap.

Hal's rocking chair. Photo by Eunice David.

Hal never felt that he was superstitious, but that was definitely his go-to chair whenever he had a writing assignment. That chair remains in the office that Hal and I shared in our Los Angeles apartment, and if I shut my eyes tightly I can still conjure up Hal sitting there with that special look on his face that he always got when he was dreaming up a lyric: his eyes would become slits, and his lips would move to some imagined words. Whenever we travelled with friends, they learned not to talk to Hal when he got that look on his face. They'd turn to me and say, "Oh, Hal's working." He just seemed to zone out and get into his writing mode. It obviously worked for him.

Hal may at one time have written his lyrics on a typewriter, but after we were married he always wrote them longhand on a legal pad, and then (struggling to read his writing), I would transfer them to the computer. When writing to a melody a collaborator had written, he would listen to a tape or cassette of the music over and over again until he had it in his head. Then he would start to write the lyrics on his note pad, rarely referring back to the music. If he was writing the lyrics first, he told me that he always had a "dummy" melody in his head so that he could get the right rhythm.

On his website, www.haldavid.com, Hal states that, one thing a lyricist must learn is to not fall in love with his own words. "Once you learn that, you can walk away from a lyric and look at it with a reasonable degree of objectivity. Often I discard a good line because it is inconsistent with the basic idea. If the line happens to be witty or sad in a particularly fresh way, it hurts me to take it out. But that's part of the pain of writing."

I had many friends in Los Angeles, where I grew up and had lived all of my life, all of whom loved Hal on sight when I started introducing him around at the end of 1987. His late wife Anne had not liked the glamour and glitter of Hollywood, quite often preferring to remain in New York when Hal came west for work. So he had never had a chance to make many friends in my part of the world before we met. But once we began seeing each other on a regular basis, Hal stayed in L.A. for longer and longer periods of time, and we started on quite a round of social activities, since all my friends were anxious to get to know him. One night, a few months after we'd met, we were out to dinner with our matchmakers Babe and Herbert Eagle and another couple. They started talking about going to Indian Wells in the California desert for New Year's Eve, rather than staying in town. I thought it would be great fun for us to go with them, but Hal didn't say a word. I guess he had to think it over for a while, because it wasn't until a few days later that he asked if I would like to come with him and our friends. My bag was packed practically before he got the words out.

We had a wonderful time playing tennis, eating, and driving around the area. Babe's brother, Bob Dickerman and his wife Madeline, long-time friends of mine, lived at The Lakes, a gated community in Palm Desert appropriately named for their killer golf course with many lakes. Hal took one look at their home and others nearby and, with Bob egging him on, he decided to start looking for a place to buy in the same community.

When I first met Hal I was struck by what a gentle man he was - a true gentleman. Oh, he had his faults, he had his idiosyncrasies, he had his likes and dislikes, but overall, he was a gentle, unassuming man. And he was a very fair man. In both his professional and personal life, he made a great effort to make sure that everything was just and right. He was especially considerate of the feelings of his two sons since they were adopted, and he wanted them to understand his deep feelings of love for them.

When Hal proposed, he actually got down on one knee (he could still do that in those days) and in the old-fashioned way, asked me to marry him. He was sixty-six. I was sixty. He had been married to Anne for thirty-nine years when she passed away. I'd been married twice - once when I was very young to Bob Hirsch, a man I helped put through college, who was the father of my two sons, and later, to Bif Forester, who thought he was God's gift to women. Shortly after my divorce from Bif, I met King Hirsch, the "tall, dark and handsome" man of my dreams, and was with him until he died from complications of a stroke, just one month before I met Hal. By the time Hal and I got together, both my sons and Hal's were long since grown, and we no longer had the responsibilities we'd had when we were younger. While my sons were growing up, I had worked as everything from a secretary and an office manager to my last and most interesting position as Zoning Director for the Newhall Land and Farming Company when they developed the City of Valencia, California in the early 1960's. Hal's career took him away from home frequently and often left raising his two adopted sons to his wife. But with our newfound freedom from so many of our former commitments, we were able to travel as much as we wanted and we did so with great enthusiasm, eventually managing to visit every single place on our combined bucket lists.

We wasted no time getting started. In April of 1988, we went to Paris, where we romantically bought my wedding band at Cartier's on the Rue de

Rennes. We must have looked in every jewelry store in Paris, but kept coming back to Cartier, which was the first store we'd stopped at.

From Paris we traveled to Amsterdam, ending up in The Hague, where Hal was representing ASCAP at a CISAC meeting (The International Confederation of Societies of Authors and Composers, which works toward increased recognition and protection of creators' rights). Hal had been on CISAC's Executive Committee, and I was proud to see what a force he still was in the organization. As a result of our attending their meetings throughout the years, we made many friends in the International community.

Hal could be a fierce advocate for what he thought was right, and proved that time and again during his years with ASCAP (American Society of Composers Writers and Publishers). He was a champion of the rights of his fellow writers and frequently "walked the halls" of congress in pursuit of those rights. Paul Williams when he was President of ASCAP, called Hal a "warrior who fought for the rights of all songwriters." Dan Foliart, a fellow ASCAP Board member with Hal, hit it right on the nose when, as President of The Society of Composers and Lyricists, he wrote that, "Hal's presence in a congressional office was always a welcomed one. He was able to articulate the salient points of the moment and enlist support from both sides of the aisle. He was the most convincing spokesperson that we, as a community, could have hoped for."

While in New York, we attended a show at Carnegie Hall, jointly sponsored by ASCAP and Carnegie Hall in honor of Irving Berlin's 100th birthday. Even though Berlin was a recluse at that time and rarely, if ever left his apartment, he was very much in charge of the show, nixing certain performers or songs, and approving others. So much so that when ASCAP offered to place a closed-circuit TV in his apartment for him to watch the show in live time, he brusquely refused, saying that he knew the songs and who would be performing them and didn't need to see it on TV.

Hal had been a member of ASCAP since 1974, when he was elected to two successive terms as their President (from 1980 to 1986). His first day on the job, he sat down behind the desk in his office in the ASCAP building at One Lincoln Plaza in New York, and realized that he had no idea what he was supposed to do. He called in Toni Winter, the secretary he'd inherited from his predecessor, Stanley Adams, and together they tried to figure out where Hal should start.

Toni suggested that Hal might want to call Irving Berlin and introduce himself. Toni placed the call through Berlin's secretary, Hilda, which was the proper protocol, and Berlin called back the next day. Berlin apparently knew of

Hal's work because he asked Hal why he wanted the job, given that he was such a good writer. He told Hal he should be writing, not wasting his time as President of ASCAP. (This from one of the men who had founded ASCAP in 1914!)

Berlin asked Hal to call him "Irving," but Hal demurred, saying he had so much respect for Berlin that he just couldn't do that. Instead, he called him "Mr. B," and continued to do so throughout their phone relationship, which lasted until Irving Berlin's death in September of 1989 at the age of one hundred and one.

When ASCAP was planning a retrospective show at Lincoln Center of the work of the authors and composers who were ASCAP members, they wanted to borrow the famous piano on which Berlin had composed his songs. Since Berlin only played on the black keys, this piano had a special lever so that songs could be written in different keys. It was called a transposing piano, and he had famously bought it for just one hundred dollars. Berlin called that piano his "trick" piano and he took it with him wherever he went, whether working in Hollywood, or even on vacation. At one time, Berlin owned three such pianos, which were popular in those years with songwriters who were not schooled in orchestration.

In his later years, the piano had been put away in storage, but Berlin graciously had someone dig it out, and it was used as the centerpiece of the ASCAP show. Hal also had a business letter that Berlin had written to ASCAP, and he asked Mr. B if it too could be showcased that evening, as an important piece of Berlin memorabilia. Berlin felt that the business letter was too mundane, and told Hal to retrieve a letter he'd written to Cole Porter, the original of which was in the Yale Library. Berlin said the letter had *"tom,"* a Yiddish expression roughly translated to mean fullness or completeness. (Hal was Jewish, but he didn't know many Yiddish words, and had to be told what *"tom"* meant.) He totally understood what Berlin was getting at once he was able to get the letter from Yale. In the letter Berlin told Porter that he had just seen one of Porter's Broadway shows, and had thoroughly enjoyed it. He ended by saying, *"anything I can do, you can do better,"* a take-off on Berlin's own lyric from his show *Annie Get Your Gun*, where Annie sang the words, "Anything you can do, I can do better." Hal was always astonished that at his advanced age, Berlin had remembered not only writing that particular letter, but that he remembered exactly where it was and what it said.

Hal was once asked to name a highlight of his tenure as President of ASCAP. He singled out that it was the Jukebox Legislation. Hal was a prime mover of that legislation that was passed by Congress, requiring the previously exempt jukebox owners to pay royalties on the music that was played on their machines. He also said that when he became President, ASCAP was way behind BMI and the Country Music world. But within a year of his presidency, ASCAP was equal with BMI, and by the time Hal left office, ASCAP had about seventy percent of the Country Music charts. Hal felt that was a very significant gain. As President, he hired a lobbyist in Washington, D.C; the first time ASCAP had such a powerful a voice in the capital. Ben Palumbo not only proved to be an important asset to ASCAP, but he and Hal became fast friends and remained so through the years, with Ben always charmingly calling Hal "Mr. President" even long after Hal was no longer President of ASCAP. Ben tells about being interviewed for the position, and at the time he didn't even know how to spell the word "copyright," much less did he know what it meant. Throughout his years as a strong advocate for ASCAP, he certainly learned what the word meant - much to the benefit of ASCAP and its members.

During Hal's presidency, ASCAP offices were opened up throughout the United States and in Europe. They were beginning to have a real presence.

In June of 1988, we found ourselves again in New York, this time for an ASCAP show at the Marriott Marquis. Hal was not a performer, but he loved to sing his own songs, and he went on to improve tremendously over the years, even performing in numerous cabaret shows. Singer/songwriter Gene Pitney once commented that even though songwriters were usually not very good singers, when they sang their own songs they left a little piece of themselves in their delivery that could never be replicated by any singer who performed the song, no matter how talented, and that was true of Hal's delivery. He always did a little two-step when he sang, which his musical director Chris Caswell dubbed the "David Hop."

In July, we attended the International Festival of the Arts in New York, at which Hal and his good friend Henry Mancini spoke on a panel about the importance of music in film, with each of them screening segments of a scene in a movie without music, then showing what a difference adding music to the same scene made. Mancini's was from the popular miniseries, *Thornbirds,* starring Richard Chamberlain, and Hal chose the "Raindrops" scene with Paul Newman and Katherine Ross cycling in *Butch Cassidy and the Sundance Kid* as his example.

Before we returned to Los Angeles, we received an invitation to go to Washington, D.C., to attend a concert to be held in the Library of Congress where the Gershwin family was to receive the Congressional Medal of Honor.

That was a thrilling event, made even more memorable when I found myself seated next to Supreme Court Justice Sandra Day O'Connor at dinner. Hal had never met George Gershwin, but he did become friends with Lenore (Lee) and Ira Gershwin, who lived in Beverly Hills, and we were delighted to hear Michael Feinstein perform at the beginning of his career on that evening.

We went on to Boston to greet my newest grandson, Dylan Forester, the first of the four grandchildren to be born while Hal and I were together. (My son Donald and his then-wife Connie were living near Boston, with my other grandson, three-year-old Jordan.) That same month we travelled to Des Moines, Iowa, where Hal's youngest son, Craig, was living. He had recently met a young girl by the name of Alicia, whom we wanted to meet. (Hal's oldest son, Jim David, was the only one of our four boys who lived in Los Angeles, so we saw him often and he and I became great pals, lunching and sharing many confidences.) And later that year, we flew to Portland, Oregon, to visit my son K.C. and his daughter Kira. These visits gave us a chance to start getting to know some members of each other's family.

Hal and Eunice, May 1988 painting by John Solie.
Permission granted by the artist.

Next it was on to Atlanta, Georgia, having been invited to the Democratic Convention, where we heard the Reverend Jesse Jackson give an impassioned speech introducing Rosa Parks and the concepts of a Rainbow

Coalition and Common Ground. From there we headed to London, Munich, and Salzburg, where we heard Herbert von Karajan conduct the Berlin Philharmonic during the Salzburg Music Festival, and then took the train to Venice. For two people who had met less than a year earlier, we were covering a lot of ground and establishing the peripatetic pattern that would last throughout our married life.

When Hal and I decided to get married, I told him I wanted to wait one year after King Hirsch died. Even though King and I hadn't been married, I felt it was the right thing to do, given the depth of my feelings for him and the years we'd been together. My friends thought I was crazy: if that great guy wants to marry you, they said, what are you waiting for? But Hal understood and respected my wishes.

So we set our wedding date for September 2 of 1988. But we didn't want to wait until then to buy a place in the desert, so in April we arranged for a real estate broker to show us around and before we knew it, we became the proud owners of a beautiful home at The Lakes, overlooking a double expanse of their tricky, water-filled golf course.

We decided that once we were married we would live in my condominium in Beverly Hills, small as it was. So one weekend, before we left for our new place in the desert, Hal put his Mountaingate condo on the market, and by the time we'd arrived at The Lakes, he received a call from his real estate broker telling him that it had just sold.

With that settled, I began planning our wedding by inviting Babe Eagle to be my maid of honor, since she had introduced me to Hal. But Babe's husband Herbert was not enthusiastic about her going to New York, where Hal's lawyer felt we should be married because Hal was still a resident of New York, and where he kept a beautiful double apartment in the Museum Tower on Fifty Third Street between Fifth and Sixth Avenues.

With Babe unable to be my maid of honor, I was at a loss, since at that time I had no women friends in New York. But when Hal mentioned that his two sons, Jim and Craig, were going to stand up for him, everything suddenly fell into place. Instead of a maid of honor, I would have two men of honor: my sons K.C. and Donald Forester. That turned out to be the perfect solution.

Hal's lawyer not only advised us to be married in New York, he even suggested the name of a judge who could perform the ceremony for us. So in August we went to New York to make final preparations and to meet her. Shortly after we arrived at the Essex House, where we'd invited Surrogate

Judge Marie Lambert for lunch, the maître d' brought over a somewhat rumpled and distracted-looking woman. We waved him away, thinking that this could not be the esteemed Judge. But indeed it was and after just a few moments of conversation, we fell in love with the witty and fascinating Judge and knew we had just met the very person whom we wanted to marry us.

Our wedding took place on the fifty-second floor of the beautiful Equitable Life Building between Sixth and Seventh Avenues at Fifty-Second Street, where many executives from ASCAP gathered, along with as many family members from both sides of our about-to-be-blended family as were able to fly to New York for the occasion.

Hal, Jim and Craig were waiting at one end of the room as K.C. and Donald escorted me up the aisle.

Judge Lambert began the service enthusiastically reading her prepared remarks, but I soon started to cry. Make that "sob." I was so overwhelmed that I just couldn't stop. Hal, thinking I was about to collapse, put a supporting arm around me and, mid-sentence, Judge Lambert stopped reading her remarks, looked right at me and quipped, "I thought this was supposed to be a joyous occasion." Through my tears, I nodded and told her how happy I was. Appearing uncertain as to whether or not to believe me, she nevertheless finished the service, and Hal and I were joined in holy matrimony.

After the ceremony, with me by now somewhat composed, we all traipsed down to the forty-ninth floor to the appropriately named Music Room, where a delicious lunch was served as we listened to Frank Renzi, a gifted pianist, perform Bacharach/David songs throughout the meal.

Since we were married in New York, we decided to hold a wedding reception for our friends in Los Angeles before the year 1988 was over. We chose the newly-opened Marriott Hotel in Century City as the venue, and, as it turned out, not only one hundred and fifty or so friends from Los Angeles attended, but friends from all over the country flew in to celebrate with us.

We'd invited Judge Lambert to attend, and she responded that she would join us. We were delighted. I had baskets of fruit delivered to the rooms where all of our out-of-town friends were staying, but I didn't see Judge Lambert's name on the list of those staying at the Marriott. I called around to several nearby hotels, but no Judge Lambert was registered. Thinking that maybe she was staying with a friend, I finally called her office in New York, only to find out that the Judge thought the reception was at the Marriott Hotel in New York! Her red-faced secretary took the blame, having read the invitation incorrectly.

During the reception, I announced that all of the songs that were to be played during the evening had been written by songwriters who were in the room with us, an announcement that got a big round of applause from our other guests. Our songwriter friends in attendance included Marilyn and Alan Bergman, John Cacavas, Sammy Cahn, Mack David, George Duning, Sammy Fain, Charlie Fox, Joe Harnell, Jerry Leiber, Mike Stoller and Johnny Mandel; David Rose, Henry Mancini and Burt Bacharach were in Aspen and could not attend, but their songs were also played.

Later that month, while still on our honeymoon, we gathered with a group of men and women who were all members of the Private Sector Section of the United States Information Agency, under the guidance of Charles Z. (Charlie) Wick, who had been appointed to his position by President Ronald Reagan. About twelve couples were asked to represent the United States on a month-long junket that would take us to six different venues: Moscow, Leningrad, Helsinki, Munich, Paris, and Brussels.

The men were selected to represent different groups in our society, such as music, book publishing, communications, and film. They were chosen for their ability to help promote the U.S. national interest to people living in foreign countries, and to broaden the dialogue between Americans and their counterparts abroad.

At our stop in Russia, we were cautioned that we should not lock our suitcases when they were left in our hotel rooms (at that time we were still able to lock our luggage when flying). This was the era of Perestroika and Glasnost, the period in the 1980's, when President Mikhail Gorbachev initiated his policy of economic and governmental reform.

Even though the Soviet Union and the United States were on somewhat friendly terms, our State Department was certain that our rooms would be bugged and our luggage searched. We were also cautioned that when leaving a U.S. Embassy in any of the countries we were scheduled to visit, we should not discuss what we'd heard there while being transported from place to place, because even though the drivers professed not to understand English, they supposedly were quite proficient in our language, and were more than likely spies for their respective countries. We were warned not to buy anything on the street, and to definitely not accept any package, letter, or anything else from anyone who might approach us. Were we paranoid? Yes, but with good cause.

Our first stop was supposed to have been Moscow, but the officials in the tower at Sheremetyevo International Airport suddenly decided that our plane, since it was coming from the United States, was not going to be permitted to land on the day we were scheduled to arrive; last-minute news to our pilot. He quickly changed our flight plan mid-air, to divert us to Helsinki, where we spent the night. The next morning we were transferred to an Aeroflot plane which was allowed to land in Moscow. That, in 1988, was definitely a no-frills, no-nonsense experience! The plane seemed old and decrepit, and none of us were certain of the skills of the pilots. What a way to start our trip.

In Moscow, we attended a production of Duke Ellington's *Sophisticated Lady,* which was jointly produced, directed, and performed by Americans and Russians. The patron for the evening was President Gorbachev's wife, Raisa, whose couturier had designed the costumes for the show. Much to our delight and surprise, when reading the program, we saw that Paul Chiara was the arranger and that Frank Owens was the conductor, both of whom were long-time friends of Hal's. When the show was over, we went down to the pit to see them, and they were delighted to see us there. Paul told us how remarkable the Russian musicians were; they had memorized the complicated Ellington jazz score by heart, even before rehearsals began.

At each stop during our trip, we met with the U.S. Ambassadors who briefed us on the political and economic situation. After the show in Moscow, there was a reception at Ambassador Jack Matlock's residence, where Frank Owens was playing the piano. As a tribute to our recent marriage, Frank played a medley of Hal's love songs, encouraging many of our fellow travelers to crowd around the piano for a sing-along. Louise Wheeler, our group leader from the State Department, loved to sing, and in every country we visited, she always requested an orchestra to play "Raindrops," rightly figuring that was one song that everyone knew. That song was a perennial favorite in Europe, and over the years we heard it played on more different instruments, in more different locations, countries, planes, busses and/or restaurants than we could count.

While we visited with Mrs. Matlock, she explained that listening bugs had been imbedded inside the walls of the Embassy when it had been built by Russian construction workers. It was such a serious situation that the Americans had to move out because they couldn't conduct any confidential business there, so were forced to use another office building as their Embassy. The residence was also bugged, and as a result, Mrs. Matlock was only allowed to hire American workers, and frequently had to make the beds herself, since there weren't enough "secure" maintenance people who could staff the building.

In all the embassies we visited, we were delighted to see representation by contemporary American artists, many of them from California. In particular, we saw works by Vasa and Laddie John Dill, artists whose work I owned long before I met Hal. Hal was not as enamored of contemporary art as I was, but once he saw so much of it gracing the walls of American Embassies all over the world, he developed a growing appreciation for it.

There was a huge USIA-sponsored cultural expo in progress in Leningrad, and while there, we were given tickets which we were told we could hand out to people who might have done us a special favor while we were in town, using the tickets like a tip. Those tickets would enable a recipient to go to the head of the line, which would have been a six-hour wait otherwise. The expo was housed in a massive building with booths staffed by young Americans who spoke fluent Russian showing off displays of American wares ranging from farm implements to electronics. The display that I thought was the most ingenious was a very large Xerox machine which was spewing out thousands of copies of the American Bill of Rights, printed in Cyrillic and eagerly being grabbed up by the thousands of Russians who flocked to the expo. What a good way to spread the word.

The local people we met in Leningrad were friendly and outgoing, much more so than the people we'd met in Moscow. But when we got to the airport in Leningrad, on our way back to Helsinki, the people working there were regimented and militant – and very intimidating. I found myself looking over my shoulder on occasion hoping there would be no glitches and that there would be nothing to delay our departure. So I was startled and admit that my heart skipped a couple of beats when we heard Hal's name being called out. But the voice had an American accent - a southern accent to be exact. It turned out to be Lanier and Karla Temerlin from Dallas, Texas, long-time friends of Hal's. They were traveling on business for the Pepsi Cola Company with Leo Tolstoy's grandson, who was on the staff of their advertising company which was based in Texas, and who still had great contacts in Russia.

When our Aeroflot flight from Leningrad finally landed in Helsinki, the passengers spontaneously started applauding, and great sighs of relief could be heard throughout the plane. I guess I wasn't the only one to feel so anxious about leaving. In those days, Russia was an interesting place to visit, but definitely not a place to linger for any length of time.

The U.S. Ambassador to Finland was Rockwell Schnabel, who happened to be from Southern California. While we were in Helsinki, he hosted our group at the home and studio of the famed Finnish architect Eliel Saarinen, which was built in 1902. Saarinen was one of the innovators of the minimalist movement, and his place offered great warmth, a unique use of space and material and what could be called "high tech" design, having a very recognizable Finnish flair: a stunning combination of elements. Ambassador Schnabel was a most genial host. His wife was back in Northridge, California, supervising the finishing touches on the Frank Gehry-designed home they were building there, because when President Reagan's term of office ended in a few months, so would Schnabel's appointment as Ambassador.

I remember during that junket, going to the studio in Munich where Radio Free Europe, which was under the auspices of the USIA, was broadcast and hearing people at microphones around the room speaking every language under the sun. They had a wide array of news-gathering monitors and mind boggling displays of equipment used to transmit information to the far corners of the world.

The head of the R.F.E. agency, A. Ross Johnson, invited us all to an Italian restaurant which he casually announced had been Adolf Hitler's favorite eatery. I'm not sure that would have been our first choice had we known that beforehand. In fact, the service was pretty bad, which I'm sure would not have been tolerated by Adolf.

Ambassador and Mrs. Joe Rogers were our representatives in Paris and being from Nashville, they were very familiar with, and very complimentary about, Hal's music. It turned out that they and Hal had many friends in common, so that made our visit there special. I think they were as excited to have us in Paris, as we were to be there.

Hal had been on one of these USIA trips before, and during his previous stop at the Ambassador's residence in Moscow, Mrs. Arthur Hartman, the-then-Ambassador's wife complained to him that they had no piano at the residency, and were therefore not able to entertain properly. When he returned to the U.S., Hal contacted the people at Steinway and arranged for a piano to be shipped to Russia as a gift for our Embassy. That was the sort of thing that the members of the USIA did. Hal represented the music industry. Other areas represented were book publishing, movies, advertising and similar areas that could be of help to our embassies overseas. When we visited with Shirley Temple Black, who at the time was the U.S. Ambassador to Czechoslovakia, she mentioned that she did not feel that the movies that were shown in that country accurately portrayed the American way of life. Through the USIA, Hal was able to see that a wider variety of movies were shown there.

The USIA once made a movie about Hal's life, showing how a child of immigrants to the United States could achieve success. Hal's parents both came to the United States from Austria when they were young children. The movie was titled *Hal David: Expressing a Feeling*. By law, it was only shown in Europe, but in 1985 Congress passed legislation allowing it to be shown in the United States as well. Hal was very proud that there had been a bill with his name on it passed by Congress regarding that video. Footnote: In case anyone wishes to read it, it is H.R. 2068, Section 212: Distribution within the United States of the USIA Film Entitled *Hal David: Expressing a Feeling*.

When the movie was being made and the camera crew joined Hal on a tour of the area where he grew up, they realized how badly the area had deteriorated from when Hal was a boy. It had always been a lower-middle class neighborhood, but now the building where his father's restaurant had been, housed a very seedy-looking bar, and the neighborhood where he had enjoyed such a wonderful childhood was totally blighted. Hal and the crew were afraid to get out of the car and passed on filming the site that was formerly David's Delicatessen. But, worse than that, when they went to Thomas Jefferson to film Hal at the high school from which he'd graduated, they were greeted by fierce-looking police dogs patrolling the halls, staring at them menacingly. Even though they'd gotten permission to do the filming there, no one had informed them about the dogs, who fortunately, turned out to be manageable enough to allow the filming to proceed.

For the last stop on our USIA junket we flew to Brussels, where we spent the whole day at NATO receiving a complete briefing of the world situation on subjects ranging from politics to currency and defense. We were able to ask NATO officials from all over the world, including the recently elected head of NATO, the former German Defense Minister Manfred Worner, who was visiting there at the time as many questions as we could think of, and believed that our provocative questions were answered candidly. We wondered how much of the forward planning being done there would come to fruition, especially the plan to unify money to be used jointly by a wide group of European nations starting in 1992. That currency was going to be called the "euro."

Long before I knew Hal, I'd been appointed by Deane Dana, a Los Angeles County Supervisor, to serve as a Commissioner to the Los Angeles County Music and Performing Arts commission. My name was suggested to Dana because of my experience in having served on the boards of numerous arts organizations over the years.

One morning after Hal and I returned from the USIA trip, I drove downtown in October for my monthly meeting. On arriving, I was told that there was an urgent message for me from my husband. Naturally my first thought was that Hal was ill. But when I reached him on the phone he said, "How soon can you get back home?" It turned out that President Ronald Reagan was going to be signing the Berne Convention into law at the Beverly Hills Hotel, and Hal and I had been invited to watch the ceremony. The Berne Convention dealt with copyright and intellectual property law and Hal had testified before Congress numerous times on the importance of those issues.

I'm sure I broke every law in the book driving back from downtown Los Angeles to our apartment in Beverly Hills to pick up Hal. Hal and I had front row seats as we watched President Reagan sign that significant bill into law. It meant a great deal to songwriters as well as filmmakers, authors, and anyone else who owned intellectual property. It was a landmark occasion, and we were proud to have witnessed it being born.

Just a month later, Hal and I travelled to South America for a CISAC meeting, this one being held in Buenos Aires, Argentina. A few days prior to the meeting we took a side trip to Iguazu Falls, waterfalls being one of my favorite things. The Falls were spectacular, justifiably considered one of the great natural wonders of the world. We saw them from the Argentinian side, as well as from Paraguay, but I knew that at some point in time we'd have to come back to see them from the Brazilian side, said to provide the most spectacular view. And so we did, many years later.

In the late 1980's, the cab drivers in Buenos Aires were renowned for trying to gouge their passengers. Most hotels advised their guests to ask a driver beforehand what the fare would be, and to not pay the drivers until they arrived back at the hotel, so the doorman could oversee the transaction. But the drivers had gotten wise to that, and they had tricks up their sleeves. One night we were returning from dinner with our friend, the composer/conductor Morton Gould, who had a reputation for having unbelievable mishaps with New York cabbies. So when our driver stopped a block or so before our hotel and pointed to a red light on the dashboard indicating that something was wrong with his car and that it could not go any further, we weren't at all surprised, having Mr. Cab-Driver-Jinx with us. The driver insisted that we pay him twice what we knew the fee was supposed to be. When we tried to argue with him, he just threw up his hands and pointed to our hotel, indicating that we should start walking, because his car was not working. No sooner had we gotten out of the car, but the door slammed behind us, and miraculously, the driver took off at the speed of lightning, with his taxi in perfect working order. Another lesson learned the hard way!

We were in and out of New York early in 1989, and also took an extended trip to Australia and New Zealand. While we thoroughly enjoyed ourselves there, we didn't go just on a whim. A year prior to our trip, John Sturman, the beloved head of the Australian performing rights society, APRA, told me that Hal was going to be honored by APRA at their annual gala, asking me to keep it a secret.

We arrived in Australia in May of 1989, with Hal thinking he'd only been invited to present some of the awards at the annual APRA event, which, was the ruse to get him there, but which he was actually going to do.

Since we were going to be in Australia, we decided to go to New Zealand, prior to arriving in Sydney. I was something of a daredevil when I was young, learning to fly at an early age, and always willing to take all sorts of risks, including a parachute jump. Hal was much more conservative in that area than I was, but since we'd been married I'd taken him along with me on some pretty harrowing adventures. So it was, that in Queenstown, New Zealand, Hal grudgingly accompanied me on a Helisuper Jet ride over the Shotover River.

The Superjet pilots were real daredevils, swooping as close to the mountains as they could get, while flying at a very precarious angle almost as though they intended to land vertically on the side of the mountain. Once the pilot was sure our stomachs had jumped up into our throats, he would swoop down to land in the river. Hal was a little green when we finally came down but he was a good sport about it.

When we finally arrived in Sydney, we were ensconced in the beautiful Regent Hotel overlooking the Sydney Opera House and bridge, brilliantly lit at night with hundreds of lights; a magnificent sight to see.

The morning of the awards gala, Hal was interviewed on Australian radio. The interviewer, evidently trying to be provocative, rather sneeringly asked Hal, (while "I'll Never Fall in Love Again" was being played in the background), How do you feel today about lyrics like "What do you get when you kiss a guy, you get enough germs to catch pneumonia? After you do, he'll never phone ya." Hal never skipped a beat and just calmly looked at him and pointed out, "Those lyrics have held up pretty well all these years, haven't they?" The engineer sitting next to me in the sound-proofed booth actually started applauding.

Then it was time for the awards banquet. The ceremonies went smoothly, and after Hal handed out the last award, he stepped down from the stage and started to make his way to our table. Behind Hal's back a huge screen rolled down, and a wonderful video chronicling his accomplishments began to unfold. There were pictures of Dionne Warwick being interviewed, along with many others who had worked with Hal, and videos of different artists singing Hal David lyrics that they had helped to make famous. I could see the uncertain look on Hal's face as he approached our table; he thought the evening was over, and he wondered why his music was being played. At that point, The Honorable Clyde Holding, Federal Minister for the Arts and Territories of Australia called Hal back to the stage. When he returned to the mike, he was absolutely speechless as the whole audience rose as one to honor him. It was a very touching moment, and I was glad I'd managed to keep it secret all year.

When we returned to Los Angeles, Hal went to the studio of talented photographer Vicki Milhich (who was once married to the Yugoslavian artist Vasa, a good friend of ours), to have a new head shot taken. It came out just great, and we've used it ever since to send an autographed copy to fans, for program books for shows that Hal has been in, etc. - it is ageless.

Hal has been asked to write songs about unusual subjects from time to time. Take, for example, "A House is Not a Home," which was written for the Joe Levine movie of the same name about the infamous madam, Polly Adler, whose house was definitely not a home. Hal especially enjoyed Luther Vandross' version, and fondly remembered that once when Luther spotted us in the audience of a charity event he came right to the edge of the stage, knelt down, and sang it directly to Hal and me.

Hal always said that he never got the easy assignments. But in June of 1989, he was given a real challenge when he was asked to write English lyrics for a melody that was going to be written by a Japanese composer, Katsuhisa Hatori to commemorate the peace that followed the bombing of Hiroshima toward the end of World War II. But Hal agreed to do it and we soon found ourselves on our way to the opening of an International Festival in Hiroshima, Japan. The song was to be played for both the opening and closing sessions,

Hal.
Photo by Vicki Milhich.

and Hal was donating all proceeds from it to a charitable organization in Hiroshima that helped Japanese children.

In Tokyo we were met with great ceremony by a large delegation, and whisked to a room where a huge traditional Japanese banquet awaited us, including lengthy toasts made by everyone in the room, and reciprocated by us. The toasts were fine, but getting up from the floor each time one was given was the equivalent of a good aerobic workout and our legs were really sore by the end of the evening.

Once in Hiroshima, we were taken on a tour of the extensive Festival grounds, which covered many acres and were filled with a wide variety of colorful Disneyland-type rides and an equally wide variety of Asian products and displays of technology.

The Peace Museum on the festival grounds was devoted entirely to graphic descriptions of the aftermath of the Atom bomb, grisly reminders of what happened to both people and structures. Hal and I realized that we were the only Caucasians in the building, and I wanted to run away and hide somewhere. But then I realized that, just as the Holocaust must be remembered, Hiroshima too cannot be forgotten, in the hopes that valuable lessons may be learned from it. It was that positive theme that Hal chose to reflect in the lyrics he wrote:

Trees have learned how to grow
Streams have learned how to flow
I know that if we learn how to be kind
We will find happiness to share

Make the child understand
Start by touching his hand
I know that if we're taught the ways of love
There'll be love here and everywhere

Hiroshima, hear my song
Singing out to every girl and boy
Hiroshima, hear my prayer
May the world we give them give them joy - Hiroshima

Time makes everything heal

Faith has much to reveal
I know that love can spread its wings and fly
Through the sky
Reaching everyone

Dreams are filling my heart
Hope is ready to start
I know that love can day by day increase
Bringing peace - peace to everyone

Hiroshima, hear my song
Singing out to every girl and boy
Hiroshima, hear my prayer
May the world we give them give them joy – Hiroshima

The song was sung by a chorus of young children, all in different native costumes, and with their sincere, innocent faces and sweet young voices, it was very moving. A recording was made by two young Japanese singers, and Hal was told that it did very well in the Asian market.

In August we took a Black Sea cruise and spent our first wedding anniversary aboard the ship, docked in Odessa, Russia. The chef prepared a special Russian meal for us, with plenty of caviar to commemorate the occasion, along with borscht, a fish soup called ukha, and some jellied pieces of pork called kholodets. Naturally the meal would not have been complete without pirozhki, topped off with fried curd fritters called syrniki. Since we were unfamiliar with most of the selections, and not sure we really liked some of them, the accompanying vodka we consumed was a big help.

We continued to seesaw back and forth between Los Angeles and New York, enjoying ourselves in each city and widening our circle of friends. But one particular east coast event stood out that year. In October, at the height of the leaf- peeping time, Hal was asked to perform at a fundraiser for the Berkshire Theatre in Stockbridge, Massachusetts. The show was called *Thanks for the Melodies* and featured ASCAP members singing songs from Broadway shows they'd written. Each songwriter was asked to bring someone who had appeared in the show to perform with them. Hal brought Jill O'Hara, who had been the ingénue in the original production of *Promises, Promises,* a musical, written by Burt Bacharach and Hal David, with a book by Neil Simon, *Promises, Promises* is based on the 1960's film *The Apartment,* which starred Jack Lemmon and Shirley Maclaine. The original Broadway production had premiered in 1968, with Jerry Orbach as Chuck Baxter, the lead, and Jill O'Hara, playing Fran. Orbach, who later went on to star as Det. Lennie Briscoe in the long-running TV show Law and Order, won the Tony for Best Performance by a Leading Actor in a Musical, and Marian Mercer won a Tony for Best Performance by a Featured Actress in a Musical. Burt Bacharach also won the Tony that year for Outstanding Music.

The first song Hal wrote for that show was "She Likes Basketball," and he had a reason for that. He explained that from the time he accepted an assignment until he finished it, he would go through a number of emotional stages. At the beginning, he'd be very excited, and couldn't wait to get started. Then, when it was actually time to start, he would become terrified, fearing that he wouldn't be able to do it. So while the first lyric he wrote wasn't always the one that wound up being the most important, just writing it calmed his fears enough so that he could continue working with some degree of calm and relaxation.

Hal was on the track team when he was in high school, but he'd joked about his delusions of grandeur because he wanted to be a basketball player, and given that he was only 5'10", that didn't happen. He said he always thought he was meant to be 6'7", and that led him to come up with the lyric for that first song he wrote for *Promises,* "She Likes Basketball."

Hal and Burt had written a song for the opening of the second act which they thought was great. Producer David Merrick liked it, as did choreographer Michael Bennett and everyone connected with the production. The only problem was that the preview audiences in Boston didn't like it! Burt and Hal were supposed to come up with a song for the new opening scene Neil Simon was writing to replace it, but Burt suddenly got so sick that he was hospitalized with pneumonia. Merrick was frantic because they needed the new song "yesterday" and he even threatened to bring in another composer to write a song for that one scene. Hal, not wanting anyone else brought in did what he did best: he sat down and started writing a lyric, to reassure Mr. Merrick that a song was in the works.

In the scene for the song, Fran has taken some sleeping pills after the breakup of an affair. She is revived, and as she strums a guitar, she sings a song.

Hal, once again drawing on life for his inspiration, obviously had the hospitalized Burt in mind when he wrote the much maligned, yet unforgettable rhyme, of "pneumonia" and "phone you:"

What do you get when you kiss a guy?
You get enough germs to catch pneumonia.
After you do, he'll never phone you....

Once Burt got out of the hospital, he sat hunched over at the piano, wrapped up in a warm coat, and pounded out the memorable melody to "I'll Never Fall in Love Again." The first night it was sung it stopped the show, receiving a standing ovation, and soon became a huge hit.

Hal remembered the months when *Promises, Promises* was on the road before coming to Broadway as a series of marvelous moments and not-so- marvelous hotel rooms. There were no temperamental outbursts, no arguments, and no petty jealousies. Everyone respected and got along with each other. Hal felt that all of his collaborators were not only nice guys but that they were exceptionally talented. Unashamedly stage-struck, he always hoped that he'd get tapped to write another Broadway show, intense as the experience was.

But Burt, being the perfectionist that he was, was unhappy with the experience because the songs sounded different at every performance. Neither of them ever did another Broadway show together, although Hal tried a couple of times with other composers. One was for a show called *Brainchild*, to which Michel Legrand wrote a beautiful score, but the show closed during out of town previews.

Still pending, but probably never going to be produced on Broadway, are *The Chosen,* and *Turning Point,* both of which Hal wrote with Charles Fox, and *Lady for a Day,* which he wrote with Charles Strouse.

The original show *Promises, Promises* ran for one thousand two hundred and eighty-one performances, with the cast album winning the Grammy Award for best cast recording. Two of the songs from the show, "I'll Never Fall in Love Again" and "Promises, Promises," became big singles hits for Dionne Warwick, and "Promises, Promises" won her a Grammy. The 1968 show, produced by David Merrick, was directed by Robert Moore and brilliantly choreographed by Michael Bennett. A national tour, starring Melissa Hart as Fran, toured throughout the United States during the 1970's.

In 1969 the show was performed at the Prince of Wales Theatre in the West End of London. That production starred Tony Roberts and Betty Buckley, and ran for five hundred and sixty performances.

One of the touring shows was produced at the Goodspeed Opera House in Connecticut in 1993, starring Evan Pappas and Juliette Lambert.

Encores!, the New York entity which produced great American musicals in concert form, showcased *Promises, Promises* at City Center in March of 1996 starring Christine Baranski and Martin Short. Howard Wassel's review in the *New York Daily News* of that show, in part, read, "Neil Simon's book is a marvelous springboard for comic performances by Christine Baranski, Dick Latessa, and Terrence Mann. Kerry O'Malley makes the heroine far more appealing than I remember her thirty years ago. But the true hero is the totally adorable Martin Short who makes the cynical woebegone hero irresistible. The score is superbly served by conductor Rob Fisher, both in its flashy exuberance, and the quiet handling of its hit song, "I'll Never Fall in Love Again."

The Reprise Theatre opened their first season in Los Angeles in 1997, with *Promises, Promises,* starring Jason Alexander as Chuck, Karen Fineman as Fran, and Jean Smart as Marge. It was so successful that they performed it twice that same year.

Promises had its first Broadway revival in 2010, with that production starring Sean Hayes and Kristin Chenoweth. It performed to sold-out houses at the seventeen-hundred-and-sixty-seat Broadway Theater. Fans applauded wildly when two Bacharach-David songs were added to the score: "I Say a Little Prayer" and "A House is Not a Home." Both songs, big hits previously recorded by Dionne Warwick, were given to Kristin Chenoweth to perform in the show to round out her role.

While in New York, after the Berkshire Theatre Production, we attended a memorial for Joe Raposo, held at the Pierre Ballroom. Joe, a longtime friend of Hal's, was perhaps best known for his work on the children's television series *Sesame Street,* and for writing the theme songs for *The Electric Company, Shining Time Station, Three's Company,* and *The Ropers.* Liz Smith, the gossip columnist for the *New York Daily News* was the Mistress of Ceremonies. Jim Henson, who created the characters on *Sesame Street,* and the journalist Walter Cronkite both recalled their fond memories of Joe.

Hal had written several songs with Joe, including "America Is," which was played during the opening ceremonies for the refurbished Statue of Liberty gala in 1986. Pat Collins, Joe's wife, asked Hal to be interviewed for a video which was being made about Joe. In an interview with Merv Griffin, many years earlier Hal had said how excited he was when he was asked to write the song for the re-opening of the Statue of Liberty, given that his parents had come from Austria to the States through Ellis Island when they were quite young.

This evening, Hal told about writing a song with Joe for First Lady Nancy Reagan's Foster Grandparent program. When the program was launched it was suggested that it would be a good idea to have a song to go along with her book about the program, *To Love a Child*. She had her agent contact Hal to see if he would write it. Hal loved the idea and contacted Joe Raposo to compose the music to his lyric. When the song was finished, Hal called the First Lady and said that he and Joe would like to come to Washington, D.C. to play the song for her. But she replied that they'd gone to the trouble of writing the song for her and they shouldn't have to be the ones to travel; she would come to them.

Prior to her visit to Hal's office in the ASCAP building in New York, Secret Service men scouted out the building, and commandeered one of the elevators exclusively for Mrs. Reagan's use. Then they thoroughly checked the ASCAP offices, and Hal's office in particular, to make sure that the First Lady would be comfortable and safe.

Only then did she arrive to listen to the song and her heartfelt response was caught on film: she was so affected that she actually cried.

Afterward, it had to be decided who was going to sing the song. Nancy, without any hesitation, recommended Frank Sinatra, who was immediately brought into the project.

Before the year 1989 was out, we had the privilege of meeting and spending some quality time with Doris Kearns Goodwin, the Pulitzer Prize-winning presidential biographer, historian, and political commentator. Hal was especially interested in getting to know Doris because he was such a history buff. Even though she was a few years away from writing Team of Rivals, we knew the Civil War period was of interest to her, as it was to Hal. Doris and her husband Richard Goodwin, who was an advisor and speechwriter to Presidents Kennedy and Johnson, were renting the Brentwood, California home of friends of ours while Richard was working on a movie based on his experience as special counsel to the Legislative Oversight Subcommittee of the U.S. House of Representatives.

Richard, while still a very young man, had uncovered the scandal that arose regarding answers being fed to contestants on the game show *Twenty-One*, causing networks to cancel quiz shows and prompting Congress to pass amendments to the Communications Act of 1934, preventing anyone from again fixing quiz shows.

The movie that Richard was working on, which came out in 1994, was titled *Quiz Show*.

The well-known Broadway producer Alexander Cohen asked Hal to appear on a television special he was putting together titled Night of a 100 Stars. The show was going to be filmed live on May 5, 1990 at Radio City Music Hall. But Hal had already committed to being the keynote speaker on May 4 in Los Angeles at an Independent Music Conference dinner, and had already written his speech. Cohen, however persisted, arranging for a driver to pick us up in Los Angeles right after Hal's speech, and put us on the red-eye to New York, which we good-naturedly agreed to take (we were young then). From JFK, we were whisked to our apartment where we quickly freshened up, before dashing the few blocks over to Radio City so Hal could have a quick rehearsal.

I always found it great fun to be involved in Hal's rehearsals, and I had a grand time in the Green Room, talking with all the celebrities who were waiting for their rehearsal times. Katherine Hepburn, whom I had always admired, left me tongue tied, even though I was dying to ask her about Spenser Tracy.

In the number that Hal was in, which had been conceived by Karen Sherry and Bill Harback, songwriters were seated at gleaming white pianos which were hydraulically raised from below stage level to form a pyramid. Beside each piano was a singer who had made one of the writer's songs popular. The songwriters would play the piano, and the singers would sing, making the whole thing very glamorous and exciting. The only problem was that Hal couldn't play the piano. But with a little coaching by Karen and me, he looked very convincing on TV as he faked it, moving his hands over the keys, and bopping in time to the music as though he was really playing.

Some of the others writers in the scene, besides Hal were: Charles Strouse, Marilyn and Alan Bergman, Cy Coleman, and Diane Warren. Some of the singers were Marilyn McCoo, B. J. Thomas (for "Raindrops") Carol Channing, Debbie Boone, Peggy Lee and Gladys Knight. That segment of the show was a real smash! It was the hit of the two-hour special, as far as I was concerned.

Hal and I both got a kick out of what happened when we walked out of the stage door after the rehearsals. A fellow standing there with a stack of sheet music in his arms, approached Hal and said, "I know you're somebody. But will you just tell me your name?" Taken aback, Hal gave the fellow his name, and he immediately separated out at least ten pieces of sheet music of Hal's songs and asked for Hal's autograph on each of them. For a long time, I teased Hal by telling him that with that, I was finally persuaded that he was "somebody."

In May, when we were in D.C. for the annual show that ASCAP produced as a thank you to legislators who helped songwriters with intellectual property rights, I was with Hal and the Board members of ASCAP as they "walked the halls" of Congress, having just accompanied Hal when he and Henry Mancini had talked to a group of Senators, showing scenes from movies with and without music. (It was a program similar to the one they presented for the New York City Festival of the Arts.) From there, we had dashed to the Senate building where Hal and Hank, along with a group of other songwriters, were going to visit Ted Kennedy in his office. I was sitting alone outside of Kennedy's office when Ben Palumbo, the ASCAP lobbyist, came to tell me I'd been invited into Kennedy's inner sanctum.

The songwriters crammed into the office on that auspicious occasion were Lyle Lovett, Burton Lane, Sammy Cahn, Henry Mancini, Marilyn and Alan Bergman, Johnny Mandell, Cy Coleman, Hal David and Mike Stoller: quite an impressive group by anyone's standards!

Kennedy said, "Listen, you guys, I know why you're here, and I'll do everything I can to help you. Now what I really want is to hear some of your songs." With that, each writer sat down at the piano Kennedy had had arranged to have brought into his office, and played a few "and then I wrotes." Cy started off by playing some of his own songs, and then said, "Okay, Hal, now it's your turn" and with that, Cy accompanied Hal as he sang "Raindrops," with everyone, including Kennedy, joining in.

It was quite a high-powered private cabaret show that Kennedy managed to make happen right there in his office that day.

On our way to board a cruise ship which would take us through the magnificent fjords of Norway, we stopped in London because we'd been invited to have dinner with Andrew Lloyd Webber and Sarah Brightman, who were married at the time. Upon arriving at Andrew's three-hundred-and-fifty-acre estate called Sydmonton Court in Hampshire which was about an hour and a half drive out of London, Andrew greeted us at the door with a big hug for Hal, saying that Hal was someone he had always admired, and had always wanted to meet. Of course that endeared him to me and I sincerely told him what a fan of his I was, which Hal corroborated telling him I'd seen Evita more times than I could count.

We found Andrew charming, but had no answer when he asked us why we thought his shows had been so severely panned by New York critics, especially Frank Rich of *The New York Times*. Hal could only add his compliments to mine about Andrew's works, and Andrew seemed genuinely touched. With all of Andrew's tremendous success, he seemed really hurt by those negative reviews, even though his shows went on to great success in spite of them.

Andrew gave us a tour of his home, pointing out some of his favorite paintings and antiques. We had a "simple" family dinner at a long refectory table in the kitchen, an enormous yet cozy room with a huge restaurant-sized cooking area where the chef was slaving over the proverbial hot stove and there were two in help waiting to serve us. Andrew and Sarah seemed a bit preoccupied during dinner, but we thought they were possibly distracted by all the work facing them for some upcoming show.

Given their interaction with one another, it should not have been a surprise when only a few days later we learned, while we were on the ship, that they had separated. Our visit to Sydmonton Court may have been the last time that Andrew and Sarah had been together.

August found us invited to the Occidental Petroleum offices of Armand Hammer in Westwood, California, for a luncheon to meet Senator Al Gore, who was making his first run for President. No doubt our names were on the guest list because Gore knew Hal from having worked with him on some copyright matters.

Hammer's offices in a high-rise building at the corner of Wilshire and Westwood Boulevards were beautiful, but the big attraction was the zillion-dollar private art collection that was housed there, before the Hammer Museum was built. Armand Hammer was a remarkable, energetic man. He was then well into his nineties, and had just flown in from Washington, D.C. on his private jet, in time to host this luncheon. When the speeches were over, he suggested we all linger over our coffee and visit with Al Gore, even though he himself was headed back to the airport to return to D.C. to finish whatever business he had there. It rather put us "youngsters" to shame.

Our second anniversary was fast approaching, and we could hardly believe that the time had gone by so quickly. Hal and I were deliriously happy, and having the time of our lives. I still felt like pinching myself to make sure that I wasn't dreaming about the wonderful life we were leading. Whenever we had a party, or a special gathering, Hal always told our guests that he had never been happier in his life. My life was full of love both for and from my husband, and my friends who had been through thick and thin with me in the past were very happy for me now.

So it was seemed time for a celebration. I went right back to the Equitable Building where we'd been married, and planned a big second anniversary party. The hundred or so people whom we invited had a great time, dancing to the music that had been written by many of the people in the room. We hadn't expected it, but friends spontaneously got up to make warm and funny comments about Hal and me: Hal's friends Abby and Aaron Schroeder spoke about their long friendship with Hal, and how happy they were to now have me in their lives, and Richard Rosenthal turned the tables and spoke about his long standing friendship with me and how happy he and his wife Hinda were to count Hal amongst their friends, and how happy they were for us in our new life.

Hope Warner, in from Los Angeles with her husband Lee, spoke in the warm and charming way that only she could, and joked about my telling her how I had met someone whose name I didn't recognize, even though she knew who he was! Louise Wheeler from the USIA office and Bill Harwood, both in from Washington, D.C. told some delightful stories about having spent time with us when we were on our honeymoon with the USIA group in Russia and the other countries we visited at that time. A magical night indeed!

It was during this period of time that Hal and Charles Strouse started working on the score of a musical based on a Damon Runyon story about Apple Annie that they hoped was going to be produced by Peter Tear, who, even though he was a first-time producer, assured them that he had all the money secured. However, as of this writing, some twenty-five years later, the show has still not been produced; but the music that Charles and Hal wrote for its colorful characters remains wonderful.

One song in particular that Hal and Charlie wrote for the show became one of my favorites, and Hal sang it for me whenever we had a party or some special event.

It was called "Too Young to be Old." The title tells the story, which I felt fit us to a tee.

> We've been around, we two
> That doesn't mean we're through
> We may be too old to be young
> But I'm sure we're too young to be old.

> We're not two kids, I know
> Who says we still can't grow
> We may be too old to be young
> But I'm sure we're too young to be old.

> It's not how they do it in the movies
> It's not how they do it in a play
> It isn't how they tell it in a love song
> But in real life it happens this way.

> Don't let this chance go by
> Love should be worth a try
> We may be too old to be young
> But I'm sure we're too young to be old.

Our next trip in 1990 took us, with friends, from New York to Lucerne, to Zurich, then on to Prague, where we had an appointment to meet with Shirley Temple Black, former child movie star who, when just a curly-haired little girl, had saved the Fox studios from bankruptcy in the 1930's. When we met with her, she was serving as the U.S. Ambassador to Czechoslovakia.

We arrived in Prague just in time to check into the Diplomat Hotel and change for the opera. The opera house was everything we had anticipated: rococo and gilt to the nth degree.

At the first interval, we drifted into the ornate lobby, which was crowded with elegantly dressed people milling around. Suddenly, from out of the crowd, we heard someone calling "Hol, Hol." We couldn't imagine it was meant for us, but as Hal turned around, he recognized a big, burly fellow barreling towards us with his arms outstretched.

It was Boris Pankin, formerly head of VAAP in the USSR. VAAP was the Russian Performing Rights Society. Boris had been the head of VAAP when Hal was President of ASCAP, so they had come in contact with each other frequently. Boris had entertained Hal in Moscow, and Hal had the opportunity to reciprocate when Pankin came to the United States.

Here he was bearing down on us with a huge smile on his face. He embraced Hal in a big bear hug and then we were introduced all around. He explained that he was now the Ambassador to Czechoslovakia from the USSR.

That was certainly an unexpected welcome to Prague. Hal realized later that Boris had spoken to us in perfect, if slightly accented English. All the time Hal knew him in the past, he'd always used an interpreter, claiming not to understand our language. Now Hal recognized what a ploy it had been since Pankin understood and spoke English very well.

Czechoslovakia had just achieved its independence, after having been under Soviet rule for over forty years. The spirit of the people was remarkable. Everyone we met on the street was friendly, and seemed to have a happy and optimistic outlook. Stores were well-stocked with consumer goods, and people were converting state-owned stores and restaurants to privately-owned establishments. Many told us that although they were somewhat short on capital, they were getting groups together so they could buy their own businesses. The future looked promising.

We were told that we had been allocated only fifteen minutes with Ambassador Black, but it turned out that Madame Ambassador was just as welcoming as she could possibly be, with her still distinctive dimples reminding us of her childhood image of yore, and she asked so many questions about Hal's work that we were with her for more than an hour.

At some time during that hour, Hal and I mentioned that we were going to the Old Royal Castle, the former Prague Palace, to be part of a contingent presenting then-President Havel a medal of honor. Ambassador Black said she was aware of the event, but had not received an invitation to attend. In fact, she confided to us that she was somewhat put out that she hadn't been invited, having been told that it was for "artists" only, not politicians. After we left, we tried to get her an invitation based on her movie work, but I guess someone in charge didn't think it qualified as "artistic" enough, so we were unsuccessful.

We joined a small group gathered in front of the Cathedral of Saint Wenceslas at the appointed time and were duly escorted into the jewel of a castle that sat high on the hill above the city. It was ornate - gilt and crystal in the very best of taste. It made me want to whisper in awe, it was so elegant.

Before long, President Václav Havel strode down along an Oriental carpet, right in my direction. When he got close, I held up my camera as if to ask if it was okay to take his picture. He gave me a big friendly smile and nodded, so I started snapping away and caught a great spontaneous shot of him and Hal.

A professional photographer had been hired to take a group picture of those presenting the award. I decided that rather than be in the picture myself, I wanted to get my very own group picture, so I found what I thought was just the perfect spot to get the best shot. The professional photographer wasn't too happy with me because that turned out to be the very spot that he wanted. In retrospect, I'm surprised I wasn't kicked out of there. Later on, ASCAP kept requesting the group photo from the photographer, but it never arrived. When they learned that I had taken my own group picture, they asked if they could use it for the ASCAP newsletter. Not only did they use it, I even got credit for it!

For many years, Hal was on the Artist's Committee of the Kennedy Center Honors. We spent the most glamorous three-day December weekends in D.C. for about ten years in a row, the highlight of which was always the black tie dinner hosted by the Secretary of State, held in the beautiful State House, where the honorees received their medallions.

I recall at one dinner, Senator Dennis Webster DeConcini from Arizona who sat next to me said, "We legislators spend the night looking at all you celebrities and you celebrities spend all night looking at us!" He was right.

At one of these dinners, Hal was seated next to Mrs. Rex Harrison. They were chatting about an album that Rex had just completed for Columbia Records and she mentioned a few of the songs that were on the album, one of which was "Everyone's out of Town." When Hal told her that he and Burt had written it, she said it was Rex's favorite, and called across the table to tell her husband that Hal had written that song. Out of that chance connection, Hal and Rex became good friends.

On the second day of the event, brunch was followed by a late afternoon visit to the White House before going on to the Kennedy Center for the Honors show.

The White House was always elegantly decorated for Christmas with a huge Christmas tree laden with gorgeous ornaments dominating the entrance and with the Marine band playing stirring holiday music: The whole building was aglow with twinkling lights and elaborate Christmas décor. After partaking of the buffet of hors d'oeuvres we were ushered into a large room with a dais at one end. There the President and First Lady would be seated along with the honorees, and the President would introduce the honorees once again. Finally, before leaving for the Kennedy Center, we would have the opportunity to go through a receiving line, where we were able to shake the President's hand and have a picture taken with him.

I remember one year we saw the Bush grandchildren peeking out through the bannister at all the guests. And a highlight from another year was the conversation we had with Pamela Harriman, who was on her way to Paris after being appointed by President Bill Clinton as Ambassador to France. She said she was quaking in her boots at the job ahead of her, but at the same time she was really looking forward to the experience. There was always something exciting to remember from each of the years we attended those events, as for example in 1990, when George H.W. Bush was President and we patiently waited in the long receiving line with all the others. It was protocol to shake the President's hand, turn for the photo op with the President and First Lady, and then move on quickly so the next people in line could have their turn. But this time, when we were introduced to President Bush, he gustily sang out a snippet of "Raindrops" holding up the line to the consternation of those people in charge but to the delight of those around us.

ASCAP annually hosted a black tie dinner to honor composers who wrote film music. The year that Elmer Bernstein was honored, Burt Lancaster told how he got into films, many of them with music by Elmer. Hal and I had our picture taken with Lancaster, but didn't notice his wife, Susie, who had been standing on the sidelines.

I only learned that Susie had been there a good twenty-two years later, when, both being widows, we became great pals.

It was my pleasure to host a birthday luncheon for my mother at Hillcrest. They were always thrilled when they spotted George Burns entering the Club.

Burt Lancaster and Hal David.
Permission to use granted by Jane Payne, trustee, Burton Lancaster 1988

They'd giggle and carry on like teenagers whenever they saw him. So one year I asked George if he would come over to the table to say hi to the "girls," and he agreed to do so. When he arrived, he wanted to know who the birthday girl was. When my mother timidly raised her hand, he winked at her, and giving her a big kiss said, "So, what are you doing tonight, kid?" My mother and her friends dined out on that one for years.

On January 16th, 1991, Hal and I were having dinner at one of our favorite New York restaurants, Shun Lee Palace, on East Fifty Fifth Street. As we were finishing our meal, the captain quietly went from table to table, saying "It has begun." He was referring to the Gulf War. Problems in the Middle East had been escalating rapidly, and economic sanctions which had been approved and implemented by the United Nations had failed to stop Saddam Hussein from invading Kuwait, torturing their citizens, and trying to take over their oil wells in order to control the world markets.

We were riveted by the news over the next few days and watched our television sets almost 24/7 as "Desert Storm" raged.

That first night, I couldn't sleep, and almost every half hour or so I would pad out of bed to watch some horror unfolding before my very eyes. It was hypnotic. Rather than having to wait for newspaper headlines, we were right there, embedded with the reporters, as they ducked bullets, dealt with blackouts, and surreptitiously reported from hidden command posts, even though Hussein had banned their broadcasts. It was a very sobering experience. We may not have won the war, but the Gulf War had united America in a wave of patriotism not seen since WWII. If nothing else, it did accomplish that.

Like many others, Hal and I decided to boycott France and French products since France would not let our planes fly over their airspace, which would have been a big help to us and our allies. Some people stopped buying French perfume and clothes and food made in France, and at one point there was even a plot afoot to call "French Fries" "Freedom Fries." The boycotting didn't last too long, however; French products were just too irresistible. But we did decide that we wouldn't vacation in the South of France that August as we had been doing for the past few years.

The day after Desert Storm started, when we flew back to Los Angeles we were searched at the airport more carefully than ever before and our luggage was more thoroughly screened than usual - a forerunner of what was to come in the years after 9/11.

The ASCAP Board was scheduled to meet in Los Angeles just a few weeks later in February, and they debated as to whether or not have their east coast members fly during this troubling time. They finally decided to stick to their plan to present the Los Angeles tribute to the late, great composer Jimmy Van Heusen. Artists in that show included Frank Sinatra, Bob Hope, the McGuire Sisters, Angie Dickinson, and Sammy Cahn. Frank Sinatra insisted on being the first performer on stage and said he was going to start singing at 7:30 on the dot, even if the audience wasn't fully seated by then, and he added that he would only agree to one picture being taken, and that would be with Hal David, even though Morton Gould was the president of ASCAP at that time. Bob Hope and Stanley Adams (a former ASCAP president) managed to get into the photo with Sinatra and Hal and, as can be seen, Sinatra was smiling, so I guess their presence in it was okay with him.

Hal, Frank Sinatra, Stanley Adams, and Bob Hope.
February 14, 1991: Memorial tribute to Jimmy van Heusen. Photo courtesy of ASCAP.

Toward the end of the year we travelled to China where Hal was going to be a judge at an Asian Song Festival in Shanghai. I had been to China with a Young Presidents Organization group in the early 1980's, and at that time, the trip had been arduous. The hotels were filthy; towels were in shreds and changed haphazardly; linens were dingy; the rooms were dark and small, and service practically nil. Conditions were not a great deal better on this trip, except that we were traveling under the auspices of the Chinese government so we were treated with great respect.

Because of our USIA connection, we let the State Department know where we were going whenever we travelled outside of the country, which we frequently did. When they learned that we were going to be in Peking (as it was still called then), they asked Hal if he would mind sitting in on some copyright negotiations between the Chinese and United States governments. The Chinese were considering entering into copyright agreements similar to those most other countries have with each other, but they weren't quite ready to accept all the conditions which would be incumbent upon them. Hal, who was considered to be quite an expert on this subject, agreed to meet with the Chinese officials, and a luncheon was planned, to be attended by all the negotiating parties (with me included).

We first met with the U.S. Ambassador to China, Mr. J. Stapleton Roy, who was grateful to Hal for agreeing to help with this sticky matter, who coached both Hal and me regarding some of the issues that were being negotiated.

At the luncheon, the people from the Embassy tried their best to explain to the people attending the luncheon just who Hal was, but we could tell that what they were saying meant nothing to the Chinese delegation. Finally, one of the English-speaking Chinese lawyers wrote "Raindrops Keep Fallin' on My Head" in Chinese symbols, and passed it around the room. Suddenly big smiles appeared and heads began to nod in recognition.

At one point I signaled to the translator: I wanted to show everyone the watch I was wearing which, on its face, had a picture of a couple riding on a bicycle. When I pushed a button, "Raindrops" played as the second hand jiggled back and forth, keeping time to the music. The Chinese were intrigued by this and the composers grew even more excited when Hal explained that he received a royalty from the watchmakers in exchange for allowing them to use the music. As one composer told us when the Chinese government wanted him to write a song, he was told to do so and he was then paid a small sum of money just that one time. The song could then be played forever, but he received no royalties for it. When Hal explained the way it works in the United States, the composers and writers in the room were ready to sign on the dotted line.

About a month later we read that the Chinese government signed the Berne Convention agreement, and we felt pleased at the idea that we may have influenced their decision to do so at that luncheon. Maybe I even had a small hand in encouraging them to sign.

After sightseeing in China, we flew to Shanghai. As well as being asked to be a judge at the Asia Song Festival in Shanghai, Hal was asked to write the English lyrics to a song which was going to be performed at the opening night ceremonies. He called it "Sky Never Ends," and in it he describes how there is no place too far for love to reach, not even the sky. Hal always had love in his heart.

There were twenty-one Asian countries represented in the Festival, with most of the contestants appearing in their colorful native costumes. The Festival lasted two nights. After the first night, we noticed that people on the street were staring at us, we assumed because we were Westerners. However, we learned, much to our delight, that it was Hal they were staring at, because the first night's event had been televised, and people had recognized him as the sole Caucasian judge at the Festival. He had literally become an instant celebrity throughout China.

In fact, as we were leaving Shanghai, we were picked up by a driver who had been somewhat hostile to us at the airport upon our arrival. It was as though it was a bother for him to take us to our hotel. We were rather taken aback by his attitude at the time, and somewhat leery that we had that same guide to take us to the airport upon our departure. But this time he greeted us with much bowing and many apologies, and told us he hadn't realized what an important person he had been assigned to pick up. He said that he was not only impressed with Hal, but he was very proud of himself as well, because he considered that the government had given him a very high honor by selecting him to drive us.

We were closely regimented during our trip, watched over by government guides who had certain areas and certain things they were obligated to show us. Hal always liked to visit schools, especially where they teach music to young children. But when we asked our guide about doing that, we were told that it was not on our schedule. At the Mayor's lunch, we again mentioned our desire to the interpreter assigned to us, and he came up with a plan.

He suggested that the next day we tell our guide that we were tired and wanted to spend some time on our own. During that time, our interpreter would come with a car and driver and he would take us where we wanted to go. So that morning, with some trepidation we told our official guide that we would not need her services for several hours. We weren't sure that our new friend, the interpreter, would show up, but not only did he show up, but what he had arranged for us far exceeded our hopes. There was no "Children's

Palace," in Hangzhou, but our friend had arranged for us to visit a school which specialized in teaching music to exceptionally gifted youngsters. It was impressive to see the proficiency of the very young students, all of them virtual prodigies. The teachers were very proud, and had the students perform a special concert just for the two of us.

While attending a party at a friend's home in New York, Michael A. Krauss, a television producer, came running over to Hal and said, "I've always wanted to see you again to thank you for saving my life." Hal had no idea what Michael was talking about, but it turned out that many years ago, Michael was in Los Angeles prior to taping a show, and his assistant left him in a lurch, not knowing who was supposed to do what. Celebrities who were scheduled to appear on his show suddenly cancelled at the last minute, and Michael was at his wit's end, until he happened to see Hal walking into the Beverly Wilshire Hotel, where he was on assignment for a movie. Michael told Hal his predicament, and Hal agreed to do the show for Michael in San Diego, quickly returning to Los Angeles to finish his movie assignment. So, lo those many years later, there was Michael Krauss, thanking Hal for saving his skin. Michael had everyone at the party stopped mid-sentence, listening to his story. He was there with his wife, then *Good Morning America's* Co-host, Joan Lunden.

Back again in Los Angeles, Hal and Burt were honored by the National Academy of Songwriters with a star-studded program featuring Dionne Warwick and Peter Allen and hosted by Paul Williams. The talented songwriter Arthur Hamilton, who wrote "Cry Me a River," produced the show, which was reviewed in the Los Angeles Times as follows:

> The National Academy of Songwriters' sixth
> annual 'Salute to the American Songwriter' at
> the Wilshire Ebell Theatre Thursday night was
> the kind of carefully produced, well-paced,
> talent-packed show that the Emmy and Oscar
> and Grammy extravaganzas promise, but too
> often fail to deliver...

It had indeed been a wonderful show, with the performers describing how much both Burt and Hal had influenced their careers, and how respected they were by their peers.

New Year's Eve, 1991, found us aboard an airplane on our way to our first of the five African safaris that Hal and I ended up taking together.

After a stopover in London, we flew on to Nairobi, where a pilot was waiting to fly us into the bush. The pilot said that he had some incidental expenses for the plane, which we had not paid for in advance, and he needed cash in the local currency for the payment. I could see Hal's face turn white, and realized his predicament. We'd been warned prior to coming to Africa that it was imperative that one wear a money-belt to keep cash and valuables safe. So now Hal had this money belt tied securely around his waist, under his pants, and the question was, how was he going to get the U.S. money out of his belt to get it exchanged? There was no men's room available where we were, in order for Hal to get to his money belt in private. I waited outside with our luggage while Hal went into the bank. I would have loved to have snapped a photo of him undoing his pants while waiting in line at the cashier's cage, because that is exactly what he did. He and the pilot came out laughing because, apparently, it wasn't the first time someone had been caught, literally, with his pants down.

We took the short flight from the Nairobi airport to the bush, where a car from the camp was supposed to meet us. When we landed on the dirt airstrip, there was not a single person in sight, but that didn't stop the pilot from taking off: he obviously had someone else to ferry. We just stood there with our luggage on the dirt at our feet, hoping we were where we were supposed to be. Fortunately, we soon saw the dust of an approaching car coming toward us, and we both breathed an audible sigh of relief.

Our friends, with whom we were traveling, and Anne Kent Taylor were waiting for us in camp. Anne was the daughter of the man who had founded the luxury travel company Abercrombie & Kent in 1962; Colonel John Kent. Now Anne's brother, Geoffrey headed the company. Anne had helped us plan the whole trip, arranging for her mother's favorite driver and guide to take us around while we were in Kenya. In fact, while planning the trip, it sounded so good to her that she and her husband Jim Taylor decided to join us in the bush for the first part of our safari.

The safari was a photographer's delight, and in those days, when I was using film, rather than a digital camera, I had a ton of canisters to bring home with me.

We were in East Africa at the perfect time for the migration of hundreds of thousands of the animals from the Serengeti Plains in Tanzania to Kenya's Masai Mara National Reserve. There were animals as far as the eye could see, slowly moving to their destination, traveling hundreds of miles, many of them with their newborn babies struggling to keep up. Hal and I went on four safaris after this one but, by far, experiencing the migration topped them all.

Even though the team of Bacharach and David had been receiving honors together, they hadn't worked as a team in ages. But early in 1992 Burt and Hal got together after their long hiatus when Dionne Warwick persuaded them to write a song for the new CD she was recording, *Friends Can Be Lovers.* "Sunny Weather Lover" didn't climb the charts as the Bacharach/David songs of yore had done, but just the fact that the trio was back together again made headlines in the *Los Angeles Times,* as well as in the trade papers. Hal said that he was so used to working together with Burt and Dionne that it felt just like going home for Thanksgiving (always his favorite holiday).

They also wrote a song for Bette Midler's 2000 movie about the writer Jacqueline Susann, *"Isn't She Great,"* which co-starred Nathan Lane.

Hal wasn't writing as steadily as he once did, since the proverbial phone calls requesting his services did not come as often as they used to. But on occasion a request still came to him and when it did, he was like a race horse: he couldn't wait to get started on the project.

Lalo Schifrin, the talented Argentine composer, pianist and conductor, as well as a good friend, was asked to write a song for the opera star Jose Carreras to sing at the closing ceremonies of the Olympic Games in Spain. The song was then going to be put into Carreras' new album, which already had one million copies presold. Lalo asked Hal to write the lyrics.

I went into the recording studio with Hal in April. We were very excited because the session was with a live orchestra, with Lalo conducting. I thought the lyrics were extraordinary; as usual Hal had a message for the world. The song was called "Share the Dream" and in it, Hal exhorted listeners to open their hearts, to listen to the laughter, and bring joy to one another.

April, 1992 brought a trial of four policemen who had been video-taped savagely beating a black man named Rodney King, whom they were trying to arrest. They claimed he was high on PCP and didn't stop the car he was driving when they ordered him to do so. When they were finally able to stop him, he still tried to get away from them; they claimed they were trying to restrain him.

Near the arrest scene, a man was trying out his brand-new video camera for the first time and when he heard the disturbance, he aimed his camera in that direction, and caught the entire action on film. That video of Rodney King being beaten was played over and over and over again on the local and national news programs and it inflamed everyone - especially the black community of Los Angeles. Thus, during the trial there was a tremendous amount of TV coverage and a great deal of interest was generated regarding the outcome.

The verdict came down on the afternoon of April 30th, exonerating the four policemen, which immediately sparked a widespread riot in the South Central area of the city. People started burning buildings and looting stores (mostly liquor and gun stores) and overturning cars, etc. We sat glued to our television sets and actually saw close-up pictures of the havoc being created, and of people running out of stores carrying TV sets, electronic equipment and even big chairs and sofas. Liquor stores were completely emptied and then burned, and food stores were also wiped out before being set afire.

Parties on the west side of town were cancelled, as were charity events. In fact, the whole city was put under a three-day curfew. It was a very frightening time. The May 1st headline in the *Los Angeles Times* stated:

LOOTING AND FIRES RAVAGE LOS ANGELES
25 dead, 572 injured, 1,000 blazes reported

The article went on to say that the combat zone stretched from downtown, through South Los Angeles, and toward the Westside (where we lived). The interior of the landmark Art-Deco Bullock's Wilshire building, which was one of the most beautiful buildings in the city, was completely trashed. It got so bad that President Bush ordered armed troops into Los Angeles to restore law and order. People could go out during the day, but it was so frightening, that many didn't want to.

Hal had to fly into New York for a meeting for just one day, but he was reluctant to leave me because we were still under curfew. I promised him that I wouldn't go out, even during the day. It was strange to look out of our east-facing windows and see downtown Los Angeles in the distance in flames, and then to watch TV and see it all in full-color close-up.

Hal had to schedule his return from New York so that his plane would land before the evening curfew took place.

Rodney King, in an appeal for calm during the riots, famously asked, "Can we all just get along?" That question resonated, but people were not too quick to acquiesce.

On May 23rd, we drove from New York to Stamford to spend a few days with our friends Hinda and Richard Rosenthal with whom we frequently spent weekends when we were back east. We casually mentioned to Hal that they were having a few guests over, which Hal had no reason to question, since the Rosenthals entertained quite often. We went through our usual activities when in Stamford: playing tennis, eating too much, and attending a dinner-dance at the Century Country Club in Purchase, New York. But this trip was different from our previous times in Stamford because Hinda and I had planned a surprise party for Hal, whose 71st birthday was on May 25th.

We'd invited friends to drive up from the city, and not one of the fifty or so people we'd invited turned us down. Hal was completely surprised to see the first people to arrive and asked why they were there. They told him they were just passing by, and for some unfathomable reason, he bought their story. But the second couple who arrived lived in Vermont, and when Hal saw them, he finally "got it," and from then on, could hardly contain himself. As more and more friends arrived, he kept saying that he hadn't had a clue. Friends came in from Massachusetts, Tovah Feldshuh and her husband came in from New York, and so it went. There were hugs and speeches all evening long, and everyone, including Hal, had a ball. During the speeches after dinner, Tovah told everyone how Hal had provided her first chance on Broadway. She'd obviously gone on to become a big star since that early start.

On July 20th headlines proclaimed that President Havel of Czechoslovakia had resigned, a victim of post-Communist political and nationalistic fragmentation. We were surprised by this development, having believed the country was doing well and that they were happy to be out from under Communist rule, when we had been in Prague only a year earlier.

When the country was broken up into Czech and Slovakia, Václav Hovel was elected President of Slovakia.

Hal and I did not attend the symphony in Los Angeles frequently, but when we were invited to join a group going to Salzburg to support the Los Angeles Philharmonic for the first ever appearance of a "foreign" orchestra in the hallowed Marble Concert Hall of Mirabell Palace, we couldn't resist.

Jennifer Diener was in charge of the activities, which were all arranged to perfection. She assembled an interesting group of music lovers from Los Angeles, and an impressive array of dignitaries who were on the International Host Committee: Archduke and Archduchess Heinrich of Austria, Princess Marianne su Sayn Wittgenstein-Sayne, count and Countess Johannes Walderdorff, Consul General and Mrs. Christian Prosi, Dr. Gerard Mortier (the new director of the Festival) and Ms. Ilona von Ronay. We partied at Goldgasse, and at Fuschl, the hunting lodge of Princess Marianne, who insisted that we call her "Monnie."

The occasion for the L.A. Phil to be performing in Salzburg was the presentation of Olivier Messiaen's "St. Francois d'Assise;" a six-hour opera with a dinner break after the first three hours. The production was directed by the animated, highly emotional Peter Sellars and conducted by Esa-Pekka Salonen. The opera was difficult to watch at best: it was certainly not easy listening. There were eight tableaux, each recording a stage in the life of the saint, from when Francis kissed a leper to when he receives the stigmata and dies in a state of joy. But the intrepid contingent from Los Angeles braved the six hours, and bonded because of it.

After being back in Los Angeles for only a short time, we were ready for another adventure. It turned out to be a cruise along the coast of Italy that started in Positano. While there, we were invited to dinner with renowned composer Henry Mancini and his wife Ginny, who were renting the dramatic home owned by the director Franco Zefferelli. But the night we were scheduled to go, the seas were too rough to take a water taxi - and the only other way to get there was to climb down one hundred and thirty steps from the street, to get to the front door.

When we finally arrived, we were escorted into the elegantly decorated sitting room, all done in white and fairly shimmering in the subtle lighting, with huge potted plants everywhere. The Mancinis were great hosts, and it was a wonderfully unexpected addition to our trip. The only downside was that we now had to climb up those one hundred and thirty steps to get back to our hotel. But it was worth it.

We had a grand time during our ten days of cruising, but, when it was over, we were ready for our next destination: Paris. We stayed at the Hotel Plaza Athenée, the historic luxury hotel, located on the Avenue Montaigne, near the Champs-Élysées and the Eiffel Tower. The highlight of that trip, other than touring the usual wonderful Parisian sights, was when we went to an exhibit which featured forty Statues of Liberty, all dressed up by different couturiers: only in Paris!

We flew from Paris to Liege to attend a CISAC meeting which was being held in both Liege and Maastricht (Maastricht being very much in the news at that time because of the world-wide Economic Conference taking place there). Having the meeting take place between Belgium and Holland was meant to symbolically show how open the borders of Europe were becoming.

Hal had a little time to spend with me when he was not in meetings, so we drove to Bastogne, where there was a Victory Memorial Museum dedicated to events which transpired in World War II during the Battle of the Bulge. The museum had life-sized figures of General Eisenhower, General Bradley, and General Patton, plus old Jeeps, tanks, guns, and very life-like battlefield settings. It was very realistic. Too realistic. I took one look at those battle scenes and burst into tears! My first husband, Bob had been in the Battle of the Bulge (the longest and bloodiest battle of WWII), and had been captured by the Germans and held in a prisoner of war camp until the end of the war, when he was liberated by the Allied Forces. It was during the Battle of the Bulge that General Anthony Clement famously responded "nuts" to a German ultimatum for surrender.

Meanwhile, that November, the big election news back home in the States was that William Jefferson (Bill) Clinton had been elected President, relegating George H. W. Bush to a one-term Presidency.

Toward the end of 1992, Hal prepared his first cabaret show. He asked the very talented singer Freda Payne to perform with him (because she was able to sing all the difficult Dionne Warwick songs), and Corky Hale was his musical director. Hal did it as a favor to me for one of the support organizations of the Music Center, *Club 100*, of which I was a former president. The show, which was a sold-out affair, was held in the party room of the legendary Chasen's Restaurant in Beverly Hills. As a result of the tremendous success of that event, Chasen's management asked Hal and me to produce a series of cabaret shows for them, which we happily did. They proved very successful until the closure of the popular eatery two years later, in 1995.

I loved being involved in Hal's professional life, and became pretty adept at helping him manage things. It always pleased me that Hal relied on me for so many aspects of his career: he no longer had an agent, so many times I acted in that capacity for him and I loved the excitement of it.

This December at the Kennedy Center Honors in Washington, D.C., Ginger Rogers was one of the honorees. While Hal was getting our coats after lunch, I introduced myself to her and mentioned that I was Hal David's wife. She was in a wheelchair at the time, but almost jumped out of it, saying she wanted to see Hal. She told me that years earlier, they had been at a party hosted by Marylou Whitney during a Kentucky Derby event, when Hal had the nerve to ask her to dance with him. I never did learn who led, but Ginger had a vivid memory of that dance.

At one of the luncheons that weekend, we were seated with the well-known jazz vocalist Joe Williams who told us that he had recorded a special arrangement of "What the World Needs Now," and he stood up at the table to demonstrate his rendition in his low, melodious voice. Conversation at the surrounding tables stopped until Joe finished the song, to a big round of applause. Needless to say, it warmed our hearts.

In 1992 we discovered that the actress Kathy Najimy was responsible for a bootlegged production of a show called *Back to Bacharach,* for which she had never applied for the required permission. As soon as we heard about it, we flew to see it in New York, where Daryl Roth, a prominent Broadway producer who held the singular distinction of having produced six Pulitzer Prize-winning plays, told us that she was interested in producing the show legitimately. Hal and Burt approved the arrangement, and the show, now that Daryl was the producer, was appropriately re-named *Back to Bacharach and David.* It eventually opened at Club 53 in the Hilton Hotel on March 13, 1993, the night of the worst snow storm in New York City since 1913! (In fact, that 1913 storm had actually occurred on that very same date, March 13th.) There were such high winds, combined with the heavy snowfall that the papers were calling it "The White Hurricane of 1993." People had been warned to stay indoors, but we learned that Broadway shows were open, so it was decided that this show would also go on. Hal and I were relieved and pleased to find a sellout crowd in the lobby of the theatre when we arrived.

Stephen Holden's review in the *New York Times* after opening night, stated, "What lifts *Back to Bacharach and David* above the run-of-the-mill sixties nostalgia is the show's nearly perfect balance between tribute and comedy." Sadly, the show was not a major hit - unfortunately only running for six months, from March 11 to September 11, 1993.

Back to Bacharach and David had another incarnation for a limited run in 2009 at the Music Box@Fonda theatre in Hollywood. This time it fared better than any of the previous versions, with Charles McNulty, the theater critic for the *Los Angeles Times* writing that, "With such a gold mine of music you couldn't go wrong if you stood on your head and sang these classics."

We went back time and again to see the show which, was created by Steve Gunderson, who did the musical and vocal arrangements as well as the orchestrations, and with Kathy Najimy, directing (legitimately this time). Hal and I thought this version of the show had great energy, and were pleased that it had finally found its legs.

My Connecticut friend Hinda Rosenthal invited me to join her in Washington, D.C. for a luncheon sponsored by a group called "EMILY's List." The letters stood for "Early Money is Like Yeast" - it rises. There were forty-two hundred people in attendance, but since we were with the newly-elected Congresswoman Lynn Schenk, we were seated at a table quite close to the stage, where the three women Senators and twenty-eight Congresswomen who had been elected that year all gathered to receive their well-deserved applause. I saw several friends there from Los Angeles, including Roz Wyman, with whom I'd served on the Los Angeles County Music and Performing Arts Commission. Roz had been campaign manager for Diane Feinstein's successful run for Senate, and actually had quite a resume of her own. She had been the youngest person ever elected to the Los Angeles City Council, and had been influential in bringing the Dodgers from Brooklyn to Los Angeles.

The experience was thrilling for me, because it demonstrated the power that women have when they join forces and put their minds to something. As might be obvious by now, Hal and I loved to stay busy. During our marriage, in addition to being very active in philanthropic organizations, Hal was on the ASCAP Board of Directors and also on the Board of Governors of

Cedars Sinai Hospital in Los Angeles. He went to his business office on Ventura Boulevard in Studio City twice a week, frequently sat in on various other music-related meetings around town, and he also enjoyed lunching with his pals. I kept myself occupied with my own round of Board meetings, especially the Los Angeles County Music and Performing Arts Commission on which I served long before I met Hal.

The day I became President of the Commission, in 1993, I had a baptism by fire. The moment I was installed, a surprise, and extremely controversial, motion was presented, which had the entire eighteen-member Commission up in arms for about an hour and a half. One of the County Supervisors had asked a Commissioner to present the motion, so it was mandatory that we act upon it, even though the majority of the commissioners were opposed to it. The Supervisor wanted us to take $25,000 away from the Los Angeles Philharmonic and give it to a small, struggling arts group in the Supervisor's district. Although quaking and occasionally pounding on my newly-obtained gavel, I did indeed conduct the meeting (with the County Council sitting at the end of the room and occasionally nodding his head in approval at me). The final vote went the way I had hoped it would, by denying the switch, and we were able to go on to less controversial business.

Hal came downtown to be with me at the luncheon that followed the meeting, and people kept coming up to him and telling him how well I'd handled a difficult situation. I knew he was very proud of me, and to tell the truth, I was pretty proud also. I figured if I could get through that meeting, nothing would throw me!

Hal performed in Nashville, at a show called "The Legends," during Tin Pan Alley South Week. When he prepared a medley of the songs he was going to sing, he was careful to include "It Was Almost like a Song," which he had written with Nashville writer Archie Jordan. But when Hal tried to acknowledge Archie from the stage, he froze, and couldn't remember Archie's name: a serious senior moment. People in the audience, me included, were yelling Archie's name out to him, already knowing just whom Hal had written that song with. Hal finally heard us, and was able to acknowledge Archie, much to the delight of the audience. The other performers that night were Jeff Barry, Leiber and Stoller, Felix Cavaliere, Jimmy Webb, Jack Tempchin, and Bill and Sharon Rice: a pretty impressive group.

At a SHARE gala that Hal and I attended, later in in the year, we bid on and won a trip to Canyon Ranch, a health resort and spa in Tucson, Arizona. While we were there, a writer for the Calendar section of the Los Angeles Times, contacted us and set up a three-way conference call between himself, Burt and Hal, in preparation for an article he was writing about them. The fellows were scheduled to receive the ASCAP Founders Award, and he would be covering the event. Like almost everyone, he was interested in the long-ago infamous breakup of the Bacharach/David/Warwick team. Burt admitted in that article that, if he had it to do over again he never, never would have handled things the same way. But he pointed out that he and Dionne were touring again, and that he and Hal had found a touch of the old spark when they wrote "Sunny Weather Lover" for Dionne's recently released new album.

When Hal and Burt were presented the award, Morton Gould, who was then the President of ASCAP said: "We use this award to celebrate the founders of our society by honoring our most gifted contemporary songwriters, and I can't think of any team that deserves the honor more than Burt and Hal."

The article that was written for *The Times* mentioned that:

Bacharach and David's explosion of hits in the mid-60's was one of the extraordinary events in a remarkable musical decade. Going against the tidal stream of rock, they synthesized their own blend of pop, R&B, and mainstream ballads, adding quirky rhythms and interval-stretching melodies rarely heard before in popular music.

A couple of days after the ASCAP gala, Hal and I hosted a dinner party at our apartment for about fifty people. We invited Burt and his then girlfriend Jane (who later became his wife) as well as Dionne to join us. Sometime during the evening one of our guests mentioned that it was Hal's seventy-second birthday, so Burt sat down at the piano and he and Dionne belted out "Happy Birthday." It meant a lot to Hal that all three of them were once again celebrating something together.

Hal had worked on a number of projects with Senator Ted Kennedy over the years relating to the protection of intellectual property and, in fact, we had hosted a couple of fundraisers for him at our apartments, both in Los Angeles and New York. As a thank you, he invited us for dinner at the lovely home in McLean, Virginia, that he shared with his wife of just one year, Vicki. We arrived at the appointed time, only to learn that Ted would be delayed at his office for about forty-five minutes. But the always poised Vicki showed us around until Ted got there. The house was located in a prime spot, right on the edge of the Potomac River, and was a virtual museum of Kennedy family memorabilia, featuring portraits of Rose and Joseph Kennedy and pictures of all the Kennedy brothers, sisters, nephews, nieces, sisters-in-law, and brothers-in-law.

Right at the beginning of the evening, Kennedy made sure to tell Hal that he would support the songwriters on the "Life-Plus 70" copyright legislation scheduled for an upcoming vote, which Hal was going to help spearhead through Congress. After that, we were able to enjoy the rest of our visit without that elephant in the room.

Back in Los Angeles Hal was having a fine time singing, with Corky Hale as his accompanist, in cabaret shows around town, including performing at the Los Angeles Jewish Home in Encino, where my mother Miriam lived. My father, a concert cellist, had passed away in 1986, and my mother loved the security and companionship of living at the Home.

One day when they knew Hal was going to be at the Home to perform, they wheeled out a man who lived in their Alzheimer's unit. The fellow had such an advanced stage of that terrible affliction that he never responded to anything around him. He just sat in his chair all day and stared straight ahead. But when Hal started singing, he suddenly raised his arm and began conducting to the beat of the music. His wife was beside herself with joy, and with tears running down her cheeks, she explained that he used to be the musical director for Tony Martin, the singer/actor from the Golden Age of Hollywood musicals. We were told that was the first time in years he had had any response whatsoever to any kind of stimulus. Music is indeed a powerful healer.

During our stay that fall in New York for the ASCAP Board meetings I spent a considerable amount of time with Karen Sherry of ASCAP and Ben Palumbo, the ASCAP lobbyist, planning a private fundraising reception that Hal and I were going to be hosting for Ted Kennedy in our Los Angeles apartment.

There was an endless stream of calls, interruptions, and changes. But somehow or other, it all came together, and we later learned that our event raised the most PAC money that ASCAP had ever raised for a legislator at a single event. Senator Kennedy was very grateful. When he read his thank-you speech, which Vicki had helped him compose, he used some of Hal's song titles to get his message across. For example, he said that last year when he married Vicki, he made her promise, "Don't Make Me Over." At the end of his speech, he thanked everyone for coming and saying that he was glad that they

76

didn't just "Walk on By." It was Kennedy campaigning at his best and the sixty or so guests who had come to our place to meet him and to contribute to his campaign were delighted.

About this same time in 1993, Hal and the wonderfully talented composer Charlie Fox were auditioning singers for a benefit show they were about to produce. Years before, they'd written the score for a show based on Chaim Potok's book *The Chosen,* but after running into some problems with the production, they pulled out of the show. The producers brought someone else in to write new music, but the show only ran for two nights on Broadway before it closed; Hal and Charlie had obviously known what they were doing when they pulled out. They tried for years to get the rights to that ill-fated production so that they could produce their own version of it, but, sadly it never happened.

However, they did get the right to perform the show in a concert version, for one night only, as a benefit for the trauma hospital Assaf Harofeh in Tel Aviv. The story, set in 1944, is told against the backdrop of the historic events of the time, including the death of President Roosevelt, the end of World War II, and the struggle for the creation of the state of Israel. One of the characters in the show is the sister of the one of the two young boys who are the central characters in the musical. Hal and Charlie were in total agreement about all the singers and dancers they auditioned, except for the role of the sister. Hal was keen on hiring a particular young girl who had auditioned for them, but Charlie wasn't as taken with her as Hal was. But, being a good sport, and a good friend as well as a good collaborator, Charlie acquiesced, and Farah Alvin was hired.

After she was told that she had the part, Farah came up to Hal and said that she realized he hadn't remembered her, but when he had been a judge at one of the Spotlight Awards evenings (conceived by the renowned director Walter Grauman) at the Los Angeles Music Center, he had chosen her as the winner of one of the scholarships offered in the visual and performing arts fields: her category of pop singer. Years later, when Hal's show, *The Look of Love,* appeared on Broadway, there was Farah, as one of the pit singers. Three times with Hal must have been a charm for Farah, because she has since gone on to sing and act in numerous Broadway productions.

Hal was busy rehearsing for his upcoming cabaret show at the Russian Tea Room in New York, and he was preparing the remarks he was going to make when he testified in D.C. for an intellectual property bill that was being formulated, in addition to rehearsing with Charlie Fox for that one-night show of *The Chosen*. But when friends of ours, Elly and Jack Nadel, asked us if we wanted to join them on an around-the-world trip on a private jet with Travcoa, a luxury tour company, we jumped at the opportunity.

As it turned out, the Nadels were unable to join us for the first part of the trip because Jack became ill, but we were booked and had paid in advance, so we went ahead on our own. We flew to Singapore in October, meeting a few fellow travelers on the plane, easily identifiable by the spiffy travel cases that Travcoa had provided for us. We stayed at the recently renovated hotel Raffles while in Singapore, the colonial-style hotel built in 1899 by two Armenian brothers. It was named after Stamford Raffles, the founder of modern Singapore, and became Singapore's best-known icon.

A story is told that at the start of the Japanese occupation of Singapore on February 15, 1942, Japanese soldiers were astonished to see guests of the hotel dancing one final waltz in the ballroom. Hal and I didn't dance any waltzes, but we definitely did sample the renowned Singapore Slings which the bartender Ngiam Tong Boon invented, and for which the hotel is noted.

Fearless

Next we boarded the newly-built Eastern & Oriental Express for a two-day train trip through the countryside from Singapore to Bangkok, where our very own private L-1011 jet awaited us, and our real adventure began. The plane, originally designed to hold two hundred people, had been redesigned to carry 70 passengers, so it was extremely luxurious. We were assigned to seats which were ours throughout the trip, with ample room to move around and visit with our fellow travelers while airborne.

One of those passengers with whom we became good friends was Norman Shtofman and his wife Barbara. Norman was the Mayor of Tyler, Texas, and a couple of years later he grandly presented me with the Key to the City and made me an honorary citizen of Tyler at a birthday party of mine which he and Barbara attended.

Our around-the-world trip took us to Muscat, Oman, and from there, we cautiously skirted the air space over Somalia where a war lord had been shooting down American planes, and took the long flight to Cape Town, South Africa. After seeing the stunning vistas from Table Top Mountain, we visited the Cape of Good Hope, which marks the point where a ship begins to travel more eastward than southward, and then flew to Nairobi. We spent three days on safari at Governor's Camp in the Masai Mara where I was able to take the photographs of animals in the wild that I so enjoyed taking.

On one of our game runs, we came across an ostrich nest with fifteen eggs in it. Our driver got a little too close to the nest (on purpose, I suspect) and the next thing we knew our Jeep was being attacked by both the mother and father ostrich, trying to protect their unhatched babies. The ostriches were spitting at us, flapping their huge wings, and even kicking at the Jeep. The other occupants ducked under the dashboard but I, ever the undaunted photographer, kept snapping pictures and got some pretty good close ups of those angry birds.

From Nairobi, we flew to Istanbul, where the Nadels finally joined us at the Ciragan Palace Hotel, every bit as grand as the palace which formerly stood on the same grounds must have been.

Part of that leg of the trip was a five-day cruise on Cunard's Sea Goddess, with our group as its only passengers. Then we flew to Malaga, on Spain's Costa del Sol, where we boarded the ship for our trip to the Canary Islands and Gibraltar, after which we docked in Casablanca early one morning and were driven to Rabat which we toured before being treated to a fabulous luncheon, complete with belly dancers. One night on the ship there was a costume party to allow people to show off the purchases they'd made along the way. Most of our fellow travelers had bought colorful jewelry and bright native costumes. Hal and I were in a quandary about what to wear, since we'd been busy sightseeing, not shopping. So we decided we'd "come as we were," which was Hal as a tourist and me as a photographer. Much to our surprise, we won first prize that night!

All in all, we'd logged twenty-four thousand air miles on the three-week trip, and deemed it one of our more interesting adventures.

Refreshed rather than exhausted by the long trip, Hal eagerly jumped right into the final rehearsals for *The Chosen*. Even though the production was only going to be performed once, it consisted of a sixteen-piece orchestra, and the performers were going to sing and dance in makeup and costume.

The play, which was presented in the ballroom of the Beverly Wilshire Hotel, was a huge success, with many people in the audience asking Charlie and Hal why it was never produced as a Broadway show. The boys had been trying to get the rights for years, but Chaim Potok refused to relinquish them.

During rehearsals for the show Hal had been unexpectedly called to Geneva not only to represent ASCAP but also BMI (Broadcast Music, Inc. and NMPA (the National Music Publishers Association), at a WIPO conference (World Intellectual Properties), all of the organizations working to protect property rights on the legislative, litigation, and regulatory fronts. We hosted Bruce Lehman, then Assistant Secretary for Commerce, at a dinner, and included Marybeth Peters, the Registrar of Copyrights, and Ralph Oman, who represented the Library of Congress in their Registry of Copyrights department, along with Ben Palumbo, the ASCAP Lobbyist, and members of the BMI and NMPA organizations.

Hal was there to present the views of our American organizations - views that were diametrically different from the direction our government seemed to be taking. Even though ASCAP, BMI and NMPA had views that differed slightly, Hal was able to pull them all together, present their recommendations to the government representatives, and eventually win over the dissidents, which resulted in legislation being passed that was favorable to songwriters.

Hal and I had been in New York at the beginning of the year and returned to Los Angeles on January 16th, 1994. At 4:31 the next morning we were jolted awake by a powerful earthquake. At a magnitude of 6.7, it was dubbed the "Northridge Earthquake," with the ground acceleration being one of the highest ever instrumentally recorded in North America. One 6.0 magnitude aftershock occurred just one minute after the initial event, and another eleven hours later, the strongest of several thousand aftershocks in all. The death toll came to a total of fifty-seven people with over 700 injured. In addition, the earthquake caused an estimated twenty-billion dollars in damage, making it one of the costliest (to that date) natural disasters in U.S. history.

I'm an Angelina and had been through this experience before. But this was Hal's first, and he was not a happy camper. Our twenty-three story building was built to withstand an earthquake of this magnitude, being engineered to sway with the jolt. But it seemed as though the swaying of the two top floors of the building, which is where we lived, was never going to stop.

We had no electricity so were unable to raise the electric blinds in our apartment to look out to see what was happening. The phones didn't work, nor did the TV or the elevator in our apartment. I finally unearthed an old Walkman portable radio whose battery was on its last legs, but at least we were able to find out what was going on. Houses had caved in, freeways were destroyed, people had been buried in rubble, chimneys had fallen off, there were ruptured pipelines, and emergency crews were all over the place searching desperately for buried bodies. There was destruction everywhere.

When our phone service was restored, our phone started ringing immediately, with friends from all over the world calling to see how we were. Hal's office building in Studio City, was close to the epicenter, and was closed to all tenants because it had no water or phones, and the plumbing wasn't working. When Hal was finally able to get inside his office, he found file cabinets toppled over in every which direction. It took forever to get things straightened out. But at least no one had been injured.

With everyone still in panic mode after the earthquake, I was surprised when it was decided to continue with plans for a Town Hall meeting downtown. I had been invited to appear as a panelist as a representative of the Music Commission, of which I was the president. Other speakers were The Hon. Yvonne Brathwaite Burke, Chair of the Board of Supervisors of the County of Los Angeles; the Hon. Joel Wachs, Councilman of the 2nd District of the City of Los Angeles; Stephanie Barron, Curator of Modern and Contemporary Art at the Los Angeles County Museum of Art; Steven Lavine, President of the California Institute of the Arts; and Adolfo Nodal, General Manager of the Cultural Affairs Department of the City of Los Angeles. I was intimated at being on such a high-powered panel, but somehow or other I got through it, and my day was made when Caroline Ahmanson, a leading philanthropist in Southern California who was a major supporter of the arts, came up to me and said: "Eunice, you did Los Angeles proud."

In February we heard that our friend Andrew Lloyd Webber was going to be in town for an event in his honor at the Los Angeles Music Center. Only a small group was invited, which did not include Hal and me. I was pretty put out by that since I'd been raising money for the Music Center since its inception, and had even sat on many of its Boards, as well as chairing some of its biggest galas. But I decided that we'd partner with the Music Center, who was paying Andrew's air fare from London, and create a party of our own.

Although Hal and I at that time did not belong to the Regency Club, a private dining club then located at the top of the Murdock Building in Westwood, California, my former husband Bif Forester and I had belonged during our marriage, so I called them to see if we could host a party there. When they heard that our honored guest was going to be Andrew Lloyd Webber, they were delighted to allow us to use their facility.

We thought that Andrew might enjoy meeting some people in the music business who were based in Los Angeles, but we were concerned that if we invited too many of our personal friends as well, he might feel that we were putting him on display. So we invited about sixty people to the party, limiting our non-musical friends to one couple per table.

Some of the music business people we invited to that dinner were Ginny and Henry Mancini, Marilyn and Alan Bergman, Bonnie and John Cacavas, Shelby and Bill Conte, Collelette and Georges Delerue, Joyce and Arthur Hamilton, Fong and Maurice Jarre, Jack Jones, Martha and Johnny Mandel, Corky Hale and Mike Stoller, and Mel Tormé.

Everyone had a sensational time, with people networking and exclaiming they had worked with colleagues years earlier but hadn't seen them since.

The manager of the Regency Club at that time, immediately invited Hal and me to become members of the club, based on that dinner, with our glittery guest list. We did become members of the club and remained so until we joined the Hillcrest Country Club, which had tennis and golf facilities that we planned to use, besides their dining room.

Early in his career, Hal's songs started showing up on the Country charts as well as the Pops, even though he always reminded people that he grew up in Brooklyn and that when he was a young man, country songs weren't played on the radio in New York. But Hal had "The Story of My Life," which Marty Robbins recorded, "Sea of Heartbreak," and "My Heart Is an Open Book," which was recorded in Nashville and were all registering on the country charts.

As a result, Hal decided to go to Nashville, to see what it was all about. He was told to contact Buddy Killen, who ran the Tree Publishing Company, a big country music publishing house. Killen welcomed Hal to Nashville as only a gregarious country boy could. He insisted Hal stay at his beautiful home, and took him all around to meet everybody. "Everybody" included the talented young composer by the name of Archie Jordan, with whom Hal wrote the soulful "It Was Almost like a Song."

That song was made famous by country music singer Ronnie Milsap, becoming one of his greatest hits when it was released in 1977, and his eighth #1 song on the *Billboard magazine Hot Country Songs* chart. There was also a wonderful scene in the 1995 movie *The Bridges of Madison County* where Clint Eastwood and Meryl Streep were dancing in the kitchen of Streep's home while "It Was Almost like a Song" played in the background. Eastwood used a version of the song which was sung by Johnny Hartman. Hal had not even been aware that it existed before the movie came out, but he loved it.

Also on that first visit to Nashville, Hal met a young woman by the name of Connie Bradley, who was a secretary at the ASCAP office there. Later, when Hal became President of ASCAP in1980, he made Connie head of the Nashville office. She wasn't sure she was up to the job, but Hal had faith in her, and convinced her to accept the position. He always felt that was one of the better things he'd done while he was ASCAP's president. Two other major decisions he made as President were to hire John Lo Frumento, who later became the successful CEO of ASCAP, and he promoted Karen Sherry to be his personal assistant. Karen went on to become a highly acclaimed producer of ASCAP shows, Senior Vice President, Industry Affairs and Vice President and Executive Director of the ASCAP Foundation.

Hal said that it was a great thrill for him when, in 1972, he was elected to the Nashville Songwriter's Hall of Fame. At that time, he was the only non-country, New York guy whose name was listed there. He felt he had broken a barrier.

Hal had been to Israel about thirty years earlier, but I had never been there, having no special desire to go. But Hal was interested in seeing the many changes that had been made during those thirty years, and it seemed like a good window of opportunity to go since at the moment, no one was shooting at anyone or blowing things up.

We were lucky enough to have Judy Goldman, who was a writer for Fodor's travel magazine, as our guide for the two weeks we planned to be in the country in May of 1994. We started our odyssey in Jerusalem at the King David Hotel.

Judy had been born a Christian in Canada, and had come to New York to work, which is where she met and married her Jewish husband Bob, who worked in television. Soon after they were married, he was assigned to a position in Tel Aviv, with the understanding that it would be for just one year. By the time we met, Judy had converted to Judaism, they had two sons who had both served in the Israeli army, and they had been in Tel Aviv for eighteen years!

From her we learned about her adopted country from both a Christian and Jewish point of view. And because of her association with Fodor's, she was able to get us into some of the tourist attractions when they weren't open to the public. We managed to see all the requisite sights, including Herod's tomb, the Bible Lands Museum, Hadassah Medical Center (to see the Chagall windows), the Supreme Court, and the Knesset. We took the cable car to the top of Masada, and drove through Mea Shearim and walked the Stations of the Cross on the Via Dolorosa, leaving time to stop at the Western Wall (the Wailing Wall), where Hal and I separately wrote prayers on little pieces of paper and placed them in niches in the wall. And Judy took us to the Ein Gedi Kibbutz, right at the edge of the Dead Sea, where I foolishly donned the white bathing suit I had brought with me. When a group of women who were slathering the dark healing mud all over themselves spotted me, they couldn't resist, and they gleefully smeared that gooey, black stuff all over me and my white suit.

Hal, never a good swimmer, couldn't believe that he could float in the Dead Sea, but float he did, even though he hung onto a nearby post, just to be sure.

By the time we returned to the hotel, my ankle was hurting and swollen, even though I didn't remember hurting it. I did not want to go to a doctor for fear that he would make me get off my feet for a while, and I wasn't about to do that. So, with my ankle wrapped in an Ace bandage, we set off on the next day's adventures.

We'd received an invitation to visit Benny Begin, the son of Menachem Begin, a former Prime Minister of Israel. Benny was a very conservative member

of the right wing Likud party. His office was in the beautiful Knesset, but to my disappointment all cameras were held at the gate, so I didn't get any pictures.

Begin, whose party was in favor of keeping all the territories that Israel had gained during the Six Day War, told us a story to illustrate how he felt the Palestinians kept asking for more and more territory to be given up by Israel. He called it, for some reason, "The Salami Theory." A man at the beach with his young son, tells the boy not to go in the water, but the child goes in anyway. Soon the father notices that the child is in the water, so he tells him not to go past the shoreline. Again, the child ignores his father and goes further out. When the father sees that, he tells the boy not to swim too far out, etc. We got the comparison.

Of course we also toured Yad Vashem, and saw the dazzling memorial to the victims killed in the Holocaust. After the tour, we needed some solitude. so we headed back to our hotel, where, much to our surprise and delight there was a birthday cake and a bottle of wine waiting for Hal, courtesy of Judy.

Predictably, the next day my ankle was worse than ever, so I relented and asked Judy to arrange for me to see a doctor. She managed to find one willing to see me before eight o'clock that morning, so I wouldn't have to miss a minute of touring. Dr. Sherer took x-rays, poked around a bit, and then declared me fit to continue touring, only prescribing a medication which would help take the swelling down. When Hal paid him, the doctor noticed Hal's name on the check. He then proceeded to tell us that he was once in a nightclub where a woman sang a song that she said she had written with Burt Bacharach. Dr. Sherer said he didn't believe her because he knew her to be a braggart. To check out her claim, he bought the sheet music for "This Guy's in Love with You." Sure enough, there were the credits: Music by Burt Bacharach, lyrics by Hal David. Sherer told us that is why he never forgot Hal's name, and he could hardly believe that after all those years, here he was with the real Hal David right there in his office. He just couldn't get over it. Neither could we.

Hal used to tell a story about that song. When Burt and Hal gave A&M Records the song "Close to You," which launched the great career that the sister and brother act Karen and Richard Carpenter achieved, they also gave Herb Alpert (the "A," along with Jerry Moss, the "M" of A&M) a song called "This Girl's in Love with You." When Herb was preparing a TV special, he decided that he wanted to sing that song himself as a love song to his wife. But obviously the gender had to be changed. Hal hated to change a lyric, although he had changed "Message to Martha" to "Message to Michael," when Dionne wanted to record the song. It became a Top Ten hit for Dionne in 1966, so Hal was glad he made the change. It had originally been recorded as "Message to Martha" by Jerry Butler in 1962. Marlene Dietrich even recorded a German version of it in 1964.

Hal finally agreed to the changes Herb wanted, and Herb went on to record "This Guy's in Love with You," the first time he'd ever sung on a recording, and the first time Burt and Hal ever had a song which reached the coveted #1 spot in America, remaining there for four weeks in May of 1968.

Hal himself used to sing the song in his cabaret shows, as his love song to me, always pointing his finger at me when he sang the words "this guy, this guy's in love with you." The wonderful gravelly-voiced singer Steve Tyrell always sings that song when he performs in his cabaret acts, and with a twinkle in his eye, and his finger pointed right at me, I always feel very special whenever I'm in the audience and the recipient of that special attention, even though I know very well that he does the very same thing to some other lucky gal when I am not there.

As for A&M's other song "Close to You," it took seven years after it was first recorded in 1964 to reach the #1 spot on the charts. Hal recalled that when he first heard the Carpenter version he hadn't been as enthusiastic as Burt was. However, he conceded that once it became a great popular award-winning song, he quickly became quite enamored of the song.

Karen and Richard Carpenter won a Grammy for "Close to You" at the 1970 Grammy Awards ceremony in Los Angeles, where they were named the best new artist(s) of the year. They also won for the best contemporary duo for their rendition of the song. In later years, Hal used the melody of "Close to You" for many of the special material works that he later wrote for friends, changing his lyrics to fit the occasion.

But back to Israel: As my ankle healed, we went to see Jericho, the city on the West Bank believed to be the oldest city in the world, eight hundred and twenty-five feet below sea level, making it not only the oldest walled city in the world, but the lowest, and it is described in the Old Testament as the "City of Palm Trees," the place where the Israelites returned from bondage in Egypt. But a couple of days before we were scheduled to go, we read in the paper that Jericho was about to be closed to outsiders for twenty-four hours, due to the Palestinian detention of five Jews during a series of incidents.

We weren't sure if the ban was really going to be lifted, and even if it were lifted, we weren't sure if we should be going in. So our eyes were glued to the TV and to the newspapers. On the day we had planned to go, we read that the closure had been lifted, so off we went, not without a certain amount of trepidation.

As it turned out, the area was closed again a couple of days after we were there, so we were fortunate to have been able to squeeze that trip in during the short window of time that the area was open. I was glad we hadn't been chicken about taking the drive.

During our two-week stay in the Holy Land, we saw as many sights as we could, all of them historical, and all very meaningful. One of the most interesting was the Yardenite Baptismal site on the Jordan River. As we drove by, we just happened to catch flashes of white, and quickly drove over to see what was going on - in time to watch as a group of people were led into the water to be baptized.

During our stay in the Holy Land, we also had some memorable personal experiences. We were invited to tour the hospital, that benefited from the one-night production of *The Chosen* that Hal and Charlie Fox produced in Beverly Hills. During our tour of the Assaf Harofeh hospital we were led to a wall where a plaque was unveiled. The plaque had both Hal's and Charlie's name on it, in honor of the funds that had been donated to the hospital from the proceeds of that benefit performance.

Dr. Benjamin showed us through the neonatology department, which was his bailiwick. When I saw those tiny babies in their incubators struggling for every breath, I literally fell apart. But Dr. Benjamin boastfully assured us that they all would survive, and would one day be brave soldiers for Israel! Started during the Ottoman Empire, and used by the British before the Israelis, the hospital expected to serve a population of over five hundred thousand in the near future, serving both Israeli and Palestinian patients.

One day our friend Ran Kedar, from ACUM, the Israeli performing rights society, arranged for Hal to be interviewed by Ehud Manor, who was the host of one of the most popular radio shows in Israel, broadcasting over KOL Israel, the Voice of Israel State Radio. Ehud usually alternated broadcast days with Rivka Michaeli, another popular host, who had a show called Good Morning with Rivka Michaeli. When she heard that Ehud was going to interview Hal, she asked if she could co-host the show with him. They played Hal's songs, while interviewing him, and asking questions about Hal's career.

Then everything that Hal said had to be translated into Hebrew. Ehud and Rivka were wonderful hosts, making jokes with Hal and bantering back and forth. We later learned that the switchboard started lighting up like a fireworks display. We were told they'd never had so many call-ins before!

When we joined Ehud at dinner that evening, he told us that his boss decided that the show would continue to be co-hosted by him and Rivka, since it had gone over so well. As we were sitting in the outdoor seaside restaurant in Taboon in Jaffa, a Phantom fighter plane flew very low overhead, headed toward Lebanon. It made a frightening noise, and we all had a few moments of absolute panic while holding our breath, waiting for something dreadful to happen. Ehud's wife Ofra turned white as a sheet and whispered to Hal, "We live with such tension." I mentioned her comment to Ran, and his response was, "Don't you know that worrying is bad for your health?" What a way to live!

On the day before we were to leave Israel, Judy arranged a picnic lunch for us. Because it was a Saturday, the Jewish Sabbath, and she knew we wouldn't be able to find a good restaurant open for lunch, she brought a table and chairs, and even a red and white checkered tablecloth. The wife of our driver, Leon, had baked some wonderful delicacies stuffed with tuna, tomatoes, olives, and other delicious ingredients, which we completely devoured, as well as a cake she had baked.

When we were finished eating, Leon, who only spoke Hebrew, produced a paper with words his English-speaking wife had written out phonetically for him to read to us in English. At the end of the lovely sentiment which Leon expressed, he said that we now "had an Israeli friend, who would be honored to drive for us anytime we returned." How touching is that?

Anyone I've ever talked to about a trip to Israel has declared that they had the best guide ever. But we were convinced that Judy Goldman topped them all. Her love of her adopted country was commendable, and her knowledge encyclopedic. She brought the country to life for us, and seeing it through her loving eyes was a special treat.

In August we started an adventure that would last for about fifteen years. For each of those years we spent a month in the south of France, either in Cap Ferrat or Beaulieu, where we had some remarkable times, met a diverse group of people who became good friends, ate extravagantly and partied, partied, partied.

It was on our first trip to the area that we solidified our friendship with Bonnie and Bernie Hodes, who became lifelong friends, almost like family. We've since seen each other through thick and thin, always lending support, words of wisdom, and unconditional love and affection.

Our jaunts in the south of France always included drives to unique sites; a shopping spree in San Remo across the nearby Italian border, in the good old days when the lira was a real bargain compared to the U.S. dollar, and we especially liked meeting people from England, France, Greece, Hong Kong, and all over the United States.

Some of the most enjoyable evenings we had during those summers were when we drove into Monte Carlo. We'd get all dressed up and take the half hour drive into Monaco, sampling the cuisine in some of their finest restaurants and dropping a few francs at their famed casino. We frequently ran into a wonderful singer/pianist by the name of Maurizio Razori, who played in a number of different the hotels in the city. Whenever he spotted Hal, he'd start playing and singing a medley of Bacharach/David songs, much to our delight and the enjoyment of the group of friends who usually accompanied us. We met Maurizio in the early 1990's and he has stayed in touch ever since; he even sent me a very moving note when Hal passed. Our friends told us that whenever they happened to be in a restaurant where Maurizio was playing, even if we weren't along, he'd start playing a Hal David medley, which always tickled them.

We took many side trips while staying there. One day we drove to Portofino, Italy. The lure of staying at the five-star El Splendido was too much to resist, so, with another couple, we booked rooms for a short stay. One day we took in all the sights and enjoyed shopping in the picturesque horseshoe-shaped harbor, and finally climbed up the steep, winding path from the sea to our hotel. We'd planned to eat dinner in town that night, but we were so tired from our earlier activities that we decided to relax and eat at the hotel, so we could get to bed early. But that was not meant to be.

We were savoring a wonderful meal on the patio, luxuriating in the grandeur of the hotel while taking in the wonderful view, when all of a sudden we heard the pianist, who was inside, playing a short medley of Hal's songs. He had no idea that Hal was a guest of the hotel, so we were pleased to know that he was playing the songs just because he liked them. When we finished our meal, Hal stopped by to introduce himself to the pianist, who was so thrilled to meet him that he immediately started to play the "Hal David Songbook." He told us that he knew Hal's whole catalog, and we were very much afraid he was going to play the entire list for us right then and there. So there we were, falling off our feet, but unable to leave until the concert was over. Talk about conflicted feelings.

We were in the south of France the year the country was celebrating the fiftieth anniversary of the liberation of Southern France from Germany, which occurred in 1944. Pristine U.S. warships dotted the harbor of Villefranche, and young American sailors were wandering around looking at all the sights, just as we were. One day we were having lunch at La Mere Germaine, one of our favorite waterfront restaurants in Villefranche, when several young American sailors wandered into the restaurant. We asked them to join us, and offered to buy them lunch. They said that all they wanted was some of the famous French wine, and some of the famous French bread. We were happy to oblige.

On another side trip we took that year we flew to Paris where we stopped for a gourmet lunch at the Hotel de Crillon, before boarding a train for the relatively short ride to Trouville, staying at the elegantly majestic, old-world Hotel Royal Barrière in nearby Deauville. From an exclusive party at Club Régine, to the exciting Deuville horse races, where *East of the Moon,* owned by Stavros Niarcos won that year, to the Gala Racing Ball, it was definitely an exciting trip.

We especially wanted to visit the American Cemetery in Normandy. Between our visits to the German Cemetery and the American one, we stopped at Grandecamp les Bains, where we had lunch at Restaurant la Marée. We were not only surprised to find a gourmet restaurant in that little seaside town, but we were delighted at their taste in music: much to our delight, we heard strains of "Raindrops" being played in the background as we entered the restaurant.

We knew that many lives were lost on Omaha Beach during WWII, but we marveled that anyone at all had survived that fierce battle. The terrain was impossible to climb in the peaceful sunlight. One could only imagine how terrible it must have been with shells and gunfire exploding all around. Still shaking our heads in disbelief, we toured the incredibly beautiful American Cemetery, a lovely final resting place for our brave soldiers who had lost their lives in France.

Our friends Doris and Walter Goldstein kept a yacht anchored in Beaulieu and whenever they weren't out cruising on it, they invited us to join them for an outing. Our favorite annual boating expedition with them was to Lérins Island, across from Cannes and near the island where the fictitious Count of

Monte Cristo was held captive. Boats anchored near the shore so we could be picked up in a dinghy sent out by Frederick's Restaurant, whose specialty was huge lobsters dripping in butter and drenched in garlic topped by massive mounds of mouth-watering fried onions.

One of our daily routines was to have an ice cream cone every night after dinner, regardless of how lavish a meal we might have had. For Hal it was pistachio, for me, chocolate chip. We usually stopped at a little ice cream parlor in Cap Ferrat, where the owner had a quirky rule: patrons could sit at a table if they ordered ice cream in a dish, but not if they only ordered an ice cream cone. I love ice cream cones, so I ordered a dish of ice cream and separately ordered a cone. The owner had no problem with me making my own cone, as long as I adhered to his rule and bought the ice cream in a dish first.

One evening after we finished our ice cream cones, we walked home under a beautiful moon. The next morning, Hal had written the lyrics to "Over the Moon." When we returned to the States, a collaborator of Hal's, Ken Hirsch, composed a lovely melody set to Hal's lyric.

Over the moon
Looking at you, that's how I feel
Over the moon
Baby you're so unreal
Touching your hand takes me to some exotic land
Out of this world, under your spell, over the moon

Holding you tight
Makes me just feel so very loose
Light up my life
Baby, you've got the juice
Kissing your lips takes me on some romantic trips
Out of this world, under your spell, over the moon.

Although I used to get around
I never heard the sound
Of music deep in my soul
That was the way it used to be
Until you came to me
Now I hear, now I hear that music loud and clear.

Over the moon
Coming together face to face
Staying in tune
Somewhere up there in space
Feeling so fine, knowing I'm yours and you are mine
Out of this world, under your spell, over the moon.

When we returned from France, Hal threw me a birthday party at Chasen's Restaurant. He had just written "If I Could Love You More," with Archie Jordan, which he had dedicated to me. It was recorded by Engelbert Humperdinck. That was another song that Hal used to enjoy singing to me whenever we had friends over for one of our dinner/songfest parties. Archie Jordan was scheduled to sing it at Hal's memorial in 2012, but at the last minute he couldn't make it to Los Angeles and our friend Mac Davis was recruited to perform it. Mac learned it overnight, and played a stirring rendition at the memorial, accompanying himself on one of his many guitars. I was very grateful to him because the song meant so much to both Hal and me.

Our friends Bonnie and Bernie Hodes had been invited to cruise on the yacht of a businessman, Bob Lalemant, from Ghent, Brussels. They knew that Bob liked to meet new people to invite on his yacht, so they arranged for us to meet Bob's mistress Laura, with whom he'd been living for twenty-nine years. She was the one who organized the guests who joined her and Bob for their summer cruises. The Hodeses had hosted a dinner party the last time we'd been in Cap Ferrat, and Bonnie purposely sat Hal next to Laura. That did the trick: the deal was sealed that December in New York when we took Laura and Bob to lunch at Harry Cipriani.

That cruise led to an invitation every summer for the next five or six years on *Easy to Love*, Lalemant's one-hundred-fifty foot luxurious Fedship yacht. We took those cruises either before or after our stay in the south of France, and had some memorable experiences on board and at the lovely spots where we anchored, St. Tropez being one of Bob's favorite ports, Portofino being one of mine.

Bob, an amateur pianist, who loved pop music, had one ambition: to stump Hal in naming a song that he played on the piano in the salon of his ship. Not only was his ship named after a song, but all the staterooms were named after different popular songs. But in all the years that we joined Bob on his yacht, Hal always knew the title of whatever song he came up with, and most often he also knew who had written the songs and something about them. That frustrated Bob no end, and he kept inviting us back, in hopes of tripping Hal up.

We ended 1994 with a big bash at our Palm Desert home, where one of our friends brought the former child star Jackie Cooper and his wife Barbara Rae as guests. We began seeing them on a regular basis a few years later after Jackie and his wife moved into the Mirabella, the building in Los Angeles where we lived.

It was in January of 1995 that the historic Chasen's Restaurant closed its doors after sixty years of hosting movie stars, visiting dignitaries, presidents, and even the Pope. When Hal and I went there with our good friends the Brawermans to have our last bowl of their famous chili, we knew almost everyone in the place because so many of our friends wanted to be one of the last to eat in that landmark restaurant, just as we were doing. Oh, what stories those tables could tell! Ronnie Clint, who had been the manager at Chasen's for years, was hired by the Hillcrest Country Club to shape things up in their dining room, much to the delight of many club members who were Chasen's regulars. So, just as we always used to get a big hug every time we entered Chasen's, now we got a big hug as we entered Hillcrest.

I've never been a white-knuckle flyer, and in fact, have been quite calm during some pretty stormy weather and scary situations. I either fall asleep or immerse myself in an interesting book, and do not think about what is happening - often times to the consternation of friends who are flying with us, holding onto each other for dear life. But when Hal was asked to perform at a benefit for the Coconut Grove Playhouse in Hollywood, Florida, to be called "And Then I Wrote," the producers booked us on a Carnival Airlines flight from Los Angeles to Miami, since Carnival was one of the sponsors of the event.

I had some grave reservations about boarding the decrepit-looking plane when I first saw it parked on the tarmac at LAX, but bravely buckled up, and hoped for the best. My fears were not the least allayed when the pilot announced that there would be a slight delay because they had misplaced their flight plans, and would, obviously, have to find them before we could leave. Fortunately, I never heard of that airline again!

Charles Nelson Reilly was the M.C. of the concert, and others, besides Hal who donated their time and talent for the benefit were, Charles Strouse, who, with Nancy Reed Kanter sang "Too Young to be Old," in his medley (the song I so loved from Hal's and Charles' unproduced show *Lady for a Day*). Pat Cook, Cy Coleman, Sheldon Harnick, Jerry Leiber and Mike Stoller, Bea Arthur, Joe Bologna and Reneé Taylor, and Corky Hale.

The opening day of the O.J. Simpson trial officially began on January 24, 1995, with Deputy District Attorneys Marcia Clark and Christopher Darden representing the prosecution. Simpson had a whole slew of attorneys, the most flamboyant being Johnnie Cochran Jr., along with the more subdued Robert Shapiro. The lengthy and very dramatic trial was dubbed the "Trial of the Century." A great deal of controversy arose over the use of DNA, then a rather new type of evidence. TV sets were turned on constantly throughout the eight-month trial because there was always something startling or alarming going on, from Simpson's team alleging misconduct by the Los Angeles Police Department to complaints that blood samples had been mishandled. Judge Lance Ito became a reality TV star (even before that term was coined), because the trial was shown live on TV, and he was getting all kinds of press coverage. A verdict was due to come in, on October 3, so we decided to stay home that afternoon and watch the trial on TV. Apparently we weren't alone, because Domino's Pizza reported that they had a big spike in pizza orders in the fifteen minutes before the verdict, but when the verdict announcement began, those orders stopped, and not a single pizza was ordered from Domino's all across the country for the five minutes between 1 o'clock and 1:05 P.M. when the "not guilty" verdict was handed down.

Not guilty! Like many others, Hal and I were stunned because the evidence had seemed so overwhelmingly against Simpson. It was a shocking outcome which was debated over and over again for years to come, especially by Dominick Dunne, a popular investigative reporter and bestselling author.

By mid-February that year, the headlines shouted that the Dow Jones Industrial Averages had topped the four thousand mark. Federal Reserve Chairman Alan Greenspan helped trigger the gain by indicating that interest rates would hold steady at three percent, where they had been for the past three years. As a comparison, in 2011 the Dow Jones had climbed to well over 17,000 and interest rates were still low.

We heard about a trip around Scotland on a train called "The Royal Scotsman" and joined up with our friends from San Francisco, Lonna and Marshall Wais, to take the five hundred and forty mile journey through the Highlands of Scotland. But first we stopped at Greywalls, an elegant Scottish Edwardian country house, built in 1901. It was situated on the edge of the Muirfield championship golf course, with stunning views over East Lothian and the Firth of Forth (I just love that name).

During our tour around the neighboring towns, we spotted a restaurant called "Open Arms," where we booked dinner one night. That prompted Hal to tell our friends about the time we'd been in Israel and had gone to a concert at Caesarea, the ancient city located between Haifa and Tel Aviv. Archeologists unearthed an amphitheater there that they estimated once held fifteen thousand spectators. We'd taken a bus from Tel Aviv, along with our guide, and a group of others who were attending the concert. When it was over, and we were settled back on the bus, the driver turned on his radio, and we suddenly heard the dulcet tones of Jane Morgan singing "With Open Arms." Hal turned to me and said, "I wrote that song." I turned to our guide and told her that Hal had written that song. Judy turned to the bus driver to tell him about the song, and the bus driver announced, in Hebrew, over the loudspeaker, that the composer of the song that was playing on the radio had been written by a man sitting on his bus. With that, everyone stood up, right there in the bus, and gave Hal a big round of applause. We were just flabbergasted!

From Greywalls, we and the Waises headed to Edinburgh, where we were going to catch the Royal Scotsman train. Our first night there, we decided to eat at the rooftop restaurant of the Nira Caledonia Hotel, which had been highly recommended to us. As we were enjoying our first course, we heard the pianist play "With Open Arms." Hal could hardly believe his ears, especially having just told the story about "With Open Arms" to Lonna and Marshall. He couldn't resist going up to the pianist to introduce himself and to ask why that particular song had been chosen. The pianist said he just loved the song, and then produced a Hal David Songbook for Hal to sign. Even though the Jane Morgan version of the song reached #39 on the pop charts, and had a modicum of success, we never heard it again after that time in Edinburgh.

The Royal Scotsman lived up to its billing as one of the world's finest luxury train experiences: it was like a cruise, only on railroad tracks. We enjoyed the trip immensely as we traveled throughout Scotland from Edinburgh and back to Edinburgh, except when they tried to feed us haggis! In case you have never tasted Haggis, the savory pudding is beloved by the Scots but an acquired taste for almost everyone else.

After leaving the train, Hal and I rented a car in Edinburgh and, with me driving and Hal navigating all the roundabouts, we took our time before arriving at Glyndebourne, stopping overnight at three different manor houses along the way. Our friends Hope and Lee Warner met us at Horsted Place, a lovely Victorian Country House, where we stayed in order to be near Glyndebourne, and we had a grand time touring that area, as well as attending an opera, held in a six hundred-year-old country house in East Sussex, England. The original opera house, which opened in 1934, has continually been the venue for the annual Glyndebourne Festival, except during WWII, when it closed. Some people picnic on the grounds before the opera, but we opted to eat in the dining room, gazing at the opera-goers in their black tie finery, and their kilts.

We turned in our rental car, and had a driver take the four of us to London, where we had secured some hard-to-come-by tickets for Wimbledon. Known as "The British Open", Wimbledon is the oldest tennis tournament in the world, held at the All England Club in Wimbledon, London since 1877. They have a strict dress code for the players, and spectators observe the well-known tradition of eating strawberries and cream. Royal-watching can be as exciting as the tennis. In 1995, the Men's Singles winner was Pete Sampras, and the Women's Singles winner was Steffi Graf.

1995 was also the year that Hal and I took our first flight on the French Concorde, from New York to London. Flying fifteen hundred mph was a kick, and I loved the fact that we could get from New York to London in just three and a half hours: breakfast in New York, dinner in London. We were hooked after that first flight and took many Concorde flights back and forth to England or France from that time until two days before an Air France Concorde crashed in 2000, killing all passengers and crew members on board. The plane that crashed was the very same plane on which we'd just flown to Paris to start our August vacation. Although we were tempted to take another flight on the Concorde after that, we just couldn't bring ourselves to do it, and all the aging Concorde planes were retired just a few years later, never again to be rebuilt. They were just too expensive to operate.

Later, during our stay in the south of France that August, one of the highlights was the Annual Red Cross Ball in Monte Carlo, one of the dressiest galas we'd ever attended. The event was held at the Monte Carlo Sporting Club, and there too, we enjoyed watching all the "B.P.'s," including Prince Rainier, Prince Albert, and Princess Caroline, in all their haute couture finery and glittering jewelry.

There must have been something about the air in the south of France, because Hal wrote another song while we were there that year, a touching lyric which he titled "Don't Give up on Me," to which Kenny Hirsch wrote the melody. I couldn't figure out where the idea came from for this song, because we ourselves had not experienced any of the problems suggested by the lyrics.

When Hal played it at one of our dinner parties that summer, it was the hit of the party, even if it did bring tears to the eyes of our guests.

I know how much I've hurt you
How much I've let you down
The times I should have been there
When I was not around
But don't give up on me
Don't give up on me
I love you more than life, dear
So, don't give up on me

I've built my house with daydreams
The roof keeps falling in
They say that life's a gamble
I hardly ever win
But don't give up on me
Don't give up on me
I love you more than life, dear
So, don't give up on me

When I reach for the sky
I may find it's too high

Still I know if I try
There's nothing I can't do
As long as I have you

Today is all that matters
The past has come and gone
And I'll be there for you, dear
Forever from now on

So don't give up on me
Don't give up on me
I love you more than life, dear
Please don't give up on me

Hal was basically a very happy man. He'd realized his dream of becoming a successful songwriter, and he and I had a very fulfilling life. At one point though, he realized that a number of his songs had the word "blue" in them. He knew that was out of character for him, he was rarely, if ever blue. But somehow he had success with that word, so he kept using it. For example, there was "Bell Bottom Blues," written with Leon Carr in 1953, in which a woman longs for her absent sailor boy. The hit version in the United States was recorded by Teresa Brewer, and in the U.K., the song was a hit for Alma Cogan. Brewer's recording reached the Billboard Magazine charts in February of 1954, and lasted three weeks. Cogan's version was released the same year and reached #4 on the U.K. charts.

Then there was "Blue on Blue," a song of loneliness and loss of love which Hal wrote with Burt, which was first recorded by Bobby Vinton in 1963. It peaked at #3 on the *Billboard Hot 100* chart, and reached #2 on the *Easy Listening* chart. In fact, Vinton had such success with "Blue on Blue" that he recorded an entire album of blue-themed songs, which he titled, not too imaginatively, Blue on Blue.

That year, our usual side trip during our stay in the south of France was to Biarritz. We boarded a train in Monte Carlo with Lonna and Marshall Wais, not exactly as luxurious as the Royal Scotsman had been but adequate for our overnight trip. Shortly before we arrived at Biarritz, the train stopped in Lourdes to let off a group of nuns. Hal spoke to them as the train pulled into the station, in broken French, very broken. Two of the nuns laughed at Hal and in perfect English told him that they were from Brooklyn, Hal's hometown!

We'd gone to Biarritz to stay at the Eugénie Les Bain spa, where our bodies were pampered and our taste buds tantalized by the cuisine prepared by the renowned chef Michel Guérarde. Our routine was to be pummeled by the water treatments at the spa or to soak in their white mud baths in the morning, and then to go touring in the afternoon. One day, remembering the nuns we had met on the train, we decided to go to Lourdes, which turned out to be a-once-in-a-lifetime experience.

We were enormously impressed by the piety of the huge number of people who visited the site. There were people in wheelchairs, people being pulled in rickshaw-like chairs, and even people on stretchers, all gathered there in the hope of being cured of their illnesses. It turned out that we had arrived at Lourdes at a very propitious time. It was the one day, and the exact hour when they were having a grand procession of people from around the world that had come to pray and to be healed. There were thousands of them - a sea of them. There were nurses in the parade, spiritual and holy people, along with the masses who had gathered there. It was quite a sight, which will remain forever imprinted on our minds.

Hal and I had come to the realization that my condominium on Spalding Drive in Beverly Hills was not quite right for us because of the fact that it had no concierge, no front desk, and no valets; beautiful as it was, it was not a full-service building, which we realized we needed, so we moved to a slightly larger condominium on Oakhurst, still in Beverly Hills. We subsequently decided that we wanted to live on "the corridor," a few concentrated blocks of Wilshire Boulevard between Beverly Hills and Westwood Village where there were some beautiful high-rise condominiums. Hal sent me out to research the area, and I found a penthouse that we both fell in love with. By the time I saw it, it had been on the market for about two years, and we lost no time negotiating with the seller. His company had transferred him out of town, and he really was anxious to sell, but he was sticking to his guns, and would not accept the low-ball price that Hal offered.

Having lost that beautiful unit, I rather unenthusiastically went about looking for another one along the corridor, but had no luck. I think my heart was still set on the first one I'd seen.

But one night we were at a dinner party where I was seated next to a man who told me that he was a builder in the Los Angeles area. I somewhat facetiously asked him if he had any units for sale along the Wilshire Corridor. He told me that he himself didn't have any, but that a friend of his was having a cash flow problem and had a penthouse for sale somewhere on the corridor.

When I called his friend the next day, it turned out that his penthouse was in the Mirabella, the same building where I'd seen the unit I loved the previous year. Hal suggested that when I went to see the man's unit, I should also check to see if the original penthouse I'd seen was still for sale. It was!

I would have been happy to move into either one of them. We told the young man with the cash flow problem that we would make him and the other owner the same deal and that we would buy from the first person who accepted our offer. The man with the cash flow problem said that his mortgage was more than what we were offering, so that was out. By this time the company of the man we'd talked to a year ago had taken over his unit, and they were very motivated to sell. They accepted the offer we'd made the previous year, and the beautiful penthouse, with glorious views of the city, was finally ours.

We kept a pretty low-key profile in the building, but once, shortly after we first moved in, Hal asked one of his collaborators to come to our apartment to work at our piano while Hal wrote some lyrics. When Phil Spector drove up to the courtyard and gave his car to the open-mouthed valets, our reputation quickly gained in stature. Phil, the record producer and songwriter who originated the "Wall of Sound" technique, was a pioneer in the 1960's girl-group sound, and produced over twenty-five top forty hits between 1960 and 1965. He and Hal were working on a song that they planned to play for Linda Ronstadt, hoping she would record it in Spanish.

Later, we mentioned to Phil that we were going to be in New York, and he told Hal that he would meet there so they could continue working on the song, giving us the name of the hotel where he would be staying. But when we called there and asked for Mr. Spector, we were told that he was not registered. Only later did we learn that Phil liked to travel incognito, usually registering under an assumed name. This time it was "The Lone Ranger."

Years later, Phil Spector gained infamy on a murder charge and conviction under his real name, and is currently serving a long-term sentence in prison. As I mentioned earlier, Hal always had a contentious relationship with his older brother Mack, who was also a songwriter. Hal became more successful than Mack early in his career, and I'm sure that never sat too well with Mack or with Mack's wife, Bea. Hal had another older brother, Bernie, but, other than telling me that Bernie had been a brilliant artist who then became a very successful insurance agent, Hal never spoke much about him or his family; nor did he often speak about their younger sister, Barbara Bierer. I'd met Barbara and her daughter, Lynne Wilkins, but not Bernie.

When Hal and I first met, he hadn't seen or talked to Mack in several years. But he arranged for me to meet Mack and his wife Bea at dinner one evening. Mack was charming and erudite that evening, obviously on his best behavior.

I think Hal's animus toward his brother started quite early in his life. Their father died when Hal was still a young boy. While he lay on his sick bed, Hal happened to overhear a conversation that his father had with Mack, during which their father told Mack to look after Hal when he was gone. Rather than considering that their father might have had Hal's best interests at heart, Hal took this to mean that his father thought he couldn't take care of himself, and that hurt him terribly. It took him a long time to get over that overheard conversation, and in fact, I'm not sure that he ever did because he mentioned it frequently. That Mack tried to dissuade Hal from doing the one thing that really appealed to him, certainly didn't help their relationship. Hal was always sorry that neither of his parents lived to see his success in his chosen field. He felt his father especially would have wanted to know that he made it - on his own - without Mack's help.

There were other reasons for Hal's less-than-positive feelings toward his brother. Mack, who was an inveterate gambler, frequently borrowed money from Hal. Hal, was doing better financially than Mack during those years and never wanted to confront Mack with what he owed, so those debts went unpaid, and that understandably always rankled Hal, as well as his wife, Anne.

In the 1950's, Mack tried to write English lyrics to the French song "La Vie en Rose," which Edith Piaf had made so famous. But he was having trouble getting them just right. He asked Hal to help him out, which Hal was happy to do. But there was no mention of Hal's name on the credits, an omission Hal found difficult to forgive.

Hal was pleased with the results when on his own, he wrote the English lyrics to the French song "Non je ne Regrette Rien" which he titled "No Regrets. It was recorded by Edith Piaf in 1961. Kay Starr had a big hit with it in 1963, and it was dramatically sung by Shirley Bassey in 1973, and Martinique recorded it in 1985. Marion Cotillard, the French star of the 2007 movie *La*

Vie en Rose sang a touching version of the song at the end of the movie, which left many in the audience in tears.

Mack, who was living in California at the time of Anne David's death, did not come to New York for her funeral and, that, to Hal was the unkindest cut of all.

Then there was another instance that almost ended the brothers' relationship for good. Mack and his wife Bea lived at Canyon Country in Palm Springs, having moved out of the Beverly Hills area. This was back when Hal and I had our weekend home in Palm Desert at The Lakes, not too far away. One night we happened to be at an event in the desert honoring Jimmy Van Heusen, when a mutual friend of the David brothers came up to us and asked if we were planning to attend an upcoming party in the desert at which Mack was going to be honored.

We were surprised that we hadn't heard about the party before, but because the people hosting the party invited us this evening, we asked for the date and said we'd be sure to put it on our calendars.

Shortly before the event, when Mack apparently learned that Hal was planning to attend the party, Hal got a call from Mack's wife Bea, telling him that she didn't want him there. She said that Mack didn't want him there either. Hal was not willing to accept that on her say-so alone, so he insisted that she put Mack on the phone. Mack shamefacedly admitted that he did not want Hal there because he thought the event was going to be his last hurrah, and he was afraid Hal would steal his thunder if he showed up.

This proved that Mack felt even more competitive with Hal than Hal had ever realized, and that realization saddened him greatly. In fact, he was so hurt that he vowed to me that he would never see Mack again. That was the straw for Hal that broke the camel's back. That incident just about broke his heart because he felt that Mack had irrefutably hurt their relationship, not only as brothers, but as friends.

True to his word, we had no further contact with either Mack or Bea for several years. But one day Mack called and asked if Hal would come to see him the next time we were in the desert because Mack had a financial statement from ASCAP which he could not figure out, and he wanted Hal to help him read it.

Now Mack could figure out a statement with the best of them, so Hal and I knew that his request was just an excuse by Mack to reach out to his brother. I encouraged Hal to accept the invitation, which he reluctantly agreed to do. So the next weekend we joined Mack and Bea for lunch at the Canyon Club, where Hal made a pretense of reviewing the statement, and with that, Mack and Hal more or less patched things up.

Later that afternoon we received a call from Bea saying that Mack was in the hospital. Mack was known to be a hypochondriac of the first order, and Bea took him to the emergency room at Eisenhower Hospital on a regular basis. So we were not too alarmed at the news, but we did go to visit Mack in the hospital: We felt it was the least we could do, especially since Mack knew we were nearby.

Mack was released the following day, so we breathed a sigh of relief. But he was readmitted a day or two later and that time it really was the end. Mack died of heart failure on December 30th, 1993.

Hal just could not get over the fact that I had encouraged him to meet with Mack that weekend, and he kept thanking me over and over again, telling me how happy he was that he'd had a chance to reconnect with Mack before Mack passed. I hadn't had a premonition or anything of the sort; it just seemed like the right thing to do, and I was very glad that Hal had listened to me.

I'm not telling tales out of school by revealing these stories. I recorded Hal on a video, during which I asked him dozens of personal questions, which he had agreed to answer candidly. I made the video because so much was known about Hal's professional life, but very little was on record about his personal life. I always regretted not knowing more about my father's life when he was a young man. I thought maybe Hal's family would like to know more about Hal's life than they did. Hal revealed stories about his difficult relationship with Mack on that video, as he had to various friends of ours in the past, and he told me that it felt good to get those things off his chest.

Hal and I made a habit of going to La Scala, the popular restaurant in Beverly Hills, every Saturday afternoon for their renowned Leon's salad. We started to know many of the other patrons who also went there every Saturday, almost all of whom ordered the same dish, which was famously comprised of mozzarella cheese, salami, garbanzo beans, hard cooked eggs, diced pepperoncini, Greek olives, and their incomparable salad dressing. Going there was almost like belonging to a club. One day, though, we stopped in at the Hillcrest Country Club (where we were provisional members) at lunch time, and ran into friends whom we knew slightly. They invited us to join them at their table, and that started a new long-running tradition. Every Saturday from then on, whenever we were in town we would have lunch at the Club with Peggy and Walter Grauman. Peggy was a major philanthropist, who had served on many prestigious Boards. Walter, perhaps best known for his successful twelve year run as director of Murder, She Wrote, had been a B-25 pilot during WWII, having received the Distinguished Flying Cross and the Air Medal with five oak leaf clusters, for his bravery during fifty-six combat missions in the European theater. In spite of those daunting credits, Walter felt that his most significant achievement was his creation of the Music Center Spotlight Awards.

That chance meeting turned into a wonderful friendship, and we not only ate together on Saturdays, but we celebrated every Thanksgiving with our families, at Hal's and my apartment, watching the grandchildren grow from sitting in high-chairs to attaining adulthood.

One of the men we'd met on our honeymoon in 1988 when we travelled with the USIA group was Ralph Newman, a renowned authority on President Abraham Lincoln, and Lincoln memorabilia. If someone wanted to buy a Lincoln collectible, they usually checked with Ralph first.

Ralph was on the Board of Lincoln College in Springfield, Illinois, and he encouraged the College to present Hal with an honorary Degree of Doctor of Music. So in May of 1991, we headed to Springfield, where we had a thrilling time. The college really knew how to host their guests.

Our visit started with a dinner in Hal's honor at the Sangamo Club. There we met Louise Taper, who was also on the Board of the College and her husband Barry. I'd known Barry for many years, and had heard that he'd married someone who was a Lincoln collector and scholar, but we had yet to meet her. From that moment on, Louise Taper and I became fast friends.

Pat and Ralph Newman had donated a bookshop on the site of a recreation area where Lincoln's original log cabin stood, and the workers there were just thrilled to see "the famous Hal David," and every one of them stood in line to get his signature. It was really adorable, and Hal was very sweet and shy about signing all those slips of paper thrust at him. We toured the historic site of Lincoln's tomb and, for good luck, Hal ran his hand over the nose of the huge bronze bust of Lincoln, rubbed to a sparkling shine by the throngs of visitors, all hoping for good luck by touching that famous schnozzola.

Photo by Eunice David.

At the banquet held the night before the awards presentation, the music department of the college prepared a very ambitious program of a medley of ten of Hal's songs, which they not only sang, but had choreographed as well. All the kids were just thrilled and said later that they felt they were auditioning for a part in a Broadway show.

After the dinner, the Tapers hosted a lovely party at their apartment in Springfield: a wonderful way to top off the evening.

When we returned to Lincoln College the next day, we were ushered into the fitting room, where ladies meticulously made sure the gowns of the honorees fit just right. The other honorees that day were Marshall Coyne, a major philanthropist and businessman from Washington, D.C. He was the owner of the Madison Hotel in D.C., where coincidentally, we frequently stayed when we were in Washington. Ellsworth Brown, who was the President and Director of the Chicago Historical Society, was the other honoree.

Originally there was supposed to have been a prominent keynote speaker for the graduation ceremonies, but he took ill, and was unable to attend at the last minute. So the President of the College asked each doctoral candidate to speak for about ten minutes, telling something about how they got started and what they were doing at the moment. Ellsworth Brown spoke on a very high esoteric level, which passed over the heads of most of the students in attendance. Marshall spoke on the merits of big business which seemed to appeal to only a small percentage of his audience. But Hal had taken his instructions to heart, and he spoke about his early beginnings and the struggle he had getting into the music business. I could tell that the kids were with him all the way, because they laughed at the right times, and applauded frequently while Hal was speaking. Hal ended his speech by quoting a line from his song "America Is," which was *"anything you can dream, you can do. It's up to you."* What an appropriate sentiment for graduating students to hear. I thought he was right on! Back in the dressing room at Lincoln College, I was delighted to see how many graduates came by to ask for Hal's autograph.

After Springfield we were headed for an extended vacation in Europe that we'd been planning for some time. But as the time drew near for us to leave, Hal expressed disappointment that he was going to be so far away from friends and family on his milestone seventieth birthday. So without him knowing anything about it, I wrote to about one hundred friends, not only asking them to send Hal a birthday greeting, but actually sending them a mailing label and the correct postage.

When we and our friends Hope and Lee Warner arrived at Sharrow Bay Country House on Lake Ullswater in England, Nigel Lawrence, the manager, greeted us so enthusiastically that we were taken by surprise. But after we were escorted to our rooms which were in the gate house of this incredible estate, we understood why.

There were literally hundreds of letters, packages, Faxes, and telephone messages. Such an outpouring was overwhelming to Hal and even to me, since it went way beyond my hopes and expectations. It took us a good two days just to open and read all the messages. Naturally we both had to read every single item at least twice. Here is a picture of the birthday boy with only a fraction of what was sent.

Photo by Eunice David.

Our congenial hosts were Francis Coulson and Brian Sack. The property had been willed to Francis by an elderly aunt, and he and his partner Brian, who had been together for about thirty years, fixed it up to become the treasure

Photo by Eunice David.

that it was by the time we learned about the charming hideaway. They really made our stay memorable. Brian and Francis seemed especially sorry to see us leave, but aside from their incredible hospitality at the Inn, they had one very special treat in store for us before our departure. We had read about their prize-winning, spectacular English garden, so when they asked us if we wanted to see it, we immediately accepted the invitation, knowing that very few guests of the Inn were so fortunate. It was truly a marvel to see, especially since everything was in glorious bloom at that time of year.

Our ultimate goal was Cliveden, a great estate located on three hundred and seventy-six acres of private gardens and parklands along the Thames River. It is a gracious manor house, once owned by the Astors and various dukes and earls, with a checkered and even infamous history.

There were many scandals associated with various people who visited that manor house. The one Hal and I most vividly remembered was called "The Profumo Affair." In the early 1960's, John Profumo, then married and the British Secretary of State for War, had an affair with Christine Keeler, the mistress of a Soviet spy. Profumo lied to the House of Commons when questioned about it, after which he was forced to resign and the reputation of Prime Minister Harold Macmillan's government was damaged.

By the time we returned home, we were pleased to learn that we'd been approved as members of the Hillcrest Country Club. When we were interviewed by the Membership Committee, they had made it clear that Hal would be called upon from time to time to do something in the way of entertainment for the members, but we didn't realize just how soon that would happen.

Almost immediately I was contacted by the Women's Activity Committee. They wanted me to ask Hal to organize a program for their annual luncheon. Since I'd never attended one of those luncheons, I wasn't exactly sure what was involved, but Hal and I decided to do what we did best: organize a group of Hal's writer friends to perform their own songs. Not exactly an original idea, but I figured it was one which most of Hillcrest's members would not have seen before.

Hal called the show *Thanks for the Melodies* (also not terribly original, since he'd used it for the show in the Berkshires) and we recruited three teams of songwriters Jay Livingston and Ray Evans, Marilyn and Alan Bergman, Mike Stoller and Jerry Leiber. Mike's wife, the brilliant musician Corky Hale, accompanied Hal and the Bergmans on the piano.

The luncheon was meant to be for the female members of Hillcrest, but when word got around as to what the program was, the men threatened to strike unless they, too, could attend. At first the committee flatly refused to allow it, but the clamor became so loud that the club finally had to send out a flyer stating that "anyone" could make a reservation. We heard afterwards that this was the best attended luncheon they'd had in the history of the country club.

The Hillcrest Country Club had mentioned, when they invited us to become members, that they would be calling on Hal on occasion to do something for the club. That "something" turned into a series of events in which both Hal and I got involved. The one that we worked on in 1995 was a celebration of the seventy-fifth anniversary of the club. Hillcrest member Neil Diamond was the star of the show, which was held at the Beverly Hilton Hotel. There were over a thousand seats sold even before the invitations went out. Rhonda Fleming, also a member of Hillcrest, sang the "Star Spangled Banner," and with Monty Hall as the M.C., the show was off and running. Monty and Sidney Poitier, another member, reviewed the past seventy-five years of history of Hillcrest, and Hal and the Ray Charles Singers performed a musical tribute, which Hal wrote, as an ode to comedians who were members of the club: Al Jolson, George Jessel, Danny Kaye, Danny Thomas, Jack Benny, George Burns, and Milton Berle. Hal wrote another musical number, called "Hal David Remembers Hillcrest Composers," which he sang with the chorus, and then Hal sang "Raindrops" as a solo. Hal definitely paid his dues that year.

Our friends Ron Rosen (who spearheaded the whole thing), Walter Grauman, Howard Koch, and Hal were the producers of the seventy-fifth anniversary show. This group of fellows went on to produce show after successful show for Hillcrest, with a variety of themes. The last one Hal participated in was in celebration of Hillcrest's ninetieth anniversary in 2010. I was involved in that one also, creating the commemorative coffee-table book for the event.

The whole world (well, maybe not the Middle Eastern countries) was saddened to learn of the assassination of Yitzhak Rabin, the Prime Minister and Defense Minister of Israel. On November 4, 1995, a religious Zionist who was opposed to Rabin's peace initiative and the signing of the Oslo Accords, shot and killed Rabin as he was getting into his car after a speaking engagement. The shooter was arrested on the spot. In Rabin's pocket when he died was a sheet of paper with the lyrics of a well-known Israeli song, the English title of which was "Song for Peace." How ironic was that?

We ended 1995 at a wonderful musical evening at the home of Shirley and Jay Livingston. Whenever the Livingstons gathered friends to their Bel Air home, the guests would periodically get up and perform, and this evening was no exception, with Hal, Red Buttons, Selma and Army Archerd, Eydie and Pete Rugolo, Johnny Mandel, Betty Rose, Liné Renaud, and Frances Bergen and Craig Stevens in attendance, it turned into a very exclusive talent show.

After the success that Burt and Hal had with their Broadway show *Promises, Promises* in 1972, they were assigned to write a musical remake of the classic Frank Capra film *Lost Horizon,* about plane crash survivors who are stranded in the lost city of Shangri-La in the Himalaya Mountains.

When that movie, titled *Lost Horizon, the Musical,* failed, it was the first time Burt and Hal had ever been so severely panned, and it drove a wedge between them, with the strain of their relationship eventually affecting not only the two men but also Dionne Warwick. There were lawsuits flying back and forth at that time, leading the men to not see or talk to each other for many years.

In an interview for the ASCAP archives, Hal gave a short version of the breakup of the Bacharach/David/Warwick partnership. Burt and Hal were under contract to write a certain number of new songs each year for Dionne, and Burt wasn't coming up with the music so that Hal could write lyrics. Dionne felt she was going to lose ground if she didn't record regularly. Burt had become a recording artist in his own right with A&M Records, so new songs for Dionne were just not getting written and when Dionne sued both Burt and Hal, Hal's nose got out of joint because he had not been the one to slow things down.

In a *Los Angeles Times* article after Hal passed away, Burt publically took responsibility for their break-up, which I appreciated reading. I only wished that Hal could have read it, or learned how Burt felt about the situation while he was still alive. After that, whenever Burt performed, he graciously started giving Hal credit for writing the great lyrics which helped make their songs so popular. He hadn't done that during their early years of working together, hence the fact that so many people, including me, thought that Burt had written all those amazing songs by himself. The movie, *Lost Horizon, The Musical,* produced in 1973 by Ross Hunter (his first), and written by Normal Heart's Larry Kramer, almost bankrupted Columbia Pictures, who were the distributors. The movie got terrible reviews, while the soundtrack fared only slightly better, peaking at #56 on the Billboard Hot 100 list, with the song "Living Together, Growing Together" (a big hit for the Fifth Dimension) reaching #32. Diana Ross and Marvin Gaye recorded "Things I will Not Miss," from the movie, for their 1973 album *Diane and Marvin*.

The Fifth Dimension, featuring Marilyn McCoo and Billy Davis, Jr., Florence LaRue, Lamonte McLemore, and Ron Townson, was well-known for their stylish arrangements of pop, R&B, soul, and jazz. They had recorded Hal's "One Less Bell to Answer" in 1970 on their debut album. That song reached #2 on the Billboard Hot 100 chart, #4 on the Best Selling Souls Singles chart, and #1 on the Adult Contemporary chart. Barbra Streisand partially covered the song in the medley, "One Less Bell to Answer/A House is Not a Home" on her 1971 album, *Barbra Joan Streisand,* and it has also been covered by many other singers, including Dionne Warwick and Shirley Bassey, Vikki Carr, Vanessa Williams, Sheryl Crow, and recently, by Matthew Morrison and Kristin Chenoweth in the TV series *Glee*.

Hal loved telling the story about how the song title came to him. When he was invited to a party in London, the hostess said, *Don't bother to ring the bell when you arrive, just walk in. It will be one less bell for me to answer.* He said that the line took hold of him and wouldn't let go.

Club 100, is one of the support groups of the Los Angeles Music Center, of which I was a long-time board member and a two-term president. It sponsors an annual event honoring outstanding teachers in the greater Los Angeles area by presenting them with "Bravo Awards." Hal was asked to write a theme song for the event, so he got together with the talented composer Ken Hirsch, who wrote a beautiful melody to Hal's lyrics. The song, Bravo to The Teachers was played each year from then on, performed by children from one of the schools where a teacher was being honored. The lyrics indicate that one should say bravo to the teachers and bravo for the reachers.

Hal and I let the Education Division of the Music Center know that we wanted to grant a scholarship for the music teacher whose chorus was scheduled to sing the song each year, but the man in charge of the Division told us that they were not interested in our award. I always felt that he was very short-sighted, because ASCAP would have doubled our contribution, making it a very nice gift for the winning school.

When the Education Division of the Music Center turned our generous offer down, we were surprised and hurt, but we turned around and offered our funds to the ASCAP Foundation, specifying that it should go to a music instructor in residence at the Los Angeles County High School for the Arts. The ASCAP Foundation was not only thrilled with our annual donation, but matched our grant, which made it a very attractive and sought-after achievement for the Los Angeles County High School for the Arts. I'm proud to say that after Hal passed, I have continued funding the grant in both of our names.

Hal had agreed to perform at the Los Angeles Jewish Home for their big Mother's Day event. It is always billed as "the largest Mother's Day party in the world," and it probably is, with two thousand people in attendance. When Hal performed at the Home, where my mother lived, he always introduced her from the stage, and told everyone how much she enjoyed living there, and she would preen around for days afterwards. She and I always had a contentious relationship, ever since I could remember, she knew just which buttons to push to upset me, and she pushed them relentlessly. But Hal she loved! I clearly learned where I stood in my mother's heart while we were there on one of our usual Sunday visiting days, and she introduced Hal by saying, with great pride, "This is my son-in-law, Hal David." Then she pointed to me, standing next to Hal and said, "And this is his wife." All I could do was laugh, I wasn't about to give her the satisfaction of being hurt!

On May 25, 1996, I threw a big bash for Hal's seventy-fifth birthday at the Four Seasons Hotel in Beverly Hills. It was fun keeping all the details completely secret from him. Friends came in from near and far to help celebrate. Our delightful friend Joe Smith agreed to be the M.C. and when he got up after dinner, to start the show, one of his first remarks was: "Eunice is so organized that she could have run the Gulf War - and won it!" Knowing me, everyone broke up. It turned into a bigger deal than I had expected, but with two hundred twenty-five guests, I wanted it to be perfect, so I did pretty much micro-manage everything. Joe, a major figure in the music business, presided over three giant record labels, Warner Brothers, Elektra/Asylum, and Capitol Records, during his remarkable career. He was a graduate of Yale, and had started his music business career as a disc jockey. Who better to ask to help me with Hal's birthday party?

Many friends performed, and special lyrics were written for Hal that night. Our good friend Red Buttons brought the house down when he said that we all knew the names of Hal's hits, and then made up some funny titles which he said were Hal's misses. Hal sang "If I Could Love you More," reminding everyone that he had written it especially for me, and he also sang some special lyrics to the tune of "Close to You," part of which were: "On the day that she was born, the angels got together, and decided to create the perfect wife, so they created Eunice, and together now we share the perfect life." Hal was a real romantic!

Army Archerd, the late, great show-business columnist, wrote this excerpt in his column for Variety about the party:

Memories are made of this: Hal David's 75th black-tied birthday bash, given by loving wife Eunice at the Four Seasons, was one for the memory book. David was surrounded and serenaded by fellow music masters, as well as civilian admirers, all of whom had nothing but bon mots and tuneful tributes to the always-kind David. With Rudy Varone at the piano, songs by David were woven into the show by Paul Williams, emcee Joe Smith, and Burt Bacharach (playing, singing "Alfie"); Jay Livingston (three-time Oscar winner with Ray Evans) borrowed Cole Porter's music to parody-sing "You're the Top" to David. Selma and I even duetted to Hal and Eunice. Red Buttons, acknowledging Hal's hits, told of his near-misses, like "How are Things in Bora Bora," or "52nd Street," etc. Nancy Reed (Kanter) and Corky Hale on piano teamed to serenade Hal, who sang his "If I Could Love You More" to wife Eunice.

Not long after the party, we invited the Archerds, the Livingstons, and Red Buttons to dinner at Trader Vic's as a thank you for their help in making Hal's party such a success. Red had been performing in Chicago, and had a driver meet him at Los Angeles International Airport to bring him directly to the restaurant. When he came in, he was waving a sheaf of paper, saying that on the flight home he had re-written the off-the-cuff skit that he had performed at the party. With that, he got up in the middle of the restaurant, and performed the skit all over again, with some re-written song titles of Hal's "misses." Needless to say the patrons in the restaurant that night got more than the chop suey they had ordered.

Just a month later, we attended a dinner presented by The Marilyn and Monty Hall Statesman's Club for the Los Angeles Jewish Home. Guests at the dinner were all major donors to the home. Hal received their Rose Media Achievement Award, for his help to the home in presenting programs there, and for his willingness in general to lend his talent when and where needed. The award stated that it was to "acknowledge his vital role in educating the public regarding aging." Peter Marshall and Nancy Reed Kanter sang two of Hal's songs, and when Hal got up to make his acceptance speech, he sang "Too Young to be Old," not only a fitting song for the two of us, but a very fitting song for the Jewish Home, where the average - the average age of their residents is in the high nineties.

That summer, rather than going directly to the south of France for the month of August, we stopped in London to see a production of *Promises, Promises,* which played at the Bridewell Theatre from July to August. The actors all spoke and sang in broad American accents, and it wasn't until we went backstage to meet the cast that we realized they were really born and bred Brits. Jonathan Tunick, the musical arranger of the show when it first opened on Broadway, was in town working on the show *Martin Guerre*, and he and his wife Lee joined Hal and me the night we saw the show. *Promises* had been Jonathan's first important Broadway show, so it always held a special place in his heart.

While we were in the south of France, our friends Lonna and Marshall Wais invited us to join them at a "white party" at La Reserve de Beaulieu hosted by Cartier. The guests were asked to wear all white clothing, and there was also going to be a contest for the best chapeau. I had no fancy hat with me - just sunshades. Suddenly the proverbial light bulb went off in my head, and I called our office in Studio City to send me some supplies. When they arrived, I started cutting, clipping, pasting and stapling, and pretty soon I had something that I thought looked pretty good.

When I walked into the swanky party, I saw women with very expensive-looking store-bought hats, which made mine look very much like the hastily home-made creation that it was. But before I knew it, I was called up to the podium and told that I had won first prize, and I was presented with a beautiful lapis and gold Cartier clock. I quickly gave credit for the inspiration of the hat to my husband and explained that he wrote all the songs on the sheet music from which I'd made the hat. With that, many of the other guests, and musicians came up to us and asked for autographs, Hal's, not mine!

It was at this party that we first learned the Macarena, the dance craze that swept through Europe like a tidal wave. When it finally reached the shores of the USA, about a year later, both Hal and I thought we were very hip because we already knew all the moves, and were happy to demonstrate them at a moment's notice.

This year at the end of August, instead of heading right home, we and the Waises joined the "Save Venice" group on the Cunard Line's Sea Goddess for a cruise from Rome to Venice, stopping at Stromboli to see the volcano erupting, Syracuse, Sicily to see the ruins, and Taormina. We took a special side trip to Albania where Lady and Lord Jacob Rothschild were sponsors of an archeological dig. They were there to welcome us and proudly showed us around the site.

We celebrated our anniversary that year while on board the Sea Goddess, and Lonna arranged for the Italian pastry chef to bake a cake for us. Something went slightly awry in the translation because the beautifully decorated cake read

"RAINDROPES keep falling on your head." Lonna was mortified, but the chef certainly meant well.

Before returning to the States, we visited our friends in London, where Bob Lalemant, our host on the yacht Easy to Love, happened to be in town for the horseraces, and he invited us to join him for lunch at Epsom Downs, because his horse, which he had named ANOTHER NIGHT after one of Hal's songs, was running. ANOTHER NIGHT came in third, but we didn't care: it had been great fun to be there to watch him run.

What with our usual August in the south of France, the cruise with the Save Venice group, our trip to London and then on to Paris for a CISAC meeting, we were gone from Los Angeles for two months: too long for us to be away.

So we were happy to be back in Los Angeles, where we quickly got into our routine of visiting with friends and attending movies. We went to a screening of the movie *The First Wives Club* starring Bette Midler, Diane Keaton, and Goldie Hahn. It was a funny movie about three first wives who'd been dumped by their husbands for younger women. Hal's "Wives and Lovers" played throughout the opening credits, and he got a kick out of its use in the movie.

In November, the Miller Memorial Children's Hospital in Long Beach held a benefit concert in featuring Burt Bacharach and Dionne Warwick. The organizers of the event asked if Hal would come, as a surprise, to present awards onstage to Burt and Dionne.

Just before the show was due to end, Hal and I were escorted backstage, and as Burt and Dionne were taking their first bow, Hal was cued to walk on stage with the two awards. The looks on their faces as they saw who was carrying the awards to them was priceless. Burt immediately introduced Hal, and commented on what a great lyricist he was, and the audience responded enthusiastically. Back stage there were hugs and kisses all around, and photo ops galore.

The review in the *Los Angeles Times* by Don Heckman read in part, "Was there ever a better partnership between singer and songwriters than the combination of Dionne Warwick with Burt Bacharach and Hal David? Thirty years after the trio produced an extraordinary string of hits, their music still sounds fresh and contemporary…"

We had a special treat in December, to end the year. Lonna and Marshall Wais were celebrating their tenth anniversary with a big bash at Club 21 in New York, one of our favorite restaurants. Lonna had hired Mike Carney's Society Orchestra to play for the evening (Mike was the son of the wonderful comedian Art Carney, and looked very much like him). She asked if Hal would sing a medley of his songs during the evening, which he happily did.

Marshall had recently been kidnapped in San Francisco, so we were anxious to learn how he was doing. The kidnappers had asked for a half a million dollars in ransom money, and drove all over San Francisco during the eight hours that Marshall was in their van, blindfolded, while negotiating with his bankers to get the money. Finally, at the designated drop off spot, they took the blindfold off Marshall and gave him twenty dollars for cab fare to get home: he'd been taken from his home in his pajamas, and had nothing else with him.

The FBI, who had been alerted, somehow or other tracked the van down, and once Marshall was safely out of it and the money had been picked up, they crashed into the van and arrested the two kidnappers, retrieving all the money. One of the guests at the anniversary party was heard to comment: "Only Marshall could get kidnapped and make a profit on it!"

We'd been planning a trip to India with Joan and John Hotchkis, friends whom we originally met in Salzburg when we were there when the Los Angeles Philharmonic Orchestra performed. Joan was formerly president of the prestigious Blue Ribbon organization of the Music Center in downtown

Los Angeles and John, a business leader and philanthropist, served on numerous boards at the Music Center and other organizations. Before the trip, they ran into their friends Merle Miller and Peter Mullin, the 2015 Automobile Man of the Year, at the Hollywood Bowl, and suggested that they join us on the trip, to which they immediately agreed. Merle, who'd been to India many times, planned an incredible itinerary for our three-week trip.

We were a rather disparate group, and at that time were not close to the Hotchkises, and had certainly not yet traveled together. And we had only met Merle and Peter at a dinner which we'd arranged prior to leaving on this trip. But the combination was magical, and we had a memorable trip, traveling from Delhi to Varanasi to see the mystical Ganges, to Khajuraho to see the erotic carvings on the temples, to Agra to see the magnificent Taj Mahal, to Jaipur, where we stayed at the Rambagh Palace and had our ride on an elephant, and on to Jodhpur.

We found our way to Udaipur where we stayed at the Lake Palace Hotel, a two hundred fifty-year old marble palace sitting right in the middle of Lake Pichola. One of the nights when we were at the hotel, it was Peter's birthday, so we all decided to dress up in the Indian finery we'd purchased along the way. Joan and I had someone from the hotel help us drape our saris, and then we all met for a photo op so that Hal could read all the special material he'd written for Peter and the rest of us.

Joan and I had arranged for the six of us to have dinner in a little semi-private alcove at one end of the dining room. Merle read a toast to Peter in "Pidgin-Indian," which had us falling out of our chairs. We were having a grand time when suddenly other guests of the hotel started coming in to see what was going on, asking if they could take pictures of us: they wanted pictures of us - they wanted pictures of them with us - they just couldn't get enough of us. A German fellow even came over and asked if he could take our picture for the German magazine Stern, which meant "star" in English. He said he wanted to show how Americans enjoy themselves in India.

Near the end of our odyssey, Peter, Merle, Hal, and I left Thekkady for a five-hour drive to Cochin. We passed endless tea plantations, with the wonderfully graphic patterns created by the meticulous way the plants were growing, when suddenly, in a tiny little town somewhere a couple of hours away from Thekkady, we happened upon a local Hindu festival.

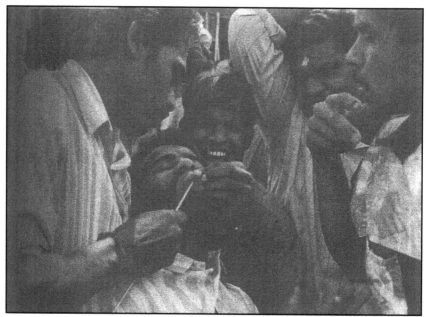

Photo by Eunice David.

We perked up immediately as soon as we saw a huge elaborately decorated elephant and heard the unique sounds of Indian music wafting through the air. We parked at the far end of town and, with cameras at the ready, ran back to that parade, as a group of locals gathered around us, sprinkling us with ceremonial colored powder: I had a head full of green hair, a yellow and red forehead, and our clothes were covered with the stuff. Peter, at 6'6", towered over everyone, and was able to get some pictures that I, at 5'3", couldn't get. The policemen, realizing that we wanted to take pictures, actually stopped the flow of traffic for us so that we could get a clear view and snap away to our heart's content.

Soon the head honcho of the village came up to us and gestured that we should follow him. He took us to see some men who were inserting long, metal rods through the lips of some of the young men we'd seen dancing around in a trance.

I was so excited that I wasn't sure I could hold my camera steady enough to get a good picture of this incredibly unusual event, but I did get one good shot and the looks on the faces of those watching the procedure was priceless. Still painted head to toe, we arrived at the Malabar Hotel in Cochin, which was a mixture of contemporary and ancient cultures. Many of the stores we passed in the Jewish section, known as "Jew Town," were originally homes of the Jewish merchants who came to India in the 1500's to settle in Mattancherry after having been expelled from Craganore. We visited a synagogue which was built in 1568 and still held some of its former splendor. An elderly man showed us around and when Hal mentioned that he was Jewish, the man said that in that case, he would open the doors to the ark and show the Torah to all the people who were visiting that day. He told us that ordinarily he doesn't let people see the Torah, only when there is someone visiting who is Jewish. He made it clear that it was all right for me to photograph the Torah, but not him, since it was a religious taboo.

We learned that at one time there was quite a large population of Jewish settlers in Cochin, but by the time we were there, there were only eighteen elderly people left.

Joan and John had returned home a few days earlier, and now Merle and Peter were leaving us. But Hal and I continued to the hillside community of Ooty for the last leg of our trip. Cochin had been hot and muggy, but in the hill country it was cool, with a nice breeze blowing. We found that driving in

India was scary at best and treacherous most of the time. Ran, our driver, said that a good driver drives with his brakes, his horn, his heart, and his luck. Fortunately for us, Ran seemed to possess all of these.

We drove through the Nilgara (Blue Mountains), climbing to about three thousand feet, with the horn blaring constantly, and our little four-cylinder Ambassador car valiantly struggling to make it up the steep grade. These roads seemed more treacherous to me than the grand Cornish in the south of France, or the Amalfi Drive in Italy.

We spent an idyllic time in Ooty, considered the queen of the Hill Stations, where they formerly housed exclusive boarding schools for the children of wealthy families because the countryside is so beautiful and the climate so comfortable. We rode in a unique cog train to the top of the mountain, which took about one and a half hours of laborious chugging. Ran met us at the end of the train ride, having spent only a half hour to get there by car, but we were glad we'd had the experience of riding up the side of the mountain in that ninety-year-old train.

Before leaving India, we stopped in at the elegant Taj Hotel Mumbai to visit Sanjay Tandan, the head of IPRS, the Indian Performing Rights Society. He was quite excited because his parents had just arranged a marriage for him which, he explained, was the only proper way of doing things.

From Hong Kong we headed to New York because Hal and Burt Bacharach were going to be presented with the Trustees Award by the National Academy of Recording Arts & Sciences. Phil Ramone, along with Herb Alpert and Jerry Moss, were also honored that night in New York.

When the ceremonies were over, the ASCAP contingent invited us dinner at Felidia's for a private celebration. The Grammy award had come in a big box, which the people from NARAS offered to send to us in Los Angeles, but Hal wasn't about to let go of it. In fact, we even carried it into the restaurant with us. When the maître d' saw it, he immediately removed the flowers that had been in the center of the table, and replaced them with the Grammy.

I was amused that my usually rather cool and understated husband was so thrilled with this award. He just couldn't stop smiling. My eight-year-old grandson Dylan Forester, a future artist and architect, sent us his interpretation of Hal receiving the Grammy, which we have treasured over the years.

At 2 A.M. on March 30th, a new grandson arrived. Adam Alexander Peter David was the beautiful baby born to Hal's son Jim and our daughter-in-law Gunilla. We were two happy grandparents as we rushed to the hospital to cradle him in our arms.

The month of June found us back in New York, where we went to see the romantic comedy movie, *My Best Friend's Wedding,* which starred Julia Roberts, Cameron Diaz, Dermot Mulroney, Rupert Everett, and Philip Bosco. It was said to be one of the two most famous Julia Roberts films (the other being Pretty Woman). Hal was delighted to have six songs in that one film. The cast album, *I Say a Little Prayer for You,* which was featured prominently in the film, was covered by Diana King, making it a Billboard Top 100 hit, and it rose to #1 in Australia.

Not long after the cast album was out, Hal received a beautiful plaque with a gold record commemorating the sale of over one million copies.

While still in New York we attended a Society of Singers show honoring Lena Horne on her eightieth birthday. Many celebrities turned out for the event, which featured five of the original chorus girls from the old Cotton Club in Harlem who had performed with Lena when she herself was in that chorus. Hal remembered having lunch with Lena Horne and a friend of his in London one time. He said he could hardly eat because he couldn't stop staring at her; she was that beautiful.

Back in the south of France for the month of August, we enjoyed our usual round of dinners, parties, and touring. We especially enjoyed going to La Pinede, a restaurant in Cap D'Ail, a little town between Beaulieu and Monte Carlo. The food was delicious, but the main attraction was the keyboard artist/singer/guitarist, Massimo Mercurio, who performed during dinner. He always sang a medley of Hal's songs whenever we walked in, but the most fun was when he brought his guitar to the table. He loved to have Hal sing along with him, which Hal thoroughly enjoyed doing. Our group also requested other songs that we all knew the words to, so that we, too, could sing along - and sing along we did, at the top of our lungs. "Volare" was one of our favorite requests at that time, and we belted out *"nel blu dipinto di blu"* with the best of them, not even knowing what we were saying. We also had a

License-out agreement by the National Academy of Recording Arts & Sciences, Inc.
Permission for use granted by Burt Bacharach
Photo by Eunice David, circa 1999

Drawing by Dylan Forester

standing request for Carole King's song, "You've got a Friend." At least we understood the words to that song. We were always the noisiest table in the restaurant, but no one ever complained, and Massimo seemed to have as good a time as we did.

That year we decided to stay at the Hotel la Voile D'Or, which overlooked the harbor at St. Jean Cap Ferrat. When we returned from touring one day, the manager greeted us all atwitter. With binoculars lifted, he kept pointing to a yacht anchored just a few hundred yards offshore, telling us excitedly that Princess Diana and her friend Dodi Al Fayad were on board. That created quite a stir in sleepy Cap Ferrat.

When we left France just a few days later for a short stay in Venice, once again with the Save Venice group, we saw headlines in the Italian papers that read: *"Favola tragica: è morta Diana."* We didn't need to understand Italian to know what that meant. That was another tragedy which caused us to watch TV 24/7, and to read every newspaper we could get our hands on, English, Italian, or French.

One night while we were still in Venice, the Save Venice group organized a very elegant dinner party at Ca'Rezzonico, a three-story marble palazzo on the Grand Canal, which is now a public museum dedicated to eighteenth century Venice. Peter Duchin and his orchestra were flown in from New York to provide entertainment and music for dancing. But the Save Venice participants got more than they bargained for because Bea Guthrie, the wife of Bob Guthrie (Randolph H. Guthrie) who was then head of the Save Venice organization in New York, asked if Hal would sing a few songs with Peter's orchestra. Both Hal and Peter were good sports about this unexpected addition to Peter's repertoire, and Hal's gig was arranged. Hal sang "I'll Never Fall in Love Again," "To All the Girls I've Loved Before," and "Raindrops Keep Fallin' on My Head," expertly accompanied by Roberta Fabriano, Peter's lead guitarist. Our friends from Save Venice were a very appreciative audience, but the one that meant the most to me was a musician with the band who got up to snap Hal's picture. I got a real kick out of that.

There were two sad deaths to report in September of 1997: Princess Di and Mother Teresa, the saintly nun who died at eighty-seven years of age.

On September 16th, back in Los Angeles, Hal threw a grand seventieth birthday party for me at the Beverly Wilshire Hotel. Jay Livingston wrote special lyrics titled "Ya Got Class," which he sang to me in his wonderfully raspy voice, Selma and Army Archerd sang some special material that Jay had written to the melody of "You're the Top," and Hal even changed the words to "Call me Irresponsible", which went like this:

> I met Eunice David one sweet day
> At a tennis court
> That was twenty years ago
> We were introduced to each other
> That's when I first looked at her
> And oh, brother
> Eunice looked so classy
> And what's more, what a chassis
> And plus that she was sassy and fun
> Later during dinner
> I knew I'd picked a winner
> And that's when I received the first clue
> That I'd be spending my life with
> Eunice - she's so pretty
> When she speaks she's so witty
> Inspires every ditty I write
> In Eunice I discovered
> My best friend and my lover
> There's no one I could ever prefer
> And that's how I fell in love with Eunice
> Forever and ever in love with her

Freda Payne sang beautifully, with Corky Hale accompanying her. My family, Hal's family, and many of our friends from near and far got up to give speeches and toasts in my honor. It was a night to be remembered. At that party Norman Shtofman, whom we'd met on our around-the-world trip, made me an honorary citizen, and presented me with the key to the City of Tyler, Texas.

Hal and I enjoyed hosting an annual "Literary Dinner" for the Los Angeles Library Foundation. When we, and Ginny Mancini, who lives in the apartment right across the hall from us, both agreed to host a dinner for the Foundation on the same night, I suggested that we pool our resources to give our guests a special treat. Iris Rainer Dart, the great comedy writer, was the guest speaker at our dinner, and after our respective dinners were over, our group of about twenty people trooped over to Ginny's, where Hal, Ginny, and Ginny's twin daughters Felice and Monica put on quite a show. The Mancini sisters sang a great rendition of "I'll Never Fall in Love Again," Hal sang a medley of his songs, and Monica sang some of her father's songs, including, of course, "Moon River." The hit of the evening was when Hal and Monica sang a duet of "Send a Little Love My Way," the song Hal and Hank had written for the movie Oklahoma Crude. There'd never been a Library dinner like that before.

A few years later, when I'd written a book, *High Rise, Low Down,* I was invited to be the guest author at a library dinner, at the home of Jane and Stephen Ackerman. Hal and I put on a dual act for them: I talked about highlights of my book, and Hal, with Chris Caswell (who had become Hal's Musical Director) accompanying him, sang a medley of his songs.

In 1998, we stopped in London prior to going to the south of France so that Hal could go to the recording studio where Dot Allison was laying down the tracks for the song "Did I Imagine You?" which she and Hal had written together. We'd invited Bobbie and Bob Greenfield to join us at the recording studio, thinking it would be a unique experience for them. In the taxi on the way to the recording studio in Hammersmith, Bobbie, who was the owner of Bobbie Greenfield Fine Arts, at Bergamot Station in Santa Monica, California, where we frequently purchased art, pulled out a transparency of a Robert Motherwell drawing. They had been houseguests of friends in Connecticut recently and while there, noticed a beautiful oil painting by Motherwell, as well as the sketch that went with it. Bobbie asked if by any chance the drawing was for sale. The owner told her that it just so happened that he'd recently bought a farm and needed some cash to buy some cows so he was indeed interested in selling the drawing. Hal and I had started a collection of nineteenth and twentieth century artist's original works on paper, so this was right up our alley. Right there in the taxi, the deal was done, sight unseen, except for the transparency. We now owned a Motherwell, just because someone wanted to buy some cows.

From England, we flew to Paris and on to Nice, where we met up with "the usual suspects," our wonderful friends with whom we so enjoyed spending the month of August. Besides taking a boat to Lérins Island for our lobster "fix," we always made a couple of trips to our favorite restaurant in Nice, Le Petite Maison, owned by the unpredictable and volatile Nicole Rubi. We wore washable clothes whenever we went to Le Petite Maison because Madame Rubi was known to shake up a bottle of Champagne and then run around the room spraying it on everyone in sight. Strange as that may seem, it really was great fun, but one had to come prepared. Newcomers were always in for a big surprise. Madame frequently called in one of the street musicians to liven things up a little. One night she called in a guitarist who started serenading us, and before we knew it, almost everyone in the restaurant got up to dance to the intoxicating rhythm of his guitar. There was one table right in the middle of the restaurant, where two people sat, trying to calmly enjoy their meal. They were suddenly buffeted by the wild, gyrating dancers, and seemed quite annoyed at what was going on around them. They immediately called to have their table moved away from the center of the floor, which had been completely taken over by the dancers. We thought they were angered by what was happening around them, but that wasn't the case at all: as soon as their table was moved, the woman got up and joined the happy throng, while her husband placidly remained right where he was, with his head down, never missing a bite of his meal.

One year later later, Bonnie and Bernie Hodes hosted a group of ten friends at Le Petite Maison. Once we were seated, someone in our party noticed Elton John sitting at the other end of the room, so Hal went over to say hello to him. But he was prevented from approaching Elton's table by a burly bodyguard. So Hal told the fellow to just tell Mr. John that Hal David said hello, he returned to our table.

A moment later, Elton appeared and was very gracious about meeting all of our friends, even coming over again to say goodbye when he left.

Then, when at the end of the evening, Bernie asked for his check, Madam Rubi came over to tell us that Elton had paid our bill. We'd heard about his legendary generosity, and tonight we were the happy beneficiaries. Hal and I found out the name of his favorite florist in Nice, and sent him a huge floral arrangement the next day as a thank you.

In 1998, the CISAC meeting was held in the eastern section of Berlin, where we stayed at the Adlon Hotel, which had been commandeered by the Nazi Party during WWII. Our room overlooked Unter Den Linden Avenue, the famous street in Berlin lined with Linden trees. A documentary that was playing on our TV as we entered the room showed that during Hitler's time, the Linden trees had been ripped out and replaced with Nazi flags flying from tall poles.

The first night we were there, there was a reception at the Schloss Bellevue, the palace of the President of the Federal Republic of Germany, who at that time was Roman Herzog. We were surprised when Herr Herzog told us that his son spoke Hebrew fluently. When we asked why, he said that his son just liked the language, and wanted to learn it. Herzog was a member of the Christian Democratic Union, and served as President of Germany from 1994 to 1999.

The Schloss, located in the Tiergarten district of Berlin, had only been the official residence of the President of Germany since 1994. It was originally built in 1786 as a summer residence for Prince Augustus Ferdinand of Prussia. The building had been badly damaged during strategic bombing by Allied Forces in 1945, and required a great deal of work to restore it to its original splendor.

When we were there, extensive building projects were taking place wherever one turned. There were big cranes dotting the city everywhere we looked. When the men were able to take time away from their meetings, a group of us went to the Cecilienhof Castle, which was where the Potsdam Agreement had been signed in 1945 by Russian General Secretary Joseph Stalin, British Prime Minister Clement Attlee, and the President of the United States, Harry Truman, dividing the city of Berlin into east and west and allowing the Communists to take over the eastern sector for a period that lasted fifty years.

We drove over the Glienicke Bridge, which was used to exchange International agents during the Cold War Period. The American pilot Gary Powers, who crash-landed his U-2 plane in Russia and was incarcerated in the SS Headquarters located in Potsdam, was exchanged over that bridge in 1962, along with an American student, Frederic Pryor in a well-publicized spy swap. In exchange, the Soviets got back their KGB Colonel Vilyam Fisher, who had been caught by the FBI and jailed by the Americans for espionage.

Our Los Angeles friends Lee and Larry Ramer generously funded the office of the American Jewish Committee in Berlin, and Hal and I had an interesting visit to their offices, hosted by the head of the committee, Gene DuBow. The organization had a wide agenda, encompassing the domestic and international concerns of the American Jewish community, maintaining twenty-one offices in cities across the United States, as well as their presence in Berlin, Jerusalem, Poland, Great Britain, and Australia. The offices overlooked a mound of earth, which we were told, was where Hitler's body was buried after he committed suicide. There was no marker, because the government didn't want it to become a shrine, or a tourist attraction, but everyone seemed to know what that "bump" was anyway.

We stayed over an extra day after our conference in Berlin had ended, because we'd received an invitation to attend a gala dinner honoring Steven Spielberg, who was receiving Germany's highest honor, the Federal Cross of Merit, for his work in preserving memories of the Holocaust. When Spielberg accepted the award, he said that he was particularly pleased to see how his film *Schindler's List* had had such a powerful impact in Germany. As he accepted his award, we could hear the haunting strains of music wafting into the ballroom. We watched as clarinetist Giora Feidman slowly walked toward the stage playing the "Theme from Schindler's List," with the music growing louder and louder the nearer he came. After he'd climbed the stairs to where Spielberg was standing on the stage, Feidman dramatically presented the clarinet to Spielberg, saying "You gave me this music, now I return it to you." Spielberg was moved to tears, as were many in the audience.

Hal was again invited to be a judge at an Asian Song Festival, which was going to be held early in 1998. The organizing committee pulled out all the stops, and showed the judges a wonderful time while we were in Manila. Hal was interviewed on TV and for newspaper articles every day that we were there, with two questions uppermost on their agendas: they wanted to know how Hal felt about the fact that Burt Bacharach was so much better known than he was, and about the failure of the movie *Shangri-La, The Musical*. His answers were that 1) "Burt is a performer, and therefore the public knows him better." But he was quick to add that he himself had a wonderful life, and didn't regret a minute of it. And 2) the musical score for *Shangri-La* has become a favorite in many circles. It was the movie that was the bomb - - not the music in it."

The judges, with me tagging along, were taken to see the Malacanan Presidential Palace. My only disappointment was that we didn't get to see the hundreds of pairs of shoes Imelda Marcos collected during the two decades that her husband, Ferdinand, was president, because they were stored in a special room in the palace which was not open to visitors.

Our friend Bernadette Charles, who was originally from the Philippines but who now lived in Hong Kong, came to visit us while we were in Manila. She had been born into one of the oldest families in the Philippines, the Borromeos, a name that opened doors for us wherever we went. Berna told us that when she was a little girl, she used to play in the Palace. Between Berna and the organizing committee of the Festival, we saw Manila in depth.

A small group of the judges were invited to go to Subic Bay and Corregidor (names out of the past because of their significance during WWII). Subic Bay became infamous during the War as the site of the 70-mile "Bataan Death March," which began, on April 9, 1942. Japanese forces captured an estimated 90,000 to 100,000 prisoners, who were forced to march sixty-five miles over treacherous terrain to the Japanese POW Camp O'Donnell in the north. Miraculously about fifty-four thousand survived the march, only to perish from disease or torture while imprisoned.

After lunch at the Subic Bay Yacht Club, developed by the family of a prominent Filipino composer by the name of Ding Dong Eduque, (Hal just loved that fellow's name), some of us boarded a helicopter and flew to the southern tip of the Bataan Peninsula to Corregidor Island, where General Douglas MacArthur made his last stand against the Japanese. It was from the dock at the tip of the island that MacArthur made his famous declaration: "I shall return!" We were sobered by the sight of the destruction that was done to the Island by the Japanese when they captured it in 1942. The area and the remaining buildings were preserved as a grim reminder of what had happened there.

The night of the Festival show, I was invited to sit next to Mrs. Fidel Ramos, the wife of the President of the Philippines, and Berna was able to join me. Mrs. Ramos was very friendly, especially when she heard Berna's family name. Mrs. Ramos was a musician herself, so she was interested in the arts, and the Asian Song Festival had a special appeal to her.

As a complete surprise to us, Hal was called up to the stage to receive a Lifetime Achievement Award from KATHA, the Filipino equivalent of ASCAP, which was presented to him by Mrs. Ramos. Hal gave a warm and gracious, if impromptu, acceptance speech, mentioning that he was the proud owner of a barong (The barong Tagalog, or simply known as a barong is an embroidered formal garment worn in the Philippines). Hal said that he'd have to come back so he could wear it again. That brought the house down. Mrs.

Ramos asked if she could have her picture taken with Hal, and then she asked if Hal would sign her program. That set off a frenzy of flash bulbs.

Eunice, Mrs. Fidel Ramos, First Lady of the Philippines, and Hal

This year the contestant from the Philippines won the first prize for best vocal, and a couple from Indonesia won the Endoh Award (presented by the Japanese delegation).

Not only did Berna show us around the city, but her brother Freddie and his wife Josephine invited us to join them at the polo matches, where both Berna's brother and nephew Sonny were playing (on opposite teams). Josephine, along with her daughter Pia, came to get us with their driver, and brought us to the prestigious Manila Polo Club, where Freddie had been a very popular past president. The current president invited us to sit in the front row to watch the matches, and we were delighted when the polo announcer repeatedly told those in attendance that Hal and I were in the audience, and suggested that members stop by to say hello - - which many did. A tape of Bacharach/David songs was played over and over during the afternoon. Freddie Sr.'s team won against Freddie Jr.'s, and we all celebrated by drinking champagne out of the silver trophy cups which they'd won.

In March we were in San Diego for the opening of a show at the La Jolla Playhouse of Bacharach/David songs directed and choreographed by

Gillian Lynne, called *What the World Needs Now*. I won't repeat what I wrote in my journal about that disaster of a show; I will only say that Burt told us that when he saw Gillian in the parking lot of the theatre after he'd seen the show, he wanted to punch her in the nose, and that the *Los Angeles Times* theater critic Laurie Winer wrote that "When Burt Bacharach and Hal David ruled the earth their songs filled the airwaves and our aching hearts and private dramas." "The trouble is, everyone seems to know that Bacharach and David are fresh again, except for Gillian Lynne, the British director, choreographer, and co-conceiver of 'World.' ...Some forty-odd numbers are showcased within Lynne's cloying and repetitive choreography and a book as stale as a biscuit wrapped in Dick Clark's bell bottoms."

In a word, the show was horrible! We were really surprised, because not long before this production, Gillian had produced a show with a similar concept that had played very well on British TV.

One day Hal received a call from a producer by the name of David Gest, saying that Hal was going to receive an award at the International Achievement in the Arts dinner. We'd never heard of the organization. In fact, at that time we'd never heard of David Gest. When Hal demured, he was told that Frances Preston (then President and CEO of BMI) was also being honored and, that she had specifically asked that she receive her award at the same time as Hal. We later learned that Gest had used the time-worn ploy of telling Frances that it was Hal who wanted to receive his award at the same time that Frances got hers and vice versa. They both fell for it.

We told Mr. Gest that we were going to an anniversary party for some close friends and could not make his event, but he was so insistent that he arranged for a driver to pick us up at the anniversary party, and return us to the party once Hal accepted the award.

I had to hand it to Gest because he had quite a roster of stars performing at the event: Dionne Warwick, Michael Bolton, the Four Tops (at least the three of them who were left), Jack Jones, Crystal Gale, and Chaka Kahn. When Hal went up to receive his award, he was handed a metal vase, with no inscription on it, and that was that! It was as though someone had gone out that morning and bought something that could be handed to him: that's probably exactly what happened. With that, we climbed back into the waiting limo and were returned to our friend's anniversary party.

David later famously married our friend Liza Minnelli in March of 2002, with stars such as Elizabeth Taylor and Michael Jackson in their wedding party. The couple separated in July 2003 amidst tremendous press coverage of their tumultuous relationship.

That year when Hal gave his annual performance at the Los Angeles Jewish Home in Encino for their huge Mother's Day event, Mary Hart was the M.C. She told a story about how when Hal was a judge at the Miss America contest held in 1970, and she, as Miss South Dakota, came in second, Hal told her not to worry because he was sure she would have a wonderful career in show business. He was obviously right.

When Hal finished his gig we had a driver waiting to take us to San Pedro, where we boarded the Crystal Harmony for a cruise to Alaska. When our ship docked in San Francisco, we were able to visit with Ruth and Chuck Adams, a couple whom we'd met on our USIA junket in 1988, as well as with long-time friends of Hal's, Audrey and Bob Sockolov (who at one time owned the Rochester Big & Tall chain of stores), so that was a very enjoyable stop for us.

One of the lecturers on the ship was Charles Champlin, a film critic and writer for the *Los Angeles Times*. One day when we were having lunch in the dining room, we happened to notice Charles and his wife Peggy sitting all alone, so we asked them if they would care to join us. They were delighted, and told us that in the ten days they'd already been on board, no one had ever invited them to sit with them. We had a wonderful time talking about movies, and telling funny stories about people whom both Charles and Hal knew.

It was while we were on this trip that we learned that Frank Sinatra, who had made Hal so happy when he recorded "American Beauty Rose," had died at eighty- two of a heart attack. There was no singer like him. Since Frank's death, when singers have tried to emulate him, they have failed: they just never got his superb timing down or his rapport with an audience. Old Blue Eyes was really one of a kind.

Toward the end of '98, Hal and I were invited to join Louise and Barry Taper on a trip to Gettysburg and, while there, to attend the Lincoln Forum, where Louise had been invited to be the keynote speaker. Hal was a big Civil War enthusiast, so going to one of the most famous battlegrounds with Louise, who owned what was considered the most spectacular and in-depth Lincoln collection in private hands, was something he didn't want to miss.

We flew into Baltimore, then were driven to Gettysburg. One of the highlights of that trip was meeting Gabor Boritt, a Hungarian who became a scholar of Lincoln and the Civil War. He actually learned English as a boy in Hungary by reading Lincoln's speeches. Gabor and his wife Liz lived in an eighteenth century farmhouse at the edge of the Gettysburg Battlefield, frequently finding artifacts that popped up from the ground, having been buried for many years. Their home was once a stop on the Underground Railroad, and also a confederate hospital. When Boritt came to teach at Gettysburg College he founded the Civil War Institute and as a result, the school created the nation's first fully funded chair for the study of the Civil War - just for him.

The Tapers, Hal, and I toured the battlefields with Gabor - not stopping at all two thousand seven hundred monuments, but getting a good sense of them, and hearing all about them from our scholar/guide. Both the Confederate army and the Union army eventually converged on Gettysburg because nine of the eleven roads in the area led there. None of the troops had proper maps of the area, and in fact, one General was said to have found a wooden map on a plaque on the side of a building, and confiscated it as a means of deciding where to deploy his troops.

We began our tour at the monument erected by North Carolina, which was designed by Gaston Borglum, the artist who spent most of his life working on Mt. Rushmore. The pose of the soldiers was reminiscent of the famous sculpture of the five Marines and one Navy corpsman raising the American flag on Iwo Jima. Gabor was so passionate about his subject that he actually had us believing that we were enlisted in the Confederate Army and advancing on the Union soldiers. We walked along the battle lines as Gabor explained practically every move made by the Confederate soldiers and every order issued by their commanders.

After lunch we toured the battlefield again, but this time from the point of view of the Union troops, again reviewing each move ordered by the Generals during that historic three-day battle. As Gabor described the smoke from the fifteen thousand guns, we could almost smell the gunpowder. The scene was brought home to us by our very own Civil War scholar very graphically and emotionally.

We also visited the cemetery where Lincoln gave his Gettysburg Address on the afternoon of November 19, 1863. The Massachusetts orator Edward Everett was the keynote speaker when the Cemetery was dedicated. It is reported that he spoke for two hours and was profoundly boring. Only as an after-thought was President Lincoln requested to speak, and the 272 word,

two-minute speech he gave has become recognized as among the most elo-
quent and earnest words ever spoken.

At one point during the proceedings at the Lincoln Forum, Harold
Holzer introduced Hal to the audience by saying that "everyone was aware
that Hal knew the way to San Jose, but now they discovered that he also knew
the way to Gettysburg." Louise, as the keynote speaker, told about her collection of Lincoln memorabilia, telling the history about the pieces, as pictures
of them were flashed on a screen.

At one of the dinners we attended, Hal was asked to sing "Happy Birthday" to a little girl who was celebrating her seventh birthday. Hal was not too
keen on doing it, but Steve Carson, who was with the Manuscript Society of
America, was also at the dinner, and said that if Hal would do it, he would
join him at the mike. When Hal returned to the table, he said that the audience may have enjoyed their rendition, but the birthday girl had her hands
over her ears the whole time he and Steve were singing. I guess one has to
choose their audiences more carefully.

Hal wrote two songs with a new writing partner, Carole King, in January
of 1999: "Music by the Angels" and "I Believe in Loving You." In deciding to write together, they were both hoping for some magic to result,
but even though the songs were recorded shortly after they were written,
nothing came of them. However, years later, when Carole received the
prestigious Gershwin Prize for Popular Song from the Library of Congress, she sang "I Believe in Loving You" at a performance at the White
House, in honor of Hal, who had received the prize the year before, but
had subsequently passed away.

From mid-February to mid-March, we traveled throughout South America
with Ambassador Lester Korn and his wife Carolbeth. Lester, co-founder of
the Korn/Ferry executive recruiting firm, had been appointed by President
Ronald Reagan to serve as Ambassador to the United Nations and as a Del-
egate to the Economic and Social Council of the United Nations.

On the way to South America, we made a brief stop in Palm Beach, where
we had a stimulating dinner which included former Secretary of State Al Haig
and his wife Pat. After I told Mrs. Haig about the journals that I had been
keeping from the first day I met Hal, she told me that although she and her
husband had certainly been in some unique situations in strange places, with

fascinating people, she was always careful not to write anything down so that there could never be any untoward discoveries or revelations. But she said that she had come to regret that she hadn't kept a record of their lives.

We tried to steer away from politics that night, but Haig made one comment that I found astute: he thought President Carter was the smartest of all the presidents we've had, but that he knew the least about politics.

We left Palm Beach the next day for the start of our month-long tour of South America. Our first stop was in Manaus, at the edge of the Amazon rainforest. Our travel agent had warned us that the Tropical Hotel, where we stayed, was not on a par with the five-star establishments that we were used to. That proved to be all too true. It did not have five stars, but I did give it four "D's": dank, dark, dreary and dirty - and also distasteful. Nothing I washed, including myself, ever dried. But we were only going to be there a couple of days, so we just chalked up our stay there as part of the adventure.

Also as part of the "adventure," our guide, Gercon, took us out on a little motorized canoe to see where some locals lived on the banks of the river. We soon found ourselves in a heavily wooded area, with the narrow waterway clogged with reeds, water-soaked logs and other debris from the forest. We sat, riveted to our seats, while the young boatman revved the engine, to try to free the propeller from all the weeds which had clogged it.

We continued to sit there for a good twenty minutes, with mosquitoes swarming around us making a banquet of our tender skins and succulent blood. Carolbeth, ever prepared, pulled out a stick of Cutter's insect repellant, instantly becoming our heroine. Finally, our boatman got out of the boat and dived down into the swamp-like water to chop at the weeds until he freed the engine and with that we slowly inched forward and little by little began to pass through the tangle of growth. Then, suddenly, with a burst of speed, we finally broke through the muck. There were people living in houses right on the edge of the area where we'd been, and one would have thought they'd have heard the noise of our struggling engine and come to rescue us, but that didn't happen.

Next, we travelled to Rio de Janerio, where, of course, we had to take a walk on the famed Copacabana Beach. But the city's most famous landmark, the statue of Christ the Redeemer, was on top of Mt. Corcovado. After boarding a tiny cog wheel train, we finally reached the top of the mountain, and were duly impressed by the vistas, and by the gargantuan one hundred-and-twenty-foot high statue; no wonder it was visible from all over the city. Locals get their bearings by glancing up at the figure of Christ: the right arm faces south, and the left arm faces north.

From Rio, we flew to Iguazu Falls, where I was finally able to view the falls from the Brazilian side, which I'd always heard was the most spectacular view. Even having seen the falls from Argentina and from Paraguay, I found that this view did not disappoint. Carolbeth and I saw them by air, from a helicopter, we went under them in a boat, and we crossed a bridge over them: any view was wonderful, no matter from what perspective.

Of course, we did the requisite touring while in Buenos Aires, from seeing the outside of the Casa Rosada, the pink executive mansion of the President of Argentina, to staring at the drawings of little children memorialized on the sidewalks in white paint. The drawings depicted children who were lost in the "Dirty War" (Guerra Sucia) which took place from 1976 to 1980 during which some five thousand children disappeared. Grandmothers still walked the area every Thursday afternoon in a symbolic search for them.

No visit to Buenos Aires would be complete without seeing the unique cemetery located in an area called La Recoleta. There are rows and rows of mausoleums forming what looks like neighborhoods of miniature, elegant mansions. The two mausoleums I just had to see, since I was fascinated by the people buried there, were those of the prizefighter Louis Angel Firpa, known as the "Wild Bull of the Pampas," which has a larger-than-life-sized statue in front of it, and that of Eva Peron, whose body had been sent to Italy for a while to keep her grave from being robbed, but was now back in Argentina. Since Andrew Lloyd Webber's show, *Evita,* was one of my favorites, I just couldn't pass that up.

We traveled on to Patagonia, where our destination was San Carlos de Bariloche, a ski area designed very much like an Alpine village due to the influence of the German, Swiss, and Austrians who first settled in the area in the 1800's. We took the ski lift to the top of Mt. Campanario, where the views were breathtaking. I almost cried at my first sight of the gleaming lakes and towering mountains. I would have sung "On a Clear Day You Can See Forever," had it been one of Hal's songs. That definitely described our views.

When we left Bariloche, we journeyed over two hundred miles on a series of lakes, through some of the most beautiful scenery anywhere in the world.

We marveled at the majestic snow-covered mountain peaks of the Andes, the lovely, lush forests, the tranquil lakes, the magnificent twelve-thousand-foot high glacier called Thunder Mountain, and the Puntiagudo and Orsano Volcanos, both dramatically covered with snow.

We stopped at Santiago, a beautiful city, with its wide avenues and beautifully planted, grassy median named after Bernardo O'Higgins, who liberated Chile from Spain in the early 19th century.

Next was Chile. Lester, because of his Ambassadorial standing, had alerted the American Embassy in Santiago that we were going to be in town. We were delighted when Ambassador John O'Leary, a Yale Law School buddy of President Clinton's, and his wife Pat arranged a dinner party in our honor at the residence, a beautiful home built during John F. Kennedy's presidency. The Ambassador invited four other couples, culled from the political and banking world, all of whom were extremely interesting. We talked about politics, the arts, travel, high finance, including the melding of the Americas, North and South, into one economic system (which the Chileans were very much in favor of), and every other subject under the sun. The O'Learys had only been there a few months, but, along with their two daughters, they were already comfortably settled in. The Korns brought a book by a Steuben artist as a house gift, and Hal and I brought a *Hal David Songbook*. Pat asked Lester if he thought Hal might be willing to autograph the book for her, and Lester assured her he would, and he did. The O'Learys were only allowed a limited number of items to bring with them from their home in Maine, and it just so happened that one item that they'd brought was a record album of Dionne Warwick singing Bacharach/David songs. Dionne had been in Santiago shortly before we were, and had signed the album cover for them. Now they were delighted to have Hal's signature on it also.

Hal and I returned to Santiago a few years later, and the O'Learys threw a real shindig for us at that time, which included people in the entertainment industry, and a pianist who played and sang Hal's songs all evening long.

One night when we and the Korns had dinner at a lovely restaurant close to the hotel, Hal asked the waiter if they had any Chilean Sea Bass available. The waiter looked puzzled but politely replied, "Sir, all of our fish is Chilean." We dined out on that story for years, with Hal always good-naturedly laughing at his gaff right along with the rest of us.

Machu Picchu beckoned, and we held our collective breaths as our pilot maneuvered our little plane between two steep mountains and landed smoothly on a narrow runway eleven thousand feet above sea level in the city of Cusco. We were being driven to our hotel with Frida, our guide, when we saw hundreds of colorfully dressed Indian women from all over the highlands. They were in Cusco to take part in a festival called "The Day of the Woman." They came from many different tribes, and each were dressed in their own colorful native costumes, almost all of them carrying infants wrapped in blankets slung over their backs. Some of the women were wearing masks and animal furs. We asked our driver to stop so that we could follow the parade and take pictures, but Frida wanted us to go to the hotel right away so we could become acclimated to the altitude, by drinking their special, calming coca tea. She said there would be plenty of time later to get our pictures. We prevailed, however, and Frida had to admit that she'd never seen such a large gathering of Indian tribes together at one time, and was as fascinated by the scene as we were. She said it was definitely a-once-in-a-lifetime experience, and we couldn't have agreed with her more.

Photo by Eunice David.

We eventually got to the Monasterio Hotel, and eventually had our coca tea, with its soothing cocaine ingredient. But it was a good thing that we'd insisted that our driver stop the van earlier, because by the time we were ready to do our afternoon touring, it was pouring rain, and all those fascinating Indian women were nowhere to be seen.

We were familiar with Machu Picchu from pictures, but nothing could prepare us for our first sight of the massive Inca ruins, after our early morning three-hour train ride. It was breathtaking.

Once we arrived at Machu Picchu, we ran the gauntlet through a narrow, steep street, lined on both sides with little shops, and hordes of vendors running after us, asking our names, and begging us to promise to buy from them when we returned. It was a real trick to get through those anxious young entrepreneurs.

We had a local guide who was trying to impart detailed knowledge to us, but Carolbeth and I only wanted to take pictures, not listen to history. However, I did learn that the area was discovered in July of 1911 by Hiram Bingham who was an academic, explorer, treasure hunter, and politician from the United States. It is believed that the original city had been built in the mid-fifteenth century, during the time the Inca leader Pachacutec ruled the land. Research suggests that the city was inhabited primarily by women, given the high percentage of female skeletons which were uncovered.

Even in this remote location, when our guide learned that Hal had written "Raindrops Keep Fallin' on My Head," her eyes lit up, and in the middle of the magnificent setting of Machu Picchu, she started singing it at the top of her lungs. Now that was one place where we didn't expect to collect any royalties.

At the end of our trip to South America, Robert Kenyan, our guide asked each of us to name our most memorable part of the trip. I said that it was our walk on the bridge over Iguazu Falls. Carolbeth agreed, even though she felt as though we were intruding on nature. Lester loved the Zodiac boat ride under one of the falls at Iguazu, but he too agreed it was hard to pick out just one special event. Hal said he'd always have in his mind's eye the picture of all those Highland women parading in their Sunday best. That was something that could never have been planned, and we were fortunate to have been in the right place at the right time to have experienced it.

Our travel agent left our little group in Peru and we and the Korns went on to Ecuador without a guide for the last leg of our trip. It turned out that we had an extremely difficult time getting out of Peru because, unbeknownst to us, the airline that we were booked on had gone out of business while we were traveling through South America and no other airline was willing to accept their tickets. In fact, our passports were temporarily confiscated by some officious airport officials and we were left standing around, completely bewildered, for a couple of hours. We eventually got it all sorted out, and were very happy when we finally secured seats on another airline. But not for long because we learned that there was rioting in Quito, Ecuador, which is where we were headed, and the city was totally shut down. People were not at work, all banks were closed, and we were told that we could expect to see police action everywhere.

When we arrived, we could see barricades on every corner, with embers of bonfires spraying up into the air and burning tires blocking roadways. There were no cars on the road, and very few people were outside; the city was like a morgue. We were concerned about our flight back to the States after we took our side trip to the Galapagos and, in fact, we were wondering if we could even get to the Galapagos.

When we stayed overnight at the hotel, prior to leaving for the Galapagos, we ate in their fancy French restaurant, and had room service the morning we left. When we went to check out, our bill shocked us: it came to a total of $47 in United States currency.

At the airport, we ran into an American who lived in the southern part of Ecuador and worked on the oil pipeline. He told us that all the American employees in his company had received a State Department advisory telling them to get their families out of the country. We mentioned that we were going to the Galapagos, and then back to Quito, and he thought we were out of our minds to continue with our plans. He was frantically trying to get air passage out of the country for himself, his wife, and their two children. But, we thought that since the American Embassy knew where Ambassador Korn was, and we hadn't heard anything from them, we were good to go. Then we learned that a group that were traveling to the Galapagos on the same boat we were going on, consisted of newspaper publishers and their wives from all over the United States - highly visible people with considerable resources, and they had not heard anything about leaving Ecuador. So off we went.

The Galapagos was everything I had hoped it would be, and then some. For a person as interested in photography as I am, it was heaven - from the giant tortoises to every other form of animal life that we saw on each of the different islands we visited, it was as fascinating, and as memorable a trip as we'd ever been on - a safari in its own way.

We returned to Quito a few days later, to total confusion and bedlam at the airport. While we'd been in the Galapagos, there had been very little communication with the outside world and, frankly, in that tranquil setting, we'd completely forgotten about the trouble in Quito. But, in retrospect, we realized that we hadn't taken it seriously enough. We were supposed to have had a tour of the city on our return, but that was definitely a no-go. There were no baggage handlers, and we all scrambled to find our own luggage; but even after finding it, we didn't know how we were going to get it from the airport to our hotel.

Finally, someone came out with a handcart, with our luggage and everyone else's piled willy-nilly on top of it. We were told that a truck was going to deliver it to various hotels throughout the city. We decided against that, and pulled out our own luggage, which we dragged through a barrier to a bus that our enterprising tour director had managed to commandeer for us.

Apparently the President of Ecuador had frozen people's money, so they could only retrieve a small percentage of their assets, causing a run on the banks and immediate gouging by retailers. The banks were now closed and gas prices had gone up one hundred sixty eight percent overnight. The propane gas which most people used for cooking was almost impossible to purchase.

Our bus went down up streets, up down streets, over curbs, around barricades, and across median strips, until finally depositing us at our hotel. Along the way we saw fires burning all around us, and people from the airport dragging their luggage through the streets, trying to make their way to their various hotels.

We didn't unpack anything at the hotel in Quito because we were leaving the next morning. As a precaution, we'd been told by the hotel staff to stay inside, but Hal wanted some fresh air so we went out to take a walk in front of the hotel. Fortunately, it started to rain, so we returned to our room. I say "fortunately" because Lester had been trying frantically to reach us by phone. He'd heard from the our Embassy telling him that the American Airlines flight we had planned to take the next day had been cancelled, but the airline was sending a special plane to Quito specifically to pick up any American citizens still remaining in the city. A bus was coming for us in twenty minutes. We didn't need the twenty minutes allotted us. We just grabbed our luggage and were in the lobby and waiting in mere seconds.

Once we were on the bus we were told that 1) we'd be able to get to the airport, 2) the plane was definitely coming for us, and 3) we had reserved seats on it. But because of all the barricades, the bus couldn't get too close to the airport so, luggage and all, we had to make a dash for it by foot in the pouring rain. We finally managed to leave Ecuador at about eight that night. We didn't exactly get down and kiss the ground when we arrived in Miami at midnight, but we did breathe a big sigh of relief, and were very grateful to be back on American soil.

We were told to wait for a bus from the Marriott Hotel, where we were being put up overnight, but we'd never had much luck with hotel busses in the past, and, par for the course, this one never showed up. It was quite a sight to see Hal in the middle of the road, flagging down an off duty taxicab, and then convincing the driver to take us to the hotel.

When we were back in Los Angeles, friends suggested that we see a movie we had not previously heard about called *A Walk on the Moon*. It was a story about a young family with two children who are in a rut. The grandmother's role was played by our friend Tovah Feldshuh. Halfway through the movie I nudged Hal and told him they were playing his song "Wishin' and Hopin' " in the background. He couldn't quite hear it, and thought I was wrong. But, happily, when we watched the credits at the end of the movie, which we always did even if Hal did not have a song in a movie, there it was, "Wishin' and Hopin' " by Bacharach and David. To make things even sweeter, when we got to the lobby of the theatre, they were playing "Walk on By." Dusty Springfield had a top 10 hit with "Wishing and Hopin'" in 1964. It had first been recorded by Dionne in 1963, and charted in France at #79. New York disc jockey Joe Lacey started playing it as a single in '64 and that really helped it reach #6 on the Billboard Hot 100. Then Burt himself recorded a version of the song on his debut Kapp Records album *Burt Bacharach Hitmaker!*

On May 25th, Hal's birthday, we headed to London because Hal was going to be awarded the Ivor Novello Award, named after the Cardiff-born entertainer, David Ivor Davies, better known as Ivor Novello. He was a composer, singer, and handsome matinee idol who became one of the most popular British entertainers in the twentieth century.

Pleased though Hal was, we really didn't know who Ivor Novello was or why the Ivor Novello Award was as important as it was. One day, shortly before that trip, we ran into noted pianist and singer Michael Feinstein. He had heard about Hal's upcoming honor and he invited us to his home in Griffith Park, where he had a huge collection of music memorabilia and comprehensive information on a wide variety of composers and other musical personalities, so he was able to show us material about Ivor Novello, and the awards carrying his name.

The Ivors, as they are nicknamed, are presented annually by PRS for Music as a way of recognizing and rewarding Britain's songwriting and composing talents. The award itself is a beautiful bronze sculpture of Euterpe, the muse of lyric poetry.

Popular song reviewers, Hal's peers in the music business, writers of magazine, and newspaper articles all agree that, together with Burt Bacharach, Hal has been responsible for some of the most enduring musical moments of the century. Their collaboration had been widely acclaimed, yet Hal's contribution was very often overlooked, or given a back seat because Burt was the performer, and was in the public eye, whereas Hal was always the guy in the back room, scribbling words on a pad of paper. But those in the know always recognized Hal's ability, and the fact that without his brilliant lyrics, there most likely would not have been the body of work that the team of Bacharach/David turned out.

Frequently, when interviewed and asked how he felt about being overlooked, Hal readily admitted that composers tend to be better known than lyricists, and he used to sight the writing team of Elton John and Bernie Taupin as examples: Hal felt that Bernie was a brilliant lyric writer, but acknowledged that Elton was the showman. He said, "Burt is a performer. He's good out in the open. That's never been my thing." But this time Hal himself was thrust into the spotlight when The British Academy of Composers and Songwriters recognized Hal for his string of landmark hits. Hal was the first non-British person to ever receive the award in the forty-four year history of the event, and consequently was interviewed by the British media almost every day. The first day we were in London he had interviews and photo sessions scheduled for 10 A.M., 11 A.M., noon, and even 1 P.M. The Berkeley Hotel provided a room just off the lobby for the reporters and photographers, who kept coming over in a steady stream. Hal even graciously gave several telephone interviews.

The Ivor ceremony was held at a luncheon, with about sixteen hundred people noisily gathered around, many of whom rushed over to us when we entered the room to congratulate Hal. Hal could not stop smiling: he was so excited. I hadn't known Hal when he received his Academy Award, but I would guess it must have been a similar experience, except that with the Oscar, one doesn't know in advance if they are going to win. This time there was a lot of advance notice and the excitement just kept building and building.

We sat through award after award being handed out, including a Lifetime Achievement award for Rod Stewart. Then suddenly a video was shown with many English artists featured on it who'd had hit records with Hal's songs. We were used to seeing videos showing American artists singing Hal's work, but this was new and exciting.

PRS's John Hutchinson began his remarks by saying that

The Ivors are often referred to, with respect and affection, as the "British songwriters' Oscar," and they have largely celebrated the creativity of British writers. Today, PRS and the Academy wish to present for the first time, this new, special International Award, which honors Hal David as an eminent music creator who is not British, but whose music has been hugely successful here, performed and recorded by British artists. But in acclaiming him, we are not only acknowledging his eminence as a lyricist, but also his active, caring, and influential contribution to the cause of international copyright protection over many years.

John then called up a singer by the name of Gabrielle, who sang her version of "Walk on By" with which she'd had a top ten hit in England. John mentioned that the song had been covered at least forty times in the U.K. since the 1960's, by artists as diverse as The Stranglers, Dionne Warwick, Transvision Vamp, and Helen Shapiro.

When Hal was called to the stage, the audience rose to offer a standing ovation. His remarks were wonderful warm and gracious and he remembered to thank all the appropriate people, even, as always, throwing in some loving words about me: a sure way to get my tear ducts working.

The ASCAP contingent hosted a lovely birthday party for Hal at L'Odeon Restaurant that evening, attended by many PRS people as well as ASCAP friends. A beautiful birthday cake was rolled out, that said "Congratulations, Hal," which brought everyone to their feet as they sang "Happy Birthday." We left London the next morning to spend a few delightful days at the Lygon Arms in the Cotswalds before returning home to Los Angeles.

Even though Hal wasn't working as much as he once had, when we got back from England he sat down with Kenny Hirsch and wrote a very touching song called "Beyond All Dreams." It features some of my all-time favorite Hal David lines.

I think this pretty much says it all!

If I could choose who I could be
Then I would choose no one but me
'Cause here I am in your embrace
And a million men would die to take my place.

I'm still deeply touched when I remember that Hal told me I was the inspiration for that song. Whenever he got up to give a toast at one of our parties, or at any other occasion for that matter, he always said that he had never been happier than he was since he and I had married. Our friends always said that Hal and I had a beautiful love affair, and I wholeheartedly concurred.

Our friends Vicki Reynolds, who was about to become Mayor of Beverly Hills for the third time, and Murray Pepper, who many old-timer Angelinos remembered from seeing him and his mother pictured in newspaper ads for their popular Home Silk Shop, were married in June. Vicki asked Hal if he would write some special material for their wedding, and then sing it and a few other of his other songs at the wedding. Vicki and Murray were together for fifteen years before they got married. The deciding factor was when two of their young granddaughters were playing together one day and one said that they were just like sisters. The other disagreed, pointing out that they were not sisters because Vicki and Murray were not married. The two little girls prevailed on Vicki and Murray to get married, so they could be related. That seemed like a pretty good reason, so the wedding was planned. At the reception, the two youngsters ran around making sure that all the guests knew it was because of them that we were all there.

It was a wonderful event, held at the Peninsula Hotel with about one hundred guests in attendance. The special material which Hal wrote and sang was to the tune of "Love and Marriage." In part, it went like this:

Vicki and Murray, Vicki and Murray
Took their time - they weren't in a hurry
Even though they waited
They knew they'd wind up being mated.

Elsewhere, he rhymed "Mayor" with "soothsayer"; (Vicki being the mayor and Murray a psychologist - a real soothsayer.

Later that summer, the newlywed Peppers and Hal and I joined friends for a few days on their yacht Mikili, which was anchored in Sardinia, and then headed to the south of France together. The Peppers were quickly embraced by our friends and it was fun to introduce them to the exciting life we led each August in the south of France with our wonderful friends.

We usually hosted a big party at the end of our stay but this year, before the Peppers left us, we decided to have it early in August. With music and singing and dancing to a violinist and an accordionist we'd hired, it was great fun.

We ended the season with a short trip on Bob Lalemant's yacht, but it was the last time we were to do so. Bob felt conflicted about whether he wanted his mistress or his wife in his life. It was getting a little too complicated for us: we couldn't keep the two women straight, so our paths parted after that voyage.

Before returning to Los Angeles, we spent a wonderful four days with Lonna and Marshall Wais traveling through Italy with their chauffeur doing the driving while we sat back and comfortably enjoyed the scenery. After a six-hour drive, we reached the charming town of Breuil-Cervinia, in the Valle d'Aosta, where we stayed at the quaint Hermitage Hotel, with its perfect view of the Matterhorn. The scenery was beyond breathtaking, and once again I had my camera at the ready.

Hal and Marshall lounged around at the hotel one afternoon while Lonna and I took three different-sized gondolas to get to the top of Mount Rosa, a sprawling glacier which is about thirteen thousand feet high. By the time we reached the summit, we were actually in Switzerland, with a border guard standing right there making sure no one crossed into their country unless they had proper papers. We could have taken the lift all the way to Zermatt if we'd had more time - and our passports.

Our drive the next day took us on roads with treacherous curves through little villages rested at the foot of towering mountains, each with their own distinctive church steeples, to Chamonix, where we got the pictures of Mont Blanc that we had hoped for, and were then off to Lausanne and the Beau-Rivage Palace, with its panoramic view of Lake Geneva.

We indulged in an eating frenzy in Lausanne: lunch at Auberge Pere Bise and dinner at Marc Veyrat. At Pere Bise we were warmly greeted by Charlyne Bise herself, and enjoyed a meal with each dish tastier than the one before it. We didn't know how we'd ever be able to eat dinner, but we not only ate at Marc Veyrat, we stayed at his small Auberge as well. The four of us agreed that the presentation of the food there far surpassed its taste. But the presentation was extraordinary, with some food being served on irregularly shaped pieces of bark, right out of the forest, complete with artfully arranged moss and flowers. To counteract those unique presentations, other food was served on simple, elegant, contemporary glass triangles rimmed in silver.

When we eventually reached Geneva, a gleaming Falcon 2000 was waiting for us, a plane the Waises were considering purchasing, and after a quick refueling stop in Newfoundland, it seemed as though we were landing at Teterboro New Jersey in no time at all.

Bernie Hodes was a long-time member of the New York Friars Club, and he was instrumental in encouraging the club to produce a show honoring Hal. There were numerous rehearsals, which Hal and I both sat through. At one of them, the elegant and debonair manager of The Friars, Jean Pierre Trebot, came up to Hal with a sheaf of papers in his hand. He said he thought it was about time that Hal joined The Friars, and handed Hal a pen there and then. Hal had, for some reason, always resisted joining the club, but now he was on the spot - so The Friars gained a new member, and we were happy that he had joined, because we spent some wonderful times there, entertaining friends and thoroughly enjoying our membership.

For Hal's show, Jill O'Hara and Jerry Orbach performed some songs from *Promises, Promises,* in which they'd starred some twenty-five years ago when it opened on Broadway. Christine Andreas, who was starring in The *Scarlet Pimpernel* when we first met her, performed "Alfie.". She's a dynamite singer, and has had great success on both Broadway and in Cabaret shows. Whenever she sings "Alfie," there isn't a dry eye in the house, and the night she sang it at The Friars was no exception. Len Cariou sang "Raindrops" followed by a rendition of "To All the Girls I've Loved Before," in which Angela LaGrecca took Julio Iglesias' part while Len, with a bandana tied around his forehead, did a spot-on imitation of Willie Nelson. Michele Lee came in from Los Angeles to sing "One Less Bell to Answer" and "A House is Not a Home," and Jose Feliciano sang the beautiful "There's Always Something There to Remind Me" and "Walk on By." He received a standing ovation, which, of course, he couldn't see. When it was finally Dionne's turn, she sang a great medley of Bacharach/David songs, and the audience would not let her leave the stage.

When she finally cried "uncle," Freddy Roman, a comedian once famously dubbed "king of the one-liners" who was the Dean of The Friars Club, presented Hal with his award. Tony Roberts, who had starred in *Promises, Promises* when it was on the road, and who'd done a great job as M.C. of the show, called all the performers back to the stage and, with the audience joining in, they sang "What the World Needs Now."

We floated back to our New York apartment on West Fifty-Third Street on Cloud Nine!

The next day we worried that we might not make it to Washington, D.C., because Hurricane Floyd had struck the east coast of the United States, triggering the third largest (up until then) evacuation in U.S. history. Our timing was good, though, because the storm abated in time to let us catch the shuttle to D.C. Hal and a wonderful group of ASCAP members were planning to perform before legislators in D.C. The impressive lineup of the show included, in addition to Hal, Alan Bergman, Maureen McGovern, Cy Coleman, Lillias White, Dionne Warwick, Rudy Perez, Jose Feliciano, Jimmy Webb, and Glen Campbell. The show titled *The Stories behind the Songs,* pretty much explains what it was about.

It was performed for a group of senators, congressmen and women, and other influential Washington people, in the Senate Caucus Room of the Russell Senate Office building, one of the grandest and most historic rooms in the nation's capital. Our event was a happy one, but in 1912, a much more somber event had taken place when a special Senate subcommittee had opened public hearings on the sinking of the Titanic in that very same caucus room.

Hurricane Floyd didn't stop us from going to D.C. but when we returned to New York the hurricane hit with all its fury. Fortunately, forty-one floors up in our apartment at the Museum Towers, we weathered the it without incident.

Wanderlust again tugged at us, and we soon found ourselves on our way to Thailand, headed for Bangkok, Angkor Wat, Cambodia, Kathmandu, Nepal, Tiger Tops, and Tokyo. We weren't sure what the political temperature would be in Cambodia, given that the U.S. had once bombed it unmercifully, so we were pleasantly surprised to find the locals very courteous and smiling, with a nod of their head in greeting, and frequently with their hands together in the praying position.

I have two diametrically opposed memories of Cambodia. One was the Tuol Sleng genocide prison, located in the heart of Phnom Penh. From 1974 to 1979, the Khmer Rouge Communist Dictator Pol Pot practically ruined the country. Sealing off the country from the outside world, he put anyone who had completed a higher education - all professionals, doctors, lawyers, and journalists, and their families, including their children into labor camps, known as the "killing fields." Millions died and an entire decade of intellectuals was decimated. The most horrible sight we saw at the museum was a map of Cambodia made out of wire, and filled with skulls of people who had actually been held prisoner there.

Fortunately, the next day brought something else that was also impactful, but in a good way: Angkor Wat. The largest Hindu temple complex and the largest religious monument in the world, it was built in the early twelfth century as the king's state temple and his own mausoleum. It has become a symbol of the country, appearing on its national flag since 1863, and is the major tourist attraction in Cambodia. We climbed up steep stairs and marveled at how much of the temple had been preserved. This landmark was definitely worth traveling all those miles just to see it.

Each stop on this trip was fascinating, offering photo-ops galore. A sight almost as fascinating to photograph as Angkor Wat was Mt. Everest, the tallest mountain in the world, its height the equivalent to the height of almost twenty Empire State Buildings.

We photographed it from the ground at every conceivable time of day, and even went up in a small twin-engine plane to photograph the mountain from the air. Seeing those treacherous-looking peaks up close made us realize why so few humans have ever conquered that foreboding range.

The most exciting portion of this trip, at least for me, was our stay at the Tiger Tops Jungle Lodge in the Royal Chitwan National Park near Katmandu, where we rode elephants into the brush looking for tigers. Actually, we knew we wouldn't see any tigers, because we were told in advance that tigers were no longer in the region, but we did see some rhinos, which were fascinating to see with their armor-like hides.

Tiger Tops seemed to embody all of the mystery and exotic flavor of Nepal, and as remote and primitive as it was, we still felt we were living in comfort. The second morning we were at the Lodge, we were given the option of taking another elephant ride, but this one starting at 5:30 in the morning, when there was a low-lying mist covering the area. Hal was content for me to take the ride and tell him all about it when I returned. I wasn't about to miss it, and it lived up to all my expectations. Riding through that misty, ghostly curtain, with only shadowy outlines of trees, brush, and tall grass, was one of the most beautiful sights I'd ever seen. It was almost mystical. And the thrill of suddenly seeing a rhinoceros, coming out of the mist just two feet away from the elephant on which I was riding, was cause for a loud gasp, but I kept my camera steady.

December found us back in New York City where we were hosting a fundraiser for our friend Ted Kennedy in our apartment. About one hundred people in the music industry attended, as well as some of our close Manhattan friends. Once the obligatory networking was over, Charles Strouse, Jimmy Webb, and Christine Andreas performed, and then Ted announced that his wife Vicki had recently given him a gift of singing lessons, and he wanted to show us what he had learned – which he did, choosing one of Hal's songs.

We were about to call it a night: we were ready to go to bed, but people were still milling around the piano so Hal got up to sing a few of his songs, with Frank Owens accompanying him, and then Betty Comden, who, with her writing partner Adolph Green wrote lyrics and screenplays to some of the most successful Hollywood musicals and Broadway shows, got up to perform a wonderful medley of her songs. Then Cy Coleman got into the act. It turned into a real songfest, with people both in and out of the music business clamoring for more and more songs.

The year and the century ended with predictions of major problems with desktop computers and the myriad of other things which we use and rely on every day of our lives that were dependent on computers, because of Y2K, also known as the Millennium bug. People were all up in arms thinking that their computers would no longer work, and companies worldwide checked, fixed, and upgraded their computer systems in the hope that they had corrected the impending Armageddon. Airports thought that they would be affected because they were almost all computerized, and that they would have to be shut down. The problem had to do with using two digits to designate a year, going from '99 to '00, because it was thought that computers would get confused between the year 2000, using the last two digits, and the year 1900, also using the last two digits. But somehow or other we all muddled through and Y2K turned out to be a non-event.

January 1, 2000. What an exciting date: a new millennium, a new century, and a new beginning, one that was marked early on by the United States turning over control of the Panama Canal to Panama. "The Canal is ours," Panamanian President Mireya Moscoso exclaimed as he hoisted the nation's flag over the canal's administration building, while thousands of balloons were released to celebrate the event.

We were in New York in February for the official public announcement that Hal had been appointed as Chairman of the Board of the Songwriters Hall of Fame, which had been founded in 1969 by songwriter Johnny Mercer and music publishers Abe Olman and Howie Richmond. Mercer was the first Chairman of the Board, a position also held by composer Sammy Cahn, and once by Frank Sinatra. Sinatra was not only a champion of songwriters, but he wrote some lyrics, also, which is why he was a member of the Songwriters Hall of Fame. He was famously quoted as saying of songwriters, "If it weren't for you fellas, I'd be pushing pencils in Hoboken."

One of the first things that Hal did when he became Chairman was to see that the Board was made up more evenly of members from BMI, ASCAP, and SESAC, the three competing performing rights societies in the United States. Another very smart move on Hal's part was to see that Linda Moran was ensconced in the president's position. Linda had been in the A&R department of RCA Records, and after joining Atlantic Records, she worked her way up to Senior Vice President. When Moran was the Senior Vice President at Warner Music Group, she was responsible for artist relations, industry relations, public affairs, corporate relations, special events, community relations, special projects, and charitable contributions for the parent company and its divisions. She knew everyone in the business, and they all knew and respected her. She was known for her unique blend of skills, honed during her many years in the music business. She was a major factor, along with Hal, in moving the Songwriters Hall of Fame forward.

In March the results of the Presidential primaries were announced: Al Gore (D), George W. Bush (R) were their party's nominees. Speaking of politics, that year we hosted a "red, white, and blue" party for Vicki Reynolds to celebrate her election as Mayor of Beverly Hills for the third time. I even found a flag of Beverly Hills, which none of our guests, who were long-time Beverly Hills residents, had ever seen before. I remember that everyone arrived on time except the guest of honor. Vicki was in a meeting at the Beverly Hills City Hall regarding the conversion of the historic Beverly Hills Post Office, which she envisioned as becoming a theatre complex - the first in Beverly Hills.

In March, we took General Mac Arthur's words to heart, and returned for another Asian Song Festival in Manila, even though the festival had been held there recently. This one was originally scheduled to be in Taiwan, but for a variety of reasons that venue wasn't feasible, so the Filipinos agreed to host the event again. Since we'd pretty much toured the areas in and around Manila the last time we were there, we curtailed our side trips. But Ding Dong Eduque, the Filipino composer whom we met a couple of years earlier, arranged to take us to the Magdapio Falls in Pangasian, a three-hour drive from Manila. We were outfitted with life vests and escorted to long, narrow canoe-like wooden dugouts called "bancas," where we sat in the low-lying shells with our legs stretched out in front of us. With two skinny boatmen rowing, we headed up stream – up, not down, forging the rapids the wrong way, dodging rocks that cropped up all along our four-mile route and getting completely soaked in the process. Frequently the boatmen had to jump out of the banca to use their hands, feet, and big wooden paddles to push us one way or the other to avoid the rocks. When too much water accumulated in the bottom of the boat, one of the boatmen would just take off his rubber flip-flop and splash the water right back into the Pagsanjan River.

We finally arrived at the Falls, a wide cascade of water, tumbling into a confined pool. We were already soaking wet, but opted not to paddle under the Falls: enough was enough. I was happy to stand on the sidelines and take pictures of others. Needless to say, the trip downstream took much less time than we'd spent going up stream, and with the rapids running pretty strong, we gained even more speed.

While we were still in Manila, we learned that Muslim separatists were holding hostages in Mindanao, just a short island hop from where we were staying. That was off-putting, to say the least because no one knew what to expect from them next. There was also a financial scandal involving the first lady of the Philippines, Luise Ejercito Estrada, and her son San Juan Mayor Jinggoy Estrada. The situation was very volatile, and we followed it closely, since we were in the Phillipines under government auspices.

The rules of the Festival specified that countries were supposed to present original songs that have not yet been published. Both China and Korea disregarded the rules, and the Festival committee planned to disqualify them, but not until their contestants had performed, because the show was to be televised, and they didn't want any gaps in the tightly timed show. The judges were told of the situation prior to the performances, and were also told to "get out of Dodge" as soon as possible in case there were repercussions once the announcement was made of the disqualifications. We did as told. Another bullet dodged.

The 2000 Academy Awards were televised in March, and we were especially anxious to see them this year because two Bacharach/David songs were going to be performed in one segment of the show which featured past Academy-nominated songs. "Raindrops" was sung by Garth Brooks, and "Alfie" was performed by Burt and Dionne. Whitney Houston was supposed to have sung the song with them, but when she came to rehearsals she was under the influence of either drugs or alcohol, and was unable to perform. That would have been some trio, had Whitney been up to it.

Hal and Burt agreed to put on a show for the Annual Henry Mancini Birthday Party, a fundraiser for the Mancini Institute. It would have been the first time the two of them had appeared on stage together. But unfortunately, Burt became ill, and was unable to perform. Hal in the meantime was rehearsing like mad with Freda Payne and his musical director Corky Hale. Freda and Corky had worked with Hal on numerous cabaret shows, so they had their script written, and were ready to go.

Jack Elliott, the head of the Mancini Institute, was prominent in the music and TV words, and had served as music director for the Grammy Awards for thirty years. So when he heard that Burt couldn't make it, he picked up the phone and called Dionne Warwick to ask her to fill in, not realizing that Hal already had the whole show planned and rehearsed. Dionne agreed to do the show, leaving Hal with the embarrassing problem of having to tell Freda that she might be replaced, which, naturally, he was loath to do. It was finally resolved when Hal asked Dionne what she was going to sing, and then he asked Freda to sing several other Bacharach/David songs. That seemed to satisfy everyone, including the audience – a great relief to Hal since he hadn't wanted to hurt either Dionne's or Freda's feelings.

As a thank you for his performance, Hal received a beautiful Lucite box with a conductor's baton in it. I thought it was one of the most unique awards that had ever been presented to him. After his death, that award went the way of all the rest of Hal's awards - - to his publishing company Casa David: read that "to Hal's two sons."

In May, everyone was once again glued to their television sets as the saga of little Elian Gonzales unfolded. He, his mother, and thirteen others left Cuba for the United States in a sixteen-foot motor boat which capsized. Elian's mother was one of the eleven people who perished. The immigration and Naturalization Service released Elian to his great uncle Lazaro Gonzalez, and that's when the problems started. Elian's father, who was still in Cuba demanded that his son be returned to him. His great uncle applied for asylum for Elian, but the authorities decided that the child belonged with his father. The matter went back and forth in the courts, with U.S. Attorney General Janet Reno upholding the court's decision to return Elian to Cuba. Television viewers were shocked as we watched while Federal agents broke the hinges off the front door of Gonzales' home, and stormed into the house where Elian was being held, and with him screaming hysterically, physically removed him from a bedroom where he had been hidden.

Elian's father came to the United States and took his son back to Cuba. Everyone breathed a sigh of relief when that drama was over and the hoop-la died down. But no one ever heard what eventually happened to Elian.

Hal was looking forward to receiving an honorary degree from Claremont Graduate University, in addition to the Doctor of Music degree conferred on him by Lincoln College in Illinois. We were going to drive to nearby Claremont on a Friday, but on Thursday I tripped on a step and my ankle swelled up to gargantuan size, and was very painful. I wasn't about to go to a doctor because I was afraid he'd put me on crutches, or even say that I could not go with Hal to the ceremony, and there was no way I was going to miss it. So, with an ankle brace purchased at a local drug store, and a cane taken out of our collection, Hal and I took off.

Dinner that Friday night was in a tent in the backyard of the home of the University President, Steadman Upham, and his wife Peggy. A contingent of our friends from Los Angeles drove out to Claremont to be with us that night: Vicki and Murray Pepper, Peggy and Walter Grauman, and Ron Rosen with his fiancée Judi Lawenda. Each of the three honorees was introduced by a different faculty member. Robert Davidoff introduced Hal, and I was pleased and proud when, during one part of his speech, he said, "Hal David has a re-markable partner in his wife Eunice David. Eunice is herself a leader in the Los Angeles arts and philanthropic world. Together and individually Eunice and Hal have animated and devoted themselves to a remarkable and inspiring range of artistic and charitable causes."

After a commencement breakfast the morning of May 12, 2000, Hal donned his robe, and we had a great picture taken of the two of us, although it clearly shows me favoring my gimpy leg.

Peggy Upham found a golf cart for me, and I was carted off in that to the VIP area to watch the ceremony which had all the pomp and circumstance that one would expect, and was elegant, touching, and stirring. The fully robed honorees and University dignitaries formed a line and proceeded down the center aisle to the stage, followed by about three hundred students, looking proud, awe-struck, and thrilled, all at the same time.

President Upham ended his remarks about Hal saying,

Claremont Graduate University is proud to honor you, Hal David, for the abundant gifts you have shared with the world. Therefore, upon the recommendation of the faculty and with the approval of the Board of Fellows of Claremont Graduate University, I confer upon you the degree Doctor of Humane Letters, honoris causa, with all the rights and privileges appertaining thereto.

By the time the ceremony was over, I was in excruciating pain, and Hal decided that we should skip the reception and head right to the Century City Emergency Hospital near our home, a good hour's drive away. Once there, I was fitted with a gel brace, and told that I had fractured a bone and had some badly damaged cartilage. The next day I called my orthopedic doctor to make an appointment to come in right away to see him. But his receptionist said that was impossible because he was fully booked. Well, I simply had to see him, so I called my friend Peggy Grauman who was a close friend of Honey Bear Brien. Not only was Honey Bear the daughter of Earl Warren, who served as the fourteenth Chief Justice of the United States, and the thirtieth Governor of California, she also happened to be the doctor's mother. Honey Bear called her son's office, and, by bypassing the receptionist, was able to get me an appointment to come in right away, where I eventually had a walking cast put on my leg, which I was told would have to remain on for a minimum of six weeks.

Hal's leg had been bothering him for some time, and, thinking it was just a pulled muscle, we headed back to Dr. Brien (this time getting in without any trouble). He suggested that Hal take some Aleve for relief. So Hal started on a regimen of Aleve, and continued on it when we went to New York for the annual Songwriters Hall of Fame gala. Since Hal was Chairman, he had a lot of work to do, but the gala went beautifully, enhanced by the surprise visit of Paul McCartney, who flew in to induct Brian Wilson into the Hall of Fame. Hal's leg continued to bother him, so he decided to see Dr. John Sarno, who was the Head of the Rusk Institute of Rehabilitation Medicine at New York

University, whom he had seen before. Sarno believed that when patients concentrate on what may be upsetting them in their unconscious, they can defeat their minds' strategy, because when the symptoms are seen for what they are, they go away. Hal first learned about Dr. Sarno when we were in the south of France one August, and Estelle and Carl Reiner came to our home for a dinner party. When Hal described his back problem, Estelle said that her close friend Anne Bancroft had been to see Sarno, and she was now living a pain-free life. When we returned to Los Angeles, there was Sarno's book, which Estelle had sent to Hal, and Hal immediately made an appointment to see Dr. Sarno the next time we were in New York.

After an office visit, Dr. Sarno's patients are required to attend a lecture during which the doctor further expounds on his theory. During this trip to New York, when Hal and I arrived at the lecture, which was held in New York Hospital, Hal said he was feeling a bit funny, and was very thirsty. He walked around for a while, but returned to his seat to hear the lecture. Soon he loosened his tie, and started squirming, which was unusual behavior for Hal. The next thing I knew he leaned over and said, "Get me out of here, I'm not feeling well."

It turned out that Hal had a bleeding ulcer from taking too much Aleve while also taking a daily dosage of aspirin (which Dr. Brien had neglected to tell him not to take with Aleve). That kept him in the hospital for an anxiety-filled four days.

Fortunately, he recovered in time for us to leave for London, as planned, where Hal and Burt were to receive the Nordoff-Robbins award. Their Silver Clef Awards raises funds for their work transforming the lives of vulnerable children and adults through music, so this was very meaningful to both Hal and Burt.

London was a whirl of parties honoring Hal, and frantic driving from one interview to another and attending social events with friends.

On the afternoon of the luncheon at the Inter-Continental Hotel, we were picked up in two limousines, which carried Burt and his wife Jane, Dionne Warwick and Hal and me. There were hordes of photographers and autograph seekers waiting outside the hotel, and they swarmed around us like flies. At the luncheon, Dionne presented the awards to Burt and Hal. The awards were then abruptly confiscated, to be returned later in the evening.

After changing for the evening back at our hotel, Burt and Dionne had to rush back to Royal Albert Hall to rehearse for the show, while Hal and I wandered around marveling at the size and beauty of the place. It was opened in 1871 by Queen Victoria and artists from all over the world have performed there.

I hardly know how to describe the show itself. The audience of four thousand people went wild with every song that was performed. The M.C. had wonderful stories to tell about each song before it was performed, setting the stage for each piece. Petula Clark performed, as did Elvis Costello, Leo Sayer - and Sacha Distel was even brought in from France so that he could appear in the show, since he'd had a major hit in his country with "Raindrops Keep Fallin' on my Head."

All through the performance, Hal and I had been seated in a box for ten, right in the middle of the Hall, overlooking the stage. Toward the end of the show, just as Burt and Dionne began to sing, an escort came to get Hal and me to lead us backstage so that Hal could be present for the finale. I was given a spot in the wings where I could see what was going on. When Burt and Dionne finished their set they got a standing ovation that seemed to go on forever. The audience was up on its feet cheering, stomping, and applauding. Then when Hal was called out, they started in all over again. The audience by this time was even whistling, and calling out Hal's name. What a wonderful moment for all three of them. I couldn't help but think that only one week ago, to the very day, we were wondering if Hal would be released from the hospital. It was a marvelous combination of prayer, determination, and good doctoring that got him to the stage this night.

The really big surprise of the evening was when Sir Andrew Lloyd Webber and his long-time collaborator, Sir Tim Rice carried the awards onto the stage and presented them to Hal and Burt. They'd been taken away from them at the luncheon, with the promise that they would get them back: what a grand way to receive them.

When the cast was called out to sing "What the World Needs Now," Hal spotted me in the wings and came over to bring me onto the stage. I sang lustily along with the pros with everyone kissing and hugging. It was a magical moment and a magical episode in our lives.

We waited until Petula Clark changed clothes, and with her and her husband Claude, we went to Annabelle's, where Ken Lieberman's party for us was in full swing. The place was jumping when we arrived at a little after 11 P.M. In fact, given the reputation of that hot spot, they were probably just getting started.

Hal had a smile on his face all night long. We didn't leave Annabel's until long after 2 A.M. but the autograph-seekers were still outside our hotel. Hal signed everything in sight, wanting to show his appreciation for the people who had been hanging around for so long. Even the stewardess on our Air New Zealand flight on our return home asked if she could have Hal's autograph.

As we were packing to leave London, we watched the men's finals of Wimbledon. Pete Sampras won, picking up his thirteenth Grand Slam Championship, breaking a record held for the previous thirty two years by Roy Emerson of Australia.

Although we didn't make an effort to keep up with the outside world, we learned that Republican presidential candidate George W. Bush announced that his running mate would be the former defense secretary Dick Cheney. Also, a disabled Russian submarine was stuck on the ocean bottom unable to rise to the surface. The United States offered help, which the Russians refused. The crew of one hundred eighteen all died because the Russians were unable to raise the ship.

When we returned to Los Angeles, we plunged right into the thick of things, working on a show for Hillcrest Country Club called *Hillcrest & Hollywood*. Monty Hall was the M.C. and the musical conductor was Jerry Goldsmith, of movie score fame, who had won an Oscar for the score of The Omen. There was a host of Hollywood stars who agreed to perform, making the show a one in-a-million, including June Allyson, Dina Merrill, Theo Bikel, Karl Malden, Betty Garrett, Gloria deHaven, Jack Lemmon, Red Buttons, Rita Moreno, Kirk Douglas, Angela Lansbury, Rhonda Fleming, and Sidney Poitier.

Once the show was over, we flew to Santiago, Chile, for a CISAC meeting. Hal dutifully attended all the meetings that were scheduled for him, and I did a little touring with the wives who had traveled to Chile with their husbands.

We contacted our U.S. Ambassador, John O'Leary to let him know we were going to be back in Santiago, and he organized a dinner for us with about twenty-four Chileans, many of whom were in the entertainment field, and he also included our American friends Jody and Ed Murphy who were also attendees at the CISAC meeting. Ed was the President and CEO of NMPA, the National Music Publishers Association. The O'Learys had hired a pianist, and had warned Hal ahead of time that they would like him to sing a medley of his songs. When Hal forgot some of his own lyrics, which he was known to do on occasion, the other guests quickly joined him in singing, supplying the words that they all knew, even if Hal didn't.

Back in New York again, we drove up to the Berkshires to visit our good friends, Hannah and Roy Schneider, who had a beautiful home there. This picture, taken on their patio, is another one of my favorites of Hal and me.

In October people all over the world were shocked to read about a small boat loaded with a bomb of some sort that blasted a huge hole in the U.S. Cole, while it was refueling in Yemen. Six sailors were killed and eleven were missing and feared dead. The headline screamed that, "a new chapter in terrorism may have begun." Around the same time, more than two hundred anti-Semitic acts of violence were reported in major cities around the world, caused by an outbreak of fighting between Israelis and Palestinians.

In October the Prime Minister of India, Inder and his wife Sheila Gujral, came to the United States, and because we had met them when we had been in India, Hal and I were invited to join them for dinner at a friend's home. At the Prime Minister's home in India, there had been armed guards at the ready and their home was behind huge walls. This time there were two bodyguards in the car in which the Gujrals arrived. While we were having drinks, the two bodyguards stood at attention in the foyer. When we left to go to Michael's in Santa Monica for dinner (coincidentally owned by the daughter and son-in-law of Ken Lieberman, on whose yacht the Mikili we used to sail), we were accompanied by a fleet of cars barreling down the freeway. It seemed a little cloak and dagger-ish to me, but no doubt it was a necessary precaution.

The conversation during dinner naturally centered on politics. We unsuccessfully tried to draw the Prime Minister out on his feelings about U.S. politics and about the violence in the mid-east, which had halted the peace process there. We were also anxious to hear his opinion about the presidential candidates but all we could get out of him on that subject was, "we want world peace." Very diplomatic!

America's presidential elections this year were really botched up with the Florida results going back and forth between George W. Bush and Al Gore. This prompted another marathon of TV watching. Katherine Harris, the Florida Secretary of State, eventually declared that George W. Bush was the new president, but that just brought on another spate of threats to file more law suits.

While all of that was still going on, Hal and I headed to London and from there to West Berlin for another CISAC meeting. From Berlin we went back to London to see some shows and visit our British friends. While we'd been gone, the election fiasco had gone all the way up to the Supreme Court, leaving them to decide who was going to be our next president. And decide they did, in favor of George Walker Bush, who became our forty-third president.

We spent a wonderful New Year's Eve at our apartment in Los Angeles with Peggy and Walter Grauman. It was quiet and very special because we were together with such good friends.

Contrary to public opinion, Hal and I weren't always traveling. In fact, some of our most treasured times were spent in Los Angeles, where we had a tradition of meeting Peggy and Walter Grauman for lunch at the Hillcrest Country Club every Saturday that we were in town.. If anyone was looking for us on a Saturday afternoon, they knew exactly where to find us. Peggy and I loved listening to wonderful stories told by Walter about his years of directing films and TV shows, and equally wonderful stories told by Hal about his years as a songwriter. Walter directed both film and television, and was perhaps best known for having directed fifty-three episodes of the television series *Murder, She Wrote,* which starred Angela Lansbury.

Another Saturday afternoon tradition, that we all treasured, was when Walter Mirisch, who has produced some of the finest and most memorable films of our time, joined us after lunching with his son Larry. Hal matched the two Walters, story for story.

One day when we were discussing all the unrest in the world, Hal told about how he came to write the song "Windows of the World," for Dionne to sing in 1962, during the Vietnam War. The song was one of Hal's favorites with lyrics unique for Hal because most of his songs were love songs. This was a protest song. Hal was afraid that his oldest son might have to go to war, and he didn't want that to happen.

One of Hal's songs, which I loved long before I knew he wrote it, was "Broken Hearted Melody." When we urged Hal to tell us about that, he reminded us that he'd written it with Sherman Edwards before he began his long-lasting collaboration with Burt. Although it was a huge hit for Sarah Vaughan in 1959, both in the U.S. and in the U.K, Sarah originally thought the song was corny. But after she received her first gold record for the song, it remained part of her concert repertoire for many years.

One day while we were having lunch with the Graumans, the singer Helen Grayco, who had been married to the zany bandleader Spike Jones, came over to say hello. Hal always reminded her that he'd written a song which she'd recorded, which she didn't remember doing. And all Hal had to prove his point was an empty record jacket of it with a big "X" on it. He kept saying that he would try to get a copy of the record, but he never did anything about it.

This time I'd heard that promise once too often, so when we got home, I got busy on my computer, and located a company in the Midwest who had an amazing supply of out-of-print records. Sure enough, they had a copy of "What Do You See in Her" which Hal had written in 1955 with Frank Weldon. They not only had the recording that Helen had done, but they had one sung by Dakota Staton, which even Hal did not know about!

When we got a cassette of the song, we immediately called Helen and played it for her over the phone. She said, "Oh my God, that's me singing."

Hal had heard so many stories over the years about the wonderful music still being performed in Cuba (by many musicians who wanted to, but could not, leave the country) that he urged me to find a way to get us there. The United States did not permit its citizens to fly directly from the United States to Cuba, but many did anyway, finding ways to get there through Mexico or some departure point other than leaving directly from the States. Doing that did not appeal to Hal, so I checked around to see how we could make Hal's wish come true. A friend in D.C. helped me get official forms from Conchord Cayo Hueso, an organization based in Key West, Florida, which since 1992 had carried food and medicine - and even musical instruments - to the Cuban people. Our papers were stamped with an official Cuban Assets Control Regulations Authorized Activities License, and we were good to go.

When some friends from New York heard about our pending trip, they asked if they could join us, so there were a total of eight on this trip, all loaded down with as much non-prescription medication that we could find, since we had declared that we were on a humanitarian mission in order to gain official entry into Cuba.

An hour and ten minutes after we left Miami Beach, Florida, we made a mad dash for Customs in Cuba, only to be stopped short and told that there was additional paperwork to be filled out. That, finally paid for and out of the way, we got through Customs and were welcomed by the sales manager of the Melia Cohiba Hotel, and whisked there in two vans: one for us, the other for our luggage. The hotel was a joint Spanish/Cuban venture. We were to learn that there were many joint ventures in Cuba with many different countries - but none with the United States.

We drove down a beautiful, wide, divided avenue with remnants of what had once been gorgeous homes, now in disrepair, lining each side of the street. Many of the buildings may have been falling down and were not being repaired due to lack of funds, but the Cubans took great pride in their ability to restore old cars. They even managed to make some parts by hand because they were no longer manufactured, in order to keep their shiny, pristine - but forty-year-old-cars running.

Our friend Henry Kimelman, who had been Ambassador to Haiti, arranged for us to have us an introduction to Vicki Huddleston, whose title was The Principal Officer of the United States Interests Section in Havana. (Since the United States did not have diplomatic relations with Cuba, there was no official ambassador stationed there, and instead of an embassy, there was a U.S. Interests Section building located in Havana.) Ms. Huddleston filled the role of Ambassador. She graciously met our little group for breakfast one morning and gave us an update on Cuba from her perspective. At the time, the average pay for a local was about thirty dollars a month, but in a peso-economy, that could go a very long way. Vicki mentioned that there had been many changes, such as a lot of construction and more cars on the road, so people in Cuba felt they were better off than before Russia pulled out.

We learned of a local synagogue that maintained its own pharmacy. So arrangements were made for us to meet a representative of the temple, who was thrilled with all the over-the-counter medications we'd brought with us. There was no rabbi in all of Cuba, but services were held anyway, with lay people performing the necessary rights and rituals. We were amused to see the names of the members of the synagogue listed on the walls - - names such as Jorge Goldstein, Manuel Blumberg, and Pelé Ginsberg.

Naturally we had to visit Hemingway's former home, which is now a museum, and we were very fortunate to obtain permission to visit Gregorio Fuentes, the real live "Old Man of the Sea" whom Hemingway wrote about. Fuentes' grandson translated for us, and we all had pictures taken with Fuentes, who sat still, smoking a big fat Cuban cigar. He was a hundred-three at the time we were there, and he passed away a couple of years later at a hundred-five!

While in Havana, we decided to charter a plane for a side trip to Cienfuegos (translation: one thousand fires). That was not an easy task, and there was quite a delay at the airport when we got there, even though we had all the paperwork in order. When we eventually were allowed to board the plane, there were two stern, suspicious-looking men sitting in the back of the plane. When we asked who they were, we were told that they were engineers who worked for the charter company. We didn't believe that for a minute, but felt that we could not kick them off the plane or we would never have been allowed to leave. In fact, we had invited the manager of our hotel and his wife to join us on this jaunt, but he was unable to receive Government permission to come with us. The thinking was that he might have tried to escape from Cuba since he would be in an airplane. Even though he had what was considered a prestigious position, he was still carefully watched at all times.

Cienfuegos was charming, with colonial houses and buildings topped by unique weathered red tile roofs. We'd only planned to stay a short time, so after some touring and a quick look at some of the surrounding areas, we headed back to Havana on our chartered plane: alone this time. I guess that since we were heading "back" to Havana, we no longer needed to be watched over.

Cuba was fascinating, and we especially loved the music being played at every possible venue - at a pharmacy, a grocery store, or just somewhere out on the street. Music was in the air at all times.

Our last stop, a short distance outside of Havana, was a tobacco factory, where we bought our allotted number of Cuban cigars to give to friends, once back in the States.

At the foot of the steps leading up to the plane we were taking on our return trip to Florida, Hal was stopped by a couple of officious men in uniform. Even though there was a long line behind him, he was told to stay where he was while they conferred among themselves, despite the people in the line, unable to move around Hal, getting more annoyed by the minute. Hal was finally allowed to board, but soon one of the fellows came to our seats and demanded Hal's passport. Naturally we were reluctant to give it up, but a nice young Cuban seated behind us, who spoke English fluently, told us that it would be okay, and that the plane wouldn't leave before the passport was brought back to us. When we asked why it was confiscated, the Cuban just shrugged and said that the officials frequently did things like that, and we shouldn't let it bother us.

But bother us it did, and we were on pins-and-needles before Hal's passport was finally returned.

George Walker Bush was sworn into office as the forty-third President of the United States, on January 20, 2001.

Since we had just been to Cuba, anything that had to do with the country interested me. I spotted an article from the Associated Press that read: "HAVANA: Fidel Castro this week fired his first verbal shot at President Bush since he took office, saying he hoped his new adversary in the White House was 'not as stupid as he seems." Bush had expressed support for the four-decade American trade embargo on Cuba, which is what brought on Castro's tirade

In February, Hal and I produced the first of what turned out to be one of the most popular benefits ever presented at the Los Angeles Music Center for the

Blue Ribbon, a major support group. Hal came up with the perfect title: The Writer, The Singer, The Song. The concept was to have six songwriters sing one of their songs, and talk about how it was created, and then have a professional singer perform a second song that the writer had written. For our inaugural event, this was our lineup:

Paul Williams	Helen Reddy
Alan Bergman	Maureen McGovern
Cy Coleman	Larry Gatlin
Hal David	Dionne Warwick
Mike Stoller	Sally Kellerman
Jimmy Webb	Rosemary Clooney

The first person I asked to be on the show was Paul Williams. Besides singing one of his songs, We've Only Just Begun, I wanted Paul to be the M.C. of the show. With his wonderful sense of humor and funny quips, he was a big hit, and every time I asked him to M.C. a show for me thereafter, he always generously said "yes."

The proceeds that first year went to the Blue Ribbon group and the Fraternity of Friends, two Music Center support organizations, as well as to the ASCAP Foundation. Karen Sherry, as Senior Vice President of Industry Affairs for ASCAP, produced the show, with Hal, Walter Grauman, Ron Rosen, and me lending our assistance.

The evening was so successful that we were asked to present our show (each with different artists) four times after that initial production, which we happily did.

Hal and I and Vicki and Murray Pepper were planning an extensive trip to China. But shortly before we were scheduled to leave, an American plane filled with secret eavesdropping equipment collided with a Chinese fighter that had shadowed it sixty-five miles off Chinese territorial waters. The damaged plane made an emergency landing at a military base on the southern Chinese island of Hainan, and the twenty-four American crew members aboard were taken into custody.

We were reluctant to go to China while Americans were being held hostage there, so we were unsure how to proceed. Hal called Richard Stites at the American Embassy in Beijing, who had scheduled a meeting for us with some Chinese composers, and Vicki called Senator Diane Feinstein's office to get her thoughts about Americans traveling to China at this time. Since we stood to lose our paid-for reservations if we waited too long to decide what to do, we were conflicted.

Stites told us that the Embassy in Beijing was on a twenty-four-hour alert, and he felt that there would be a great deal of anti-American feelings in China at this time, due to a tremendous amount of negative newspaper propaganda.

China was demanding an apology from America, and Secretary of State Colin Powell issued a statement of regret over the loss of the Chinese pilot who had bailed out of his plane, but whose body was never found. Chinese leaders were eager to avoid a hostile confrontation at this time because they were hoping to enter the World Trade Organization, and they very much wanted to host the 2008 Olympics.

President Bush kept warning China of damaged relations if the hostages were not released, and China kept demanding more of an apology than Powell's simple statement of regret. The stand-off lasted from April 4th to April 11th, when we turned on CNN to learn that the Chinese were going to release our servicemen within twenty-four hours. There were only seven days left before we were scheduled to leave. Our travel agent called to say that we had to let him know that day if we were going, so that he could alert the tour guides in China regarding our itinerary. Hal and I were in Nashville, Murray was in Beverly Hills, and Vicki was in Sacramento, so it was quite a trick to get a consensus as to whether or not we should go. But just in the nick of time, a beautiful picture of our twenty-four airmen boarding a chartered Continental plane appeared on TV, and we were able to reach Mr. Stites in Beijing, who told us that we could now feel comfortable about being in China.

So we and the Peppers left the U.S. on April 18th for China, where we spent almost a month touring, and had a marvelous time. I titled my journal of that experience "Trip of 1000 Surprises." Hal and I had been in Beijing three times, but our last visit had been ten years earlier and at that time the roads had been clogged with people on bicycles. Now we saw relatively few cyclists but a huge number of cars, trucks, and busses, creating major traffic jams and causing lengthy delays. The closer we got to town, the more we saw tall, modern buildings which, had they not had signs in Chinese on them, we'd never have been able to differentiate from skyscrapers in any large city, anywhere in the world.

Hal, Murray, and Vicki had all arranged for us to meet interesting people while we were in China. At one luncheon, a group of composers bemoaned the fact that they were still not getting royalties for their songs, which they knew they were entitled to (something Hal had been lobbying for endlessly). Another day, while we were in the China Art Gallery, looking at work of emerging Chinese artists, I heard a group of people speaking French. Since Vicki was fluent in French, I urged her to go over to see if she could find out what was going on. It turned out that we had stumbled on the opening ceremony of a joint exhibition sponsored by the Baroness Philippine de Rothschild and the China International Exhibition Agency. The show was titled "Mouton Rothschild Paintings for the Labels." What with Vicki having been the Mayor of Beverly Hills, and with Hal being who he was, we were immediately invited into the room and introduced to the people in charge, including the Baroness. That was a very special, totally unscripted experience.

Another was meeting an American, Sidney Shapiro, who had been married to a famous Chinese actress/writer for forty-five years, before she had died only a couple of years before our visit. She had been held in a detention camp for four years during the Cultural Revolution, mainly because she had been a close friend of Mao's fourth wife, Jiang Qing.

Besides being a writer in his own right, Sidney translated books from Chinese to English, and frequently was asked to translate for Chairman Mao. After we visited Sidney at his sparsely furnished home, he suggested we eat at the Gongwangu Sichuan Restaurant, which he categorized as the best Sichuan restaurant in the world. He knew what he was talking about. The décor may have been tacky (by our standards), but the food was sensational.

With that, we were ready to move on to Shanghai. We could not get over the incredible changes we saw which had taken place in the ten years since we'd been there. The city now had the most skyscrapers in the world: three thousand of them dotting the landscape, obliterating the former smaller, more ethnic-looking buildings of yore. And unlike on our prior trips, the food was superb, the accommodations were modern, comfortable, and clean, and the service was impeccable.

Our trip throughout China continued as it began, from visits with dignitaries to stops at interesting sites, such as the cave carvings in Dazu, and a memorable three-day cruise through the Three Gorges on the Yangtze River, at the end of which we toured the newly-constructed Three Gorges Dam that had displaced so many Chinese people and holy sites.

Of course, no visit to China would be complete for me without time spent on the Li River, and the Peppers were just as thrilled with the dramatic peaks surrounding the river as I had always been.

When we returned to the states, we happened across an article in the *Los Angeles Times* describing how even the family home in Shanghai of the famed architect I.M. Pei could not be saved from demolition because the city was being spruced up for a meeting of Asia-Pacific leaders, and the three-story building had to be torn down to make way for a park. The home had housed five generations of the Pei family. But that was the way things were being done in China, and nothing was going to stand in the way of their progress.

Burt Bacharach was to be awarded Sweden's Polar Music Prize in Stockholm in May of 2001, and the organizing committee had invited Hal and me to attend, so in Hong Kong, where we ended up after we left mainland China, we said goodbye to the Peppers and boarded a new 747 plane with wonderfully comfortable beds, so our flight over Siberia to London was very easy. After a two-hour layover at Heathrow, we headed for Stockholm, where we were met by a VIP service representative who accompanied us through customs and retrieved our luggage for us: that was a first. In the past, we'd frequently been met by VIP services after customs, but never actually inside the customs area. We realized that the Polar Music Prize was a big deal and the people running it obviously had a lot of clout in Sweden. This was just a few short months before September 11, 2001, so that was probably the end of such VIP service in Sweden - or elsewhere, for that matter.

One night we attended a glamorous event at the American Ambassador's residence, where Burt and Robert Moog (who had invented the synthesizer) were the guests of honor, and after that party ended, we went on to a "party after the party," at the home of Marie (the daughter of Stig Anderson, who founded the Polar Music Prize), and her successful singer/songwriter husband Tomas Ledin. They lived in a meticulously refurbished apartment built in the 1800's, which was a perfect backdrop for their extensive art collection which included Legers, Chagalls, and some contemporary Swedish artists.

The night of the big event, we arrived at the Berwaledhallen, a concert hall in the Östermalm district of Stockholm, where Burt, Robert Moog, and Karl-heinz Stockhausen (who had a career as a composer in the field of electronic music), were honored. Twelve of Burt's songs were performed that night; ten of them with lyrics by Hal David, one by Carol Bayer Sager, and one by Elvis Costello, who was one of the performers. Burt was especially gracious that evening in mentioning Hal's name as being the lyricist of those ten songs.

After the official presentations and performances, we and a small, group were invited back to the Grand Hotel where a banquet was being held. Before the banquet officially started, we were hustled into a room where there was an even smaller private reception with His Majesty King Carl XVI Gustaf of Sweden, the Queen Silvia, and the Crown Princess Victoria. All three of them were very accessible, and we were able to have lengthy conversations with them, plus a conversation with the King's sister Lillian, who started singing "Raindrops" for us, and even did a little jig!

His Majesty King Carl XVI Gustaf of Sweden with Hal and Me

At home in L.A., I hosted a great party for Hal's eightieth birthday at the Hillcrest Country Club. Instead of table numbers, I had sheet music of different songs, and guest's table cards directed them to those tables. That gave Hal the idea to talk about twenty of his songs, from his first big hit, "The Four Winds and the Seven Seas," on throughout his life in song. He had interesting comments to make about each song, describing how they came to be written, and what they meant in his life: marriage, down payment on his first house, etc.

It was at this party that Hal asked Chris Caswell to become his musical director. The most important thing for Hal was that Chris was always on time, and could always cover for him if/and when he made a mistake during a performance. Chris was a great arranger, as well as a wonderful songwriter in his own right.

Shortly after Hal's party, we flew to Portland, Oregon, to attend my oldest grandchild Kira's graduation from Linfield College in McMinnville, even though Hal had been scheduled to attend an ASCAP meeting in Australia. It meant as much to Hal as it did to me to be there to help celebrate her achievement.

I had not seen too much of Kira while she was growing up, but I never ceased to be excited about her and her accomplishments, and now she had turned into a lovely young woman on the brink of adulthood, and I was very proud.

Our sixth grandchild was born in June: Sara Ann David was born to Gunilla and Jim David, and we rushed over to Santa Monica Hospital to hold her in our arms as soon as we got the green light from her mother Gunilla, who didn't feel up to our visiting right away. I was just thrilled to have a little pink bundle to hold and cuddle.

During July and August, we had our usual incredible summer vacation with Bonnie and Bernie Hodes, starting with a driving trip from Paris to Provence, sampling the wonderful wine and food along the way. We eventually boarded our friend's yacht New York Lady for ten days, ending up at La Reserve for yet another month of eating and partying.

We decided that we needed a holiday to end our holiday, so we, the Hodeses, and Lonna and Marshall Wais headed to Majorca on the Wais's eight-passenger Challenger jet, where we enjoyed another fun-filled five days.

Lonna had seen an article about the Gran Hotel Son Net in a travel magazine, and had suggested we cap off our summer by staying there. We couldn't have imagined the grandeur of the 17th-century estate set in the Galatzo Mountains, overlooking neighboring hillsides dotted with little houses, olive groves, and vast forests of pine trees. The rooms, each with a different décor, were so beautiful that we couldn't decide whether to have room service or to go out to eat, although eating out won. Without even looking at the restaurant's menu, Bernie ordered a platter of lobster, langouste, razor clams, and mussels for all of us, and there were no complaints.

During our stay, we became friends with David Stein, the estate's owner, formerly from southern California, via Brooklyn. At one time the eighty-nine room Gran Son Net had been David's private residence but fortunately for us, he had turned into the elegant hotel we found by the time we arrived. From that first cocktail when we met David to the end of our stay, we were in his capable hands as he recommended restaurants, and even items to order on various menus, and he organized special tours for us.

By now and we'd been away from home for a long time. We were anxious to get back to Los Angeles to see our two grandchildren who lived there, to visit with our friends, and to open our mail (always the worst part of returning from any trip). But we had to get all that accomplished in a rush, because we were due to leave Los Angeles for New York on September 9th for some ASCAP business.

On Tuesday, September 11, 2001 we woke up early in our New York apartment and got dressed immediately because we were planning to take a shuttle from La Guardia to Washington, D.C. where Hal and a number of ASCAP writers were going to perform in the annual show that ASCAP hosted for legislators. In fact, we had a driver waiting downstairs to take us to the airport. But before we left our apartment, I needed to make a quick phone call to our niece, who was getting married soon and for whom Hal and I were going to stand up, since her parents had passed.

When I reached her, Alix said, "Aunt Eunice, aren't you watching television? A plane has just crashed into the World Trade Center." We turned the TV on and watched in real time as a second plane hit the second tower and burst into a fireball. From our bedroom window we could see huge clouds of smoke billowing up into the sky.

I don't need to document here the traumatic details of that dreadful time, but needless to say, Hal and I quickly sent our driver away, realizing that we were not going anywhere that day. Once again, we were glued to every television set in the apartment, unable to take our eyes off of the TVs.

Naturally the ASCAP event in DC was cancelled, and CEO John Lo Frumento urged Hal and me to try to make our way up to his home in Westchester County, feeling that we would be safer there than in Manhattan. But we just couldn't tear ourselves away.

At the beginning there was absolute silence in the borough of Manhattan: no planes were flying in the skies, no cars or taxis were on the road, no horns were honking: it was a weird feeling – surreal. But soon that silence was broken by a steady stream of fire engines and other emergency vehicles dashing south, with sirens screaming, to the destroyed site of what had once been the majestic World Trade Center towers.

Bonnie and Bernie Hodes called to ask us to join them for dinner. In spite of what happened, we had to eat, and none of us kept much food in our apartments. Most restaurants were closed because their employees could not get into the city since no busses were running and the subways were closed. Finally Bernie located a Japanese restaurant, Seryna, located at Fifty Third and Madison. The Hodeses walked over from their apartment on Sixty Third and Park, and we walked through the eerily deserted streets from our place on Fifty-Third and Fifth. Another couple joined us in the restaurant, which was totally deserted except for one other lone diner.

When we arrived at the building, we were greeted by a hand-written sign in the elevator saying: *"Due to a shortage of staff, please push the button for the floor you desire by yourself."*

President Bush addressed the nation on September 12th, and said that the attacks were a "monumental struggle of good vs. evil, and good will prevail."

The next day we met friends for lunch at the Friar's Club, and that evening, we walked over to the elegant La Goulue on Sixty Fourth and Madison, where we had dinner with other friends, and with Liza Minnelli, none of whom wanted to be alone. We were astonished to see the masses of people now out on the street and trying to get into restaurants, with or without reservations. The previous night, when the streets had been so deserted, people must have been in shock, but now they just seemed to want to be with other people. Strangers were talking to one another like old friends; everyone wanted to touch someone and in many cases, to hug one another.

Next we put our minds to the task of returning to Los Angeles. All flights in or out of the city were cancelled, and we didn't know how long that would last. By the time we tried to book a train, all seats were booked solid for the next two weeks. We couldn't even find a rental car available.

We decided to go to the American Airlines office located in the Waldorf Astoria Hotel at Fiftieth and Park to see what the situation was. There, we were greeted by a phalanx of security people at long tables, guarding the entrance. After checking our I.D.'s and searching through my purse, they finally allowed us into the lobby of the hotel, and from there, to the airline office, where we were told that we would not be able to fly home until Saturday at the earliest - four days hence. But at least they issued us tickets.

Many of our friends were starting to talk about making donations to both the Police and Fire departments, who had lost many of their brave men and women - the "first responders" who rushed to "Ground Zero" as the World Trade Center site had been designated. I enclosed a copy of Hal's lyrics to "What the World Needs Now" along with our donations, to both departments, and received lovely thank you notes from them, commenting on the relevance of Hal's lyrics.

We tried to buy some American flags to wave, or pins to put on our jackets, but those items had been grabbed up by like-minded patriots before we thought to look for them. I finally cut out some flags that had been printed in a newspaper and proudly pinned them on our jackets to wear as we walked around the city.

We were finally able to leave New York on September 15th, suddenly confronted with new rules at the airport. All sorts of items we were used to traveling with were confiscated by new, tight security, some understandably confiscated, some not. It was the beginning of a new era of airport travel, never again to be really "first class."

Nevertheless, we were just happy to get home safely, and to be able to reach out to family and friends. We had friends and family spread all over the U.S. and Europe, which prompted me to compose the following e-mail, which I sent to everyone on my contact list:

> *Dear friends: We feel the need to touch base with family and friends at this traumatic time, and are taking the opportunity to do so electronically. Our lives have changed dramatically since September 11th, and, although we by no means think "the end is near", we want to be sure to reach out to those we love and admire, and tell them how important they have been in our lives - whether it's been of short duration, or whether you've been with us through thick and thin. We wish we could gather you all together for a collective hug, but since that's not about to happen, we send you a "virtual hug", and hope that you and your families are well, and will be strong for each other and for our country.*

> *We're all going to be tested in ways we never expected and no doubt we'll face situations we never expected to have to deal with. But, dear friends and loving family members are the backbone of our society — and that's never going to change.*

We send our best wishes to all of you, and wish you well.

[EUNICE AND HAL DAVID]

I felt good about that, and the response was immediate and overwhelming. E-mail is such a great way to stay connected.

It was at about this time that Hal started to collaborate with John Cacavas, a wonderful composer, conductor and arranger, perhaps best known for his television scores. John was a close friend of Telly Savalas, and had been the main composer for the TV show Kojak, as well as many other shows. We'd spent numerous evenings at Bonnie and John's home, where they always had an interesting mix of people, and where we were treated to their gourmet cooking.

John had been asked to compose some songs for a CD which was going to be used for Library Music (music that production companies can use in their films which are not as expensive as purchasing the rights to use "standards"). He asked Hal if he would write the lyrics to his music. Hal wasn't sure if he wanted to do that because he wasn't too familiar with the genre of Library Music, but he just loves to write, and he had no other assignments at the time, so his answer was "sure." That led to a wonderful collaboration between the two men that resulted in five different, very successful CD's.

One album, entitled *In the Christmas Swing,* had all new Christmas songs on it that they wrote, including "Winter Warm," which had considerable success in a television ad for the Worldwide Jeep Cherokee. Other titles included "Blue Bird," from the CD *It's Showtime* (which was used in numerous commercials), "Moonlight Remembers," "Wishing Wells and Wedding Bells," "My Heart Remembers," and "86,400 Seconds." That last song referred to how many seconds there are in a day and how much a guy could love a gal in that period of time. A song I especially liked was "Slippin' and Slidin'," that was in an album titled *Singers and Swingers.* Jeff Hooper performed most of the vocals on the songs in a broad American accent, reverting to his very proper British speaking voice only when he wasn't singing.

I was the script girl on the five albums - all of which were recorded in London - even receiving my own "screen credit" in the liner notes of the

CDs. I'd sit in the booth and make sure that the singers sang each word correctly and that, with their British sensibilities, they totally understood the meaning of the words so they could interpret them properly.

Bonnie, John's wife, who has perfect pitch, was also there, making sure that each note played by the musicians was just right, in fact, she caught them out on numerous occasions.

All in all, the four of us had some grand times in London, going to the recording studio from morning to night, only taking time out for "tea breaks", and returning to our hotel in the evening, exhausted, but happily so, knowing that we'd done a good day's work.

Tena Clark invited Hal to come to her offices at DMI Music & Media Solutions in Pasadena, so that he could be recorded reminiscing about his career for a United Airlines in-flight program, which would be featured on all UAL flights. We subsequently heard from quite a few friends that they'd listened to the show, while flying all over the world, and that pleased us enormously.

Tena was a true phenomenon, as well as the extremely successful founder of DMI Music. Her involvement with Hal began when she was just 13 years-old, living in Mississippi. She told us that Hal was her idol. She saw his name on the back of a record label and decided to get in touch with him. He responded, and encouraged her to keep writing. Then, a few years later, she ran into him in Nashville, and he suggested that she come to Los Angeles, where he introduced her to people who could further her career. She soon became a very successful songwriter, but beyond that, she had a vision of music/marketing that involved selling music where it had not previously been sold. Her company, which she started in 1997, creates CD's and CD Rom's for a wide variety of companies and organizations.

In December, before we left New York, we made arrangements with L.A. friends of ours to go down to Ground Zero. At that time, a viewing platform had not yet been built, but we got as close as we could, and snapped a few pictures of the devastation.

We parked right next to St. Paul's chapel, which had a wall alongside the building, which had been turned into a shrine. People had put up teddy bears, flowers, T-shirts, caps, all things with an "I Love New York" theme, as a tribute to those who lost their lives. One large note we saw, which really spoke to me read: AMERICAN ends with I CAN. St. Paul's is Manhattan's oldest public building in continuous use, having opened in 1766. George Washington worshiped there. Although it is only a block away from the site of the World Trade Center bombing, it remained miraculously undamaged and 9/11 recovery workers received round-the-clock care there.

Photo by Eunice David.

Sad news came our way in December when we learned that Hal's sister, Barbara Bierer passed away. Curiously, both Hal's brother Mack and his sister Barbara passed away in the same month, albeit seven years apart.

With Barbara gone, Hal felt bereft: he himself never expected to live as long as he had, and he certainly never expected to be "the last one standing." Suddenly, he felt very much the orphan, and extremely vulnerable.

Hal told a story about his brother Barnett (who was called Bernie), who obviously never truly appreciated Hal's talent. Bernie's son was being Bar Mitzvah'd, and Hal was apparently the only David sibling who decided to attend the sacred event. So the D.J. made a big deal out of the Bar Mitzvah boy's "famous Uncle Hal," referring to Hal that way all through the evening. Finally, when it was time for the band to start playing, the D.J. announced that now they were going to play a medley of "famous Uncle Hal's music." With that, they proceeded to play only Mack David's songs! (Mack wrote such songs as "Bibbidi-Bobbidi-Boo," "I Don't Care If The Sun Don't Shine," and "Rain, Rain, Go Away"). Hal, understandably quite irked about that, asked Bernie why in the world they played Mack's songs when Mack hadn't even bothered to attend. Bernie replied that he didn't think his guests would know Hal's music! That says a lot about the dynamics of the David brothers. I never met Barnett, but since I was so fiercely supportive of Hal, I'm sure I would have disliked him on sight!

The Walt Disney Concert Hall, designed by the renowned architect Frank Gehry, was rapidly rising in downtown Los Angeles. I'd been a major supporter of the Music Center since its inception, and I sat on their main Board of Directors, as well as on the Center Theatre Group Board. When Hal and I got married, he caught my enthusiasm for the Center, and became a major donor in his own right. So we were invited to take a hard-hat tour of the new venue being built, during which we marveled at its unique shape, and enjoyed anticipating how the finished building was going to look.

Hal had given me elaborate and expensive gifts on Valentine's Day ever since we got married. But this year he started giving me something that was priceless, which he continued to give me every year until he passed. That something was a little note: here is the one he wrote in 2002.

I was so touched that it brought me to tears. I looked forward to those notes each year more than I would have looked forward to receiving diamonds or pearls (well, almost). They were real treasures.

We flew to D.C. in March, where Hal was performing in the annual ASCAP show before legislators, where Garth Brooks was going to receive the ASCAP Golden Note Award. Each of the ASCAP members who performed that evening sang one of their own songs, then added some complimentary comments about Garth.

At dinner that night, Hal and I were seated with Senator Orrin Hatch, Congressman Howard Berman, Congressman Xavier Becerra, and Senator Marie Cantwell from the State of Washington. Our friends from Los Angeles, Vicki and Murray Pepper, flew into D.C. to be with us for this special evening.

At one point, Senator Leahy, who was at the next table, came over to say hello to Hal. When he spotted Orrin Hatch at our table, he leaned down and said, "You're not going to beat up on me tonight, are you?" Apparently, they'd just had a very public donnybrook over the appointment of a judge that President Bush was trying to have confirmed, which the Democrats were trying to nix. The confirmation was blocked a few days later, but the two men were cordial to each other that night.

From early on, Hal included me in matters concerning his career because he said that he valued my judgment. He didn't always follow my suggestions, but I was pleased that he'd asked, and that it made him feel good to have me with him.

So in March, we went to the Chelsea Studios, a wonderful recording and rehearsal space on West Twenty-Sixth Street in New York. When we got off the elevator on the sixth floor of the huge, dark, sparse building, there were hundreds of hopefuls in every type of rehearsal/audition outfit imaginable: tight tights, short shorts, baggy pants, jeans, jeans, and more jeans, off-the-shoulder blouses, prim blouses buttoned high up on the neck, low blouses showing plenty of cleavage, tight T-shirts, etc. It was quite a scene. Hal and I were definitely the odd ones out, and were given a good once-over as we fought our way through the crowded hallways to rehearsal room three, where auditions for a possible show of Bacharach/David songs were being held.

We were at the studio to meet the people who were involved in producing a Broadway review of Bacharach/David music to be called *The Look of Love:* Todd Haimes, the artistic director of the Roundabout Theatre Company; David Loud, the musical director; former Broadway star Ann Reinking, the choreographer; Tom Thomson, who conceived the show; and Jim Carnahan, the casting director.

Auditions started at 11 am, and went on every ten or fifteen minutes until 4:30, with only a half-hour break for lunch (which we ate in the room,

To my love

Whether I call you Eunice
Or Jose or Little Girl

Whether your hair is long and straight
Or short and curled

Whether you're a few pounds more
Or a few pounds less

The one thing you always are
Is my happiness.

I love you very much
Happy Valentine's
Day
Your Maurvivbo

2002

with everyone comparing notes on the singers and dancers who had auditioned so far).

I found it fascinating to see how each performer presented themselves. Some came into the room with big smiles on their faces, and made some small chit-chat before performing their two numbers. Some came close to our table to sing, while others stayed as far back in the room as possible.

Hal had asked me not to make any verbal comments in front of the others, but he wanted me to take notes so we could discuss the possible cast members in private later on. I took copious notes, feeling very self-important in the process, and loving every minute of it.

The show was planned for the fall, so this was just the first step. But Hal was excited about having a show on Broadway again, after such a long hiatus.

While there, we went to see a revival of *Cabaret,* where I had my fifteen minutes of fame when Alan Cummings, who brilliantly played the emcee in the show invited me to dance with him on stage as he was returning from intermission. He asked me if it would be okay to "dip," and I told him to go for it. Cummings made a habit of inviting people to dance with him just before the beginning of the second act. I was in good company, since he'd invited Baryshnikov on stage with him one night, and Walter Cronkite another night.

I was not only involved in professional matters with Hal, but I was also asked to help with some aspects of the Songwriters Hall of Fame annual gala. Hal was the Chairman of the Hall of Fame, with Linda Moran as President. She always asked me to work with Buckley Hall Events, which coordinates large-scale events such as the SHOF Annual Gala. So each year, when we were in New York prior to the Gala, I met with them and the catering manager of the Marriott Marquis Hotel in Times Square, where we selected the meal and the wines that were going to be served at the gala. It took me a while to realize that I just needed to take a bite of each of the food selections, and a sip of each proposed wine, rather than gobbling up the entire portions that were presented to us. What fun that turned out to be, and I was happy to do it for as long as Hal was chairman of the organization.

At the first tasting I attended, I proposed a suggestion for saving time at the end of the meal, when everyone in the audience is anxious for the show to start: miniature cupcakes and various finger goodies, displayed on tiers in the center of the table, as a centerpiece, with small arrangements of flowers surrounding them.

That went over so well that the catering manager of the hotel later told me she'd suggested it to other organizations and it had suddenly become a very popular way to end a meal, eliminating time-consuming waiter service, and also eliminating the expense of an elaborate centerpiece. I brought my idea back to Los Angeles, and it became a popular way to end many a banquet in my hometown.

Larry King, the multi-talented, multi-awarded television host, asked a number of celebrities to contribute to a book he was writing, called Remember Me When I am Gone. The celebrities, including Hal, were asked to write about how they would like to be remembered. Hal came up with the following:

WHAT'S IT ALL ABOUT, HAL?

I'd like to be remembered for the lyrics that I wrote. They seemed to have lasted through the years, so I guess they touched people's hearts, and were meaningful enough for them not only to be remembered by those who heard them when they were new – but to have been rediscovered over the years by younger listeners and performers alike.

People often wrote to tell me that they remembered important milestones in their lives because of one of my songs. They proposed to their best girl to one of my lyrics, they celebrated anniversaries with one of my lyrics, they sang their babies to sleep by singing one of my lyrics.

That touched my heart, and meant a great deal to me.

We were in New York in May because Dionne Warwick was receiving an award given by the Jackie Robinson Foundation. This one was for her AIDS work, and August Busch III, the Chairman of the Board and President of Anheuser-Busch Companies, was also being honored for his leadership abilities. Dionne had asked the Foundation to have Hal present the award to her.

The entertainers that evening were Isaac Hayes, Cissy Houston, Chuck Jackson (Hal wrote his first hit song), Paul Shaffer, and Leslie Uggams; and, excitingly for us, Luther Vandross, whom Hal thought sang so well, also performed that evening. Naturally many Bacharach/David songs were on the program.

Hal wrote a three-minute tribute to Dionne, which he ended by saying: "In this fast-changing world, when songs come and go, and singers come and go, some things never change. As you can see before your eyes – Dionne is forever!"

I decided to have a bronze bust made of him as a birthday gift for Hal. I originally thought to surprise him, but my friend Nancy Mishkin, whom I commissioned to do the work, explained that she had to take numerous photos of Hal from every conceivable angle and measurements of his face and head had to be calculated. So the surprise was out, but Hal was delighted with the idea, and we were both totally bowled over by the finished product. It has been said that Nancy's work captures a moment in time, and that was certainly true in the work she did of Hal; she got his wonderful smile just right. I always loved the piece, and after Hal passed, it became even more meaningful to me as I looked at it every day, not having the real guy to gaze at.

I liked the bust so much that I commissioned Nancy to cast a duplicate of it, which I donated to the Songwriters Hall of Fame so that they could place it in their museum – whenever they got one.

Always hoping for another musical show to be produced, preferably on Broadway, Hal was eager to see what was happening with the new musical featuring Bacharach/David songs that producer Lawrence Stapleton had come up with, which he wanted to try out in Australia. So off we flew to Sydney to see what it was all about.

Stapleton met us outside of Customs in July, and settled us into the Park Hyatt Hotel overlooking Sydney Harbor and the Opera House, before starting a PR campaign the likes of which we'd never seen before. There were radio interviews, TV interviews, print interviews, pictures, pictures, and more pictures. We were even flown to Melbourne one day where Hal was interviewed by Bert Newton on their Channel-10 TV station. Burt was Australia's answer to Regis Philbin, so the show was seen by a large audience. (In fact, years later when we were on a cruise, a couple from Australia recognized us from that TV show.)

There were interviews and more interviews with Hal always managing to find something new and fresh to talk about. Then, after having been in Sydney for a couple of days, we watched our first rehearsal of *What the World Needs Now*, which, much to Hal's delight, seemed to be coming along very nicely - in its early stages.

During what little free time we had, Hal was able to confer with Steve Helper, the director of the show to make some suggestion, specifically about which songs Hal felt worked, and which did not. Steve seemed to value Hal's take on things, and to appreciate the input.

But by the time we were scheduled to leave Sydney, the show still needed extensive reworking. One of the leading men had to be replaced, the costumes were a disaster, the director was running scared because he was in over his head, and the actors were downcast. One of the producers asked if Hal would write a note to the cast to cheer them up. This is what he wrote:

TO THE WONDERFUL CAST OF "WHAT THE WORLD NEEDS NOW"

I'm leaving Sydney today with a smile on my face.

I've watched you at rehearsal and at the two previews I've been privileged to see, and I want you to know that I admire your talent, your energy, your dedication, and professionalism.

Winston Churchill spoke about "blood, sweat, and tears." Putting on a show demands all of the above and more. Fortunately for Burt Bacharach and me, our Australian producers and directors have given us a cast that's up to the task.

With all my best wishes for a great success: go for it!

Much love,
Hal David

Nonetheless, on the way to the airport, on July 31st, we received a call from the director telling us that he still had cold feet and was very concerned about the show. That was not a very positive bon voyage for us! The show never did have legs.

After we arrived in the South of France from Sydney, I spent a lot of time organizing another *The Writer, The Singer, The Song* show for the Blue Ribbon, with the invaluable help of the Internet and e-mail.

We got right down to business once we got back to L.A. Paul Williams again agreed to be the M.C. and Chris Caswell was again the Musical Director. This time the writers and singers were:

Hal David   Jackie DeShannon

Charlie Fox	Patti Austin
David Gates	Sally Kellerman
Albert Hammond	Leo Sayer
Barry Mann & Cynthia Weil	James Ingram
Paul Williams	Chuck Negron

Another great line-up, which again translated into a great show.

In September, for a big birthday party Hal threw for me at Hillcrest, he wrote some lyrics, again to the tune of *Love and Marriage,* which he often used for his special material.

> Eunice David, Eunice David
> You can write this down and then engrave it
> As I stand before you
> It's plain to see how I adore you
> Should the world start to unravel
> Everybody knows you will still travel
> More than just courageous
> Oh, you're a woman for the ages
>
> As you work at your computer
> You and your e-mail
> There is no one who is cuter
> You're my favorite female
>
> Eunice David, Eunice David
> When I get to love you how I crave it
> We belong together
> And that's the way we'll always stay
> Today, tomorrow, and forever.

It was a super evening, with Charlie Fox, Paul Williams, Corky Hale, Mike Stoller, and Nancy Kanter all performing, and friends and family getting up to make some very special heart-felt toasts to me. I couldn't decide what to do: cry or smile. So I did both.

For the most recent edition of The Writer, The Singer, The Song show, Ron Rosen had convinced Gibson Guitar/Baldwin Piano to contribute a piano to us, to help with our production. When the show was over, we donated it to the Los Angeles High School for the Arts. So in November, we drove to the school where three students performed some of Hal's songs for us, a plaque in Hal's honor was applied to the piano, and Hal was presented with a beautiful proclamation from the office of Los Angeles County Supervisor Zev Yaroslavsky. That was a lovely aftermath of the terrific show we'd produced at the Music Center for the Blue Ribbon.

To cap off the year 2002, Hal, Burt Bacharach, and Dionne Warwick were awarded the Heroes Award by the National Academy of Recording Arts and Sciences. Since Hal and Burt were working with Ann Reinking on *The Look of Love*, she was asked to present their awards to them. When she was called to the podium, she told a story about how, as a rebellious teenager, she was driving dangerously fast one day, with the car radio blaring. Suddenly she heard "What the World Needs Now" playing: the lyrics of which made her cry. She said that she had to pull over to the side of the road because she was crying so hard and she was convinced that Hal's lyrics had saved her life, because had she continued driving the way she was, she surely would have had a terrible accident. It was a touching story.

We ended the year sailing around the Cape of Good Hope with our friends the Hodeses and the Waises.

What a way to start the New Year! The space shuttle Columbia broke up on reentry into the atmosphere on February 1st, about forty miles above earth, killing all seven astronauts on board. There was another startling announcement on the heels of the news about the Columbia. Secretary of State Colin Powell, drawing on a high-tech collection of spy imagery and intercepted conversations, stated categorically that Saddam Hussein, the dictator/president of Iraq, had devised elaborate schemes to conceal weapons of mass destruction, which potentially could have devastating effects on other countries - but especially on the United States. Powell said, "Clearly, Saddam will stop at nothing until something stops him." Inspection teams had been in and out of Iraq for years, but had not found the weapons, because their searches had been so closely guarded, and they had limited access to the sites they were inspecting. Their inspections were a farce, with Hussein thumbing his nose at the USA. Our government put the country on "orange alert," with war looming once again.

When Hal and I had our home at The Lakes in Palm Desert, we commissioned many pieces of art from Indians who lived on the surrounding reservations and were renowned for their award-winning southwestern art. When we eventually sold the place, in the fall of 2000, we decided to donate our collection to the UCLA Medical Center, which at the time did not own any southwestern art. They'd been trying to do something to thank us for the donation, but it was hard to set a date because Hal and I had been doing so much traveling.

They finally pinned us down, and Dr. Michael Karpf, then Vice Provost of Hospital Systems and Director of the UCLA Medical Center hosted a lovely luncheon in our honor. We were taken on a hard hat tour of the Ronald Reagan Medical Center, which was then being constructed, and presented with a beautiful sculpture with the initials U C L A, in a very distinctive contemporary block form.

Rehearsals began in New York on *The Look of Love* in February, and Hal and I spent endless hours shuffling from one room to watch the dancers, to another room to watch the singers as they learned their parts.

One day after rehearsals we passed a touristy shop on Eighth Avenue, and I noticed some single-use cameras for sale. I couldn't resist buying one, and dashing back to the Brooks Atkinson Theater on Forty Seventh Street, to shoot this picture.

Things were heating up, and Hal was getting very excited about the show.

In the middle of rehearsals for *The Look of Love,* theater musicians went on strike, supported by all the other unions, forcing the closure of all Broadway musicals and disappointing thousands of ticket holders. Our producers were concerned that if the performers in our show could not rehearse, they would not be ready for opening night. But the stage manager of the show learned that the people constructing the set in the Brooks Atkinson Theatre were going to be able to continue working, since the union musicians had not yet started working on the show. That was a stroke of luck for us because while the performers might have been able to make up for lost time, the carpenters would never have been able to have the set ready if they were forced to quit work because of the strike.

So, the work continued, and we were able to breathe a sigh of relief on that score.

March 20, 2003: we woke to the news that the United States was at war again. We had attacked Iraq the night before, in an effort to oust Saddam Hussein.

Eunice

If there was one thing in the world
I would miss
If you went away
It would be you I ~~could~~ miss
walking hand in hand, I would miss (with you
Climbing in to ~~our~~ bed I would miss   with you
Going to a show I would miss   with you
Flying to N.Y. I would miss   with you
Flying every where I would miss   with you
Going on a cruise I would miss   with you
Going out to lunch with you I would miss
Going dinner parties with you I would miss
Making love to you I want miss

                 + so much more
           + so much more
              + so much more

I know the moment I met you
that you + I were meant to be
what I would give to ~~hold~~ hold you

Photo by Eunice David.

Baghdad was shelled repeatedly. We watched the night sky on TV as it was lit up by blast after blast from our bombs.

Because of that, the seventy-fifth Academy Awards were a muted affair under heavy security without, for the first time, the usual paparazzi/star-studded red carpet walk of walks.

The news from Iraq was anything but good. Our troops were outmaneuvered and outsmarted every-which-way by Saddam's Republican Guards, his fierce and loyal fighting forces. It was the beginning-of the end for Defense Secretary Donald Rumsfeld, who was accused by Army commanders of not sending as many troops to wage the war as they felt they needed in order to fight effectively and also to protect our troops who were already there.

In April, Saddam Hussein's statue in the center of Baghdad was toppled, signifying the end of his regime, but the war continued more fiercely than ever. And on top of everything else, no chemical weapons of mass destruction were ever found.

May 4th was opening night of *The Look of Love*'s limited run at the Brooks Atkinson Theater on West Forty Seventh Street in the heart of the Broadway theater district and the audience clearly loved it! But the next day brought a wide disparity of reviews. Howard Kissel of the *New York Daily News* found it a "marvelous trip back in time..." writing that he thought it was "beguiling and delightful," and that Ann Reinking's choreography gave the show theatrical power with its fiery dancing and blend of classic and contemporary steps." Bruce Weber's review in the *New York Times* was the opposite end of the spectrum: 'nuff said, other than I really wanted to march right over to his office and punch him out. Toni Winter, Hal's former assistant, from the days when he was President of ASCAP, called to remind Hal that even Irving Berlin got reviews like Weber's. I don't know if that helped Hal's terribly hurt feelings any, but it was nice of her to try.

I had made a luncheon date with a friend the day the review came out, but one look at Hal's face and I realized I needed to stay with him. The Hodes insisted that we join them for lunch at Fred's, located on the top floor of Barney's on Madison Avenue, a people-watching place if there ever was one. Hal didn't want to leave our apartment, but I prevailed on him to do so because I didn't want Weber to win. Once seated at Fred's, we greeted a lineup of friends and people who recognized us, all commiserating with Hal about the rotten review and assuring us that they were going to see the show anyway.

Many pointed out that since Weber clearly stated at the beginning of his review that he was not a fan of Bacharach/David music, he should not have been the one assigned to write the review!

Friends in and out of the business kept telling us that they were sure that Mr. Weber had some sort of personal agenda, although no one could figure out what it was; we'd never met him, so we knew it wasn't something we might have said to or about him. At JFK on our way back to Los Angeles, we ran into Carl Reiner and Mel Brooks, and their wives Estelle Reiner and Anne Bancroft. They had all seen the show and said they just loved it. That buoyed Hal's spirits up considerably.

Our friend Walter Goldstein finally took possession of his new yacht, which he christened Blue Belle even though all of his former yachts were called New York Lady. But because of the terrorist threats and the anti-American sentiment expressed by so many people in so many countries, he felt it would be safer to have a more generic name. Hal and I, along with four other couples, boarded Blue Belle on its maiden voyage from Venice to Croatia.

We learned in depth, from the people whom we met in Dubrovnik, about the breakup of Yugoslavia and the Bosnian War. There was still evidence on many of the scarred buildings of the fighting that had occurred, and resentment still simmered among the Serbs, Bosniaks, and Croats.

When our cruise on Blue Belle ended, the Hodeses, Hal and I left the group and spent three glorious days at Villa d'Este, exploring Lake Como, and trying to get a look at George Clooney's home through our binoculars.

We read a newspaper article before we left Villa d'Este that stated that Arnold Schwarzenegger, who announced that he would be running for Governor of California to replace a recalled Gray Davis, quipped: "Gray Davis. Hasta la vista, baby!" As a politically untested movie star, that was not an auspicious beginning - even if he did go on to win the election.

The Hodeses returned to New York, and we were driven to Forte Dei Marme to visit Bobbie and Bob Greenfield, who had spent the summer there for many years.

They introduced us to many friends they'd met there, many of them artists such as Janice and Ron Mehlman and Karen Difenbach (who was having a show in Bobbie's Bergamot gallery in Santa Monica) and her husband John, from San Francisco. Their houseguests happened to be Gina and Mike

Cerre. Mike had been one of the journalists imbedded with ABC during the Iraq war, and he had some hair-raising stories to tell. That meeting resulted in Mike eventually filming Hal for a "Person of the Week" segment on a Friday night ABC news broadcast.

We flew to San Francisco for a few days in September to visit with friends, prior to heading to Portland, Oregon, for my granddaughter Kira's wedding. We happened to be picked up at the airport by a very enterprising cabbie: he made it a point to ask his passengers what they did, and then if he thought they were interesting enough, he passed that information on to a friend of his at the Portland Tribune, a paper known for its comprehensive coverage of local news for Portland and the surrounding areas. The next thing we knew, we received a call at our hotel asking for an interview from Phil Stanford, a reporter on the paper, who had heard of our visit from the cabbie. When the article appeared in the Tribune a couple of days later, the reporter wrote that Hal was there for Kira Forester's wedding to Nick Potter, and suggested that they should play "What the World Needs Now is Love" at their wedding! And he sent best wishes to the happy couple. How nice was that?

The Walt Disney Concert Hall finally opened in October. Hal and I teamed up with some other major contributors to the Music Center for the first (of three) opening night parties. We had all been heavy-hitters at the Music Center, sitting on numerous boards throughout the years and contributing large sums to the Center. So we could hardly believe our eyes, when we saw our tickets: we were seated four rows from the ceiling in the uppermost balcony (nose-bleed time) of the theater. And our seats at the after-show dinner in the tent were at a table as far from the stage as it could possibly be. Needless to say, none of us were very happy campers, and are no longer contributors.
Burt Bacharach produced a new CD featuring Ronald Isley, the lead singer and founding member of the family music group, the Isley Brothers. It was called "Isley meets Bacharach." The album delivered striking new takes on many Bacharach/David songs, specifically designed to appeal to a young audience.

A December review on the Internet said, "For his part, Isley brings a soulful subtlety to readings of tunes like "Raindrops Keep Fallin' on My Head" and "Count on Me" (the better of two new Bacharach-Tonio K. numbers), with a cadence that glides effortlessly over these memorable melodies. He even dares to cover "A House Is Not a Home," which has become a signature slow jam for Luther Vandross, and comes away with his own stirring version," which we could listen to over and over again."

By this time, Hal and I had amassed a rather impressive collection of nine-teenth and twentieth century artists, original works on paper. The collection was hung in our apartment on the Wilshire Corridor in Los Angeles, but we decided that we wanted to donate the entire collection to the Hammer Museum. While it was still a "promised gift," the Hammer put on a show of the pieces, and in November we went to the museum to watch as Cindy Burlingham, the curator of the show and Director of the Grunwald Center for the Graphic Arts, and Annie Philbin, the Director of the Hammer Museum, supervised the installation. It is hard to describe the thrill of seeing our art going up on the walls of a museum. It validated our choices, and made us realize just how much we had accomplished in the relatively short period of time we'd been collecting (only about twelve years). The people at the Hammer did everything in their power to make the event very special, including producing a brilliant catalog of our collection.

I had been invited to join a wonderful organization called The Diadames of the Child Care League. It was composed of bright, dedicated women in support of the Mirman School, an independent, co-education school designed to meet the needs of academically gifted children. My friend Peggy Grauman was a member, and her husband Walter was producing a show for the first meeting that Hal and I were going to attend. The dinner happened to be on Veteran's Day, which prompted the theme "Uncle Sam Wants You." Hal was asked to be the featured performer that night. Among other songs that he sang that evening, Hal performed "Bell Bottom Blues," (which had been recorded by Theresa Brewer), the one about a girl who has the bell bottom blues because her sailor boyfriend is away at war, which seemed appropriate for the evening. And it wouldn't have been a show about veterans if Hal had not sung "Send a Salami to Your Boy in the Army," which many of our friends in the audience remembered from their days in the service.

On December 15th, we woke to headlines saying that Saddam Hussein had been captured after American troops found him hiding in a pit in Tikrit, Iraq. President Bush hailed the end of what he called "a dark and painful era" in Iraq. Even though, when captured, Hussein had a pistol with him, he did not put up any resistance and was described as a tired man - a man resigned to his fate.

One day our friend from Portland, Oregon, Gordon Sondland called to say that, as President of the Oregon film society, he and Oregon Governor Ted Kulongoski were going to be in Los Angeles to meet some people to talk about the idea of promoting more films made in the United States, as opposed to having them made in Canada, and even Australia. Gordon asked if Hal and I would like to meet him and the Governor for a quick drink at the Century Plaza Hotel in Century City. Naturally we were delighted to see Gordon again, and were looking forward to meeting Governor Kulongoski.

We were seated in the bar when Gordon arrived with a young man in tow. I didn't catch his name but sat talking to him for quite a while, while Hal and Gordon chatted up a storm. Eventually an aide came over and said that it was time for them to leave. I whispered to Gordon that I was sorry we had not been able to meet the Governor. Gordon looked at me as though I had lost my mind and said, "You've been talking to him for the past half hour!" I hadn't caught his name when Gordon first introduced us. Was my face red!

About this time, I was approached by three powerhouse Blue Ribbon women to talk Hal into doing another *The Writer, The Singer, The Song* show. Not only did I not have a chance of saying no, I really didn't want to. So my old gang got busy on another version of the show.

This time our line-up was:

Hal David	Herb Alpert
Carol Bayer Sager	Christopher Cross
Charles Strouse	John C. Reilly
Jimmy Webb	Marilyn McCoo and Billy Davis, Jr.
Paul Williams	Bill Medley
Bill Withers	Peabo Bryson

That was another great group of performers who turned *The W,S, S* into another great show, still a favorite of the Blue Ribbon members.

After the Hammer Museum's wonderful exhibition of our collection of drawings, the Portland Art Museum (considered one of the top 10 museums in the country) wanted to borrow our collection for their own exhibit, which was to last for four months. Their elaborate opening included a cabaret show with Hal and Freda Payne performing and Corky Hale accompanying them, a sit-down dinner, the exhibit itself, and a Q&A the next day.

We went directly from Oregon, after the opening of the art exhibit, to Washington, D.C., where Hal was video-taped for the archives of the Smithsonian Institution. Dwight Bowers, the Smithsonian Historian, had done his homework, and had such penetrating questions for Hal, and such a gracious way about him as an interviewer, that he was able to draw Hal out about every aspect of his life. I was pleased that not only was Hal's oral history going to be preserved, but that Hal's grandchildren and future generations of Davids would be able to avail themselves of it.

While we were in D.C., ASCAP arranged for Hal and me to meet Congressman Ron Lewis from Kentucky because he sat on the House Ways and Means Committee and was co-chair, along with Congresswoman Marcia Blackburn from Tennessee, of "the Capital Gains Bill," which, if passed, would benefit songwriters. Passing the bill would correct an old tax law that was unfair to people who needed or wanted to sell their own creations: music, art, books, etc. So Hal was sent in to lobby the Congressman, something he was very good at doing, and I'm happy to say that the bill eventually was passed in favor of copyright holders.

The World War II memorial had just opened in Washington, so we made time to tour the impressive site, as well as to see as many of the other Washington monuments as we could, spending as much time as possible at the Lincoln Memorial, one of Hal's favorites.

In keeping with Hal's interest in the Civil War, we then joined a UCLA Alumni group (my alma-mater) on the American Orient Express train for a week-long ride through the south, stopping in Richmond, Charleston, Savannah, and Jackson, and ending in New Orleans. One of the highlights of the trip, other than visiting the historical sites, was a stop at the Michie Tavern in Monticello, which was established in 1784. At that time it was the social center of the community. Nowadays it is the ultimate place to stop for lunch - the only meal they serve - sometimes accommodating up to sixteen hundred people a day.

There we ate a traditional Southern meal of fried chicken, black-eye peas, stewed tomatoes, muffins, cornbread, string beans, coleslaw, and peach cobbler, but we had the penultimate lunch in New Orleans at the not-to-be missed Commander's Palace, topped off by the Bread Pudding Soufflé with Whiskey Sauce that they are so renowned for.

President Ronald Reagan passed away at 4 P.M. on Saturday, June 5th, at his home in Bel Air, California. Hal and I had both met him several times over the years, and greatly admired him. And Hal had such a wonderful relationship with Nancy Reagan when he wrote the song that went with her book, that our hearts went out to her and her family at that devastating time.

Bernie Hodes, a gourmand if there ever was one, heard about a restaurant called El Bulli, located near the town of Roses, in Catalonia, Spain. Run by Chef Ferran Adria, the small restaurant overlooked Cala Montjoi, a beautiful, picturesque bay on the Costa Brava. It was described as the most imaginative generator of haute cuisine on the planet.

The restaurant was so popular during their limited season from mid-June to mid-December that it got more than two million requests for reservations, but could only accommodate eight thousand diners. That summer a group of nine of us wanted a reservation on a specific Sunday in June, the only day we could all arrange to be in the area. Not surprisingly, a reservation was impossible to obtain, regardless of whatever influence we tried to use.

When we happened to mention our predicament to our friend Bob Holder, who had been the head of the Olympics Committee when it was held in Atlanta, Georgia. Bob said that he knew a man in Spain who could arrange anything. We were dubious, but when the task was put to Leopoldo Rodes, a man supremely well-connected in many fields, whom Bob had met when the Olympics had been held in Spain, Leopoldo came through with flying colors, and our reservation was miraculously set, on the exact date that we requested.

Twenty-nine courses, and four and a half hours later, we finished one of the most adventuresome eating experiences any of us had ever had. Almost nothing we ate was what we would have expected it to be, or to taste like. The meal for the nine of us came to about thirty-six hundred dollars, and we all agreed that it was worth every penny.

While in the area, we and our traveling companions visited Forca Vella, the district known in Catalan-speaking areas as the "Call" (Jewish Quarter) in Girona, one of the most notable Jewish districts in all of Europe because it was one of the few places which allowed its Jewish community to dwell within the city walls. From there we headed to the town of Figueres, to see the Teatre-Museu Dali, a major wonder of surrealism and fantasy. Salvador Dali had been born in Figueres, but lived nearby in a beautiful village called Port Lligat.

We couldn't resist indulging in another great meal: this one at the Hotel Emporda, where Chef Josep Mercader was said to have created the current Catalan cuisine, based on a mixture of the land and the sea, of the sweet and the salty and including the staple of every Mediterranean chef, the finest olive oil available.

For the second time, we boarded the Goldstein's beautiful yacht Blue Belle, for a cruise to Barcelona where we quickly disembarked and headed right to the Joan Miro Foundation Building, stunningly designed by Josep Lluis Sert, the architect who also designed the Gallery Maeght in St. Paul de Vence, which we visited every year while in the south of France.

In Barcelona, we enjoyed the city and the tapas in equal portions, and wandered on the Ramblas along with all the other tourists, stopping at the nineteenth century Canaletes Fountain, where legend has it that all who drink of its waters are certain to return to Barcelona. It had taken me over thirty years from my first sip, but I did return!

We went on to Ibiza, Majorca, and toured the Balearic Islands, each one different and more interesting than the others, finally disembarking and flying to Madrid, where we took in a bullfight. Thanks again to Leopoldo's amazing contacts, we enjoyed more memorable meals, as well as the local sights.

Louise Taper, Hal, and I decided we wanted to see more of the United States. We'd all travelled extensively in Europe, the Middle, and Far East, but had never seen our own country in depth. What better place to start than a trip to Mt. Rushmore? Ambassador Lester and Carolbeth Korn were soon included in our plans, as was Doug Walker (later to become Louise's husband), and off we went to Rapid City, South Dakota, on the first leg of our journey, which had been crafted for us by Anne Kent Taylor (who had planned an African safari for Hal and me so many years ago), in conjunction with an organization called "Off the Beaten Path." Between them they designed a dream vacation for us.

Mike Link, our guide during our adventure, was a teacher of natural history in the graduate program of the Audubon Center of the North Woods. When he met us at the airport in Rapid City, a bond was immediately formed and we hung on his every word for the next couple of weeks.

The Hotel Alex Johnson in Rapid City, where we stayed when we first arrived, was originally built in 1928, with a Sioux Indian motif. When it was renovated in 1991, the manager of the hotel met with Lakota Medicine man Norbert Running to request a Lowanpi Ceremony, to obtain advice on how to renovate each of the seven floors of the hotel so that it would have the right feel. I was very touched by a line in their brochure which read: "Like the Sioux, the birds are believed to build round houses to teach us that we are all brothers to all living things, and because of this we should respond to our brother's visions." That set the tone for our adventure into the heartland of America.

We approached Mt. Rushmore through the town of Hermosa, over the Iron Mountain - the most scenic route. Some of our group, including me, had been to Mt. Rushmore in the past, but nevertheless, our first glimpse of it from far away was breathtaking.

Mr. Rushmore is a memorial to the birth, growth, preservation, and development of the United States. Gutzon Borglum sculpted busts of Presidents George Washington, Thomas Jefferson, Theodore Roosevelt, and Abraham Lincoln high in the Black Hills to represent the first hundred fifty years of American History.

When we eventually arrived at the actual site of the mountain, the very cores of our beings were touched. Returning in the evening to see those faces brilliantly lit up in the night, we were treated to stirring patriotic music from all eras, and all wars, with servicemen who were in the audience, both young and old, being asked to stand up and be recognized. We, right along with everyone else, were stamping our feet in time to the music, humming along, and even singing out loud when we knew the words. We heard Sousa's marches, George M. Cohan's stirring songs, Civil War songs, and other recognizable melodies. It was thrilling not only to be there, but to see all those people demonstrating their love of country.

A ranger announced that a storm was heading our way, but not one of the three thousand people in attendance that night left before the program was over, despite the downpour.

Before we left the Rushmore area, we'd seen the mountain from every angle, every turn in the road, and through every element. It was just spectacular: a dream fulfilled.

Next, we flew to Billings, Montana, and then on to the Custer Battlefield Museum and the Custer battleground, which we toured with Bill Yellowtail, who had grown up on the Crow Indian Reservation. Bill held a degree in geography from Dartmouth, and had been a rancher, educator, fishing guide, a Montana State Senator, and a Congressional candidate. It was interesting to hear about Custer's Last Stand from a Native American's perspective.

Dr. Joseph Medicine Crow was next on our agenda. He was the ninety-one-year-old grandson of Chief Medicine Crow, one of Custer's scouts. Joe held a master's degree in Anthropology and an honorary doctorate from USC. He was a storyteller par excellence, and because of his lineage, had his own unique perspective on the battle of Little Bighorn.

Our history lesson from Joe Medicine Crow took place on a modest ranch owned by Gail and Vernon Whiteman, on the bank of the Little Bighorn River, located between the Wolf Tooth Mountains and the Big Horn Mountains, the age-old heartland of the Crow tribe of Indians. Vernon was the great-grandson of Whiteman Runs Him, who as scout for the 7th U.S. Cavalry, guided Custer to his fateful encounter with Sitting Bull's Sioux at the Battle of the Little Bighorn.

We had planned to drive across the reservation when we left Garry Owen on our way to Cody, Wyoming, but our guide learned that a large group of militant Indians had blocked the way, prohibiting any white man from going across. Yes, that was still happening. We decided we didn't want to risk Custer's fate, so we prudently headed to the freeway for the long way around, rather than taking the scenic way around.

Bill Self, a prolific film and television producer, and a friend, had made arrangements for us to have a VIP tour of the Buffalo Bill Museum in Cody. The author James Michener dubbed the Buffalo Bill Historical Center "The Smithsonian of the West," with good reason. The Center is the largest history and art museum between Minneapolis and the West Coast, encompassing more than three hundred thousand square feet on three levels. Because it is located in a town with a population of only ten thousand people, many visitors (us included) are stunned when they venture inside. Nowhere else in the country is such an important museum located in such a remote location!

Naturally, since we were there, we had to attend the Cody Nite Rodeo, a part of Wyoming history. The Rodeo had been running for sixty-six years and had earned Cody the title of Rodeo Capital of the World. We were seated in the Buzzard's Roost seats, which were right above where the competitors came to stretch and finish dressing before getting into the rodeo ring. We were also right above the bucking chutes, which allowed us to see the riders positioning themselves on the animals before the gates were opened. We watched in fascination as the riders entered the different events, marveling at their skills. During the show, we thought we heard Hal's name being mentioned over the loudspeaker, but didn't pay too much attention to it. The next thing we knew, our guide Mike led a whole group of the riders up to the stands to say hello to us, and to present Hal with a funny green cowboy hat which they had all autographed for him. Many of the fellows had huge belt buckles depicting various rodeos where they'd been winners. Carolbeth asked one young man where his buckle was, and he sadly replied, "I ain't agotten one yit."

On our way from Cody to Yellowstone, we drove between the Absoroka and Bear Tooth Mountains, on the Chief Joseph Scenic Highway, through the Shoshone National Park. We stopped at Niz Perce lookout point, overlooking the scenic valley, where Chief Joseph, the Nez Perce Chief said "I am tired of fighting ... from where the sun now stands, I will fight no more - forever."

As we headed to Cooke City, Montana, population one hundred forty - we looked for a place to stop to eat, and could hardly believe our eyes when we started to drive through the couple of blocks that made up the town. There were about five thousand bikers on a "poker" run. The riders had five stops on their run, and would get a "card" at each stop. The biker with the winning poker hand at the end of the run would win a prize. All we could think of was Marlon Brando in The Wild Ones, and our first thought was to drive through town as fast as possible. But Mike thought it would be okay to stop at the Bistro Café, and we soon realized what an opportunity we would have missed had we passed up this stop. We spoke to a mix of bankers, farmers, accountants, teachers and, yes, rough-looking bikers, all of them friendly and talkative, and anxious to tell us about their annual ride.

We entered Yellowstone Park at the northeast entrance, and the first thing we saw was a huge herd of buffalo; the talisman that had been assigned to me by our guide, Mike. We stayed at The Lake Hotel, run by the Park Service in Yellowstone. It had been built in 1889, was very crowded, unattractive, box-like, and had no air conditioning in the rooms. In fact, there weren't even any TV's or radios available. We felt it was just as it should have been. One of the most touching experiences we had there was when a group of about forty men from the True Oil Company from Texas suddenly stood up at their dining room table, and with deep basso voices, sang "God Bless America." Hearing them, everyone in the dining room rose in unison and started singing along with them.

Of course, we toured Yellowstone from top to bottom, then ended this exceptional trip in the Grand Teton National Park, in total awe at the majesty of the peaks. We took a rafting trip on the Snake River, listening to the absolute quiet of our surroundings except for the melodic, gurgling sound of the river. For those couple of hours, everything but the river was completely insignificant.

Back in L.A. we were brought down to earth when we read a review of a Henry Mancini Institute musicale where they had honored Burt Bacharach. The author of the review, Richard Ginell, listed a number of songs which Burt had performed, and then said that they "all sprang from one mind in just a few years' time." Our friend Walter Grauman went beyond being annoyed and he did something about it. Here are two letters he wrote about the matter.

Mr. Richard Ginell:

Your musical review of the Mancini Institute musical honoring Burt Bacharach betrays not only your careless reviewing style but your ignorance of music as well. The review read "material ranging from "The Look of Love, "Alfie," and "Wives and Lovers" to "What's New Pussycat?", and "The Man Who Shot Liberty Valance" all sprang from one mind in just a few years of time." The above quote must have "sprung" from your lack of musical knowledge, an uncaring review, or cruelty, because far from "springing from one mind", everyone knows that the genius behind all of those songs (and many more) sprang from two minds, the other being lyricist Hal David, who together with Bacharach, wrote innumerable hit songs, most of which, over the years have become classics.

Sincerely,
Walter Grauman

Mr. Peter Bart
Vice President
Editor-in-Chief
Daily Variety

Dear Mr. Bart:

Enclosed please find a letter that I have written to Richard S. Ginell regarding his review of the "Mancini Musicale honoring Burt Bacharach" in the Daily Variety of August 17, 2004.

As a subscriber and faithful reader for the past 50 years and the subject of many reviews (some of which were not as favorable as I might have wished), I have never complained about the content. However, in light of the aforementioned review, I feel compelled to complain in writing to both you and Mr. Ginell, in the sincere hope that some kind of addition and/or correction be made and that the lyricist and co-creator, Hal David (winner of the Oscar for "Raindrops Keep Falling on my Head" and the Towering Achievement Award from the Songwriters Hall of Fame for "What the World Needs Now is Love", among many more prestigious awards), certainly deserves equal recognition by your reviewer, as well on page 20's text with pictures "Amour imbues Musicale".

Thank you in advance for your attention to the above.

Most sincerely,
Walter Grauman

There was never an acknowledgement of Walter's letters, or a correction of the writer's misconception.

In October, Governor Arnold Schwarzenegger appointed me to serve on the California Arts Council. I'd served on the Los Angeles County Music and Performing Arts Council for sixteen years, so this was a natural extension of that, and I felt very confident that I was capable of handling the job. Barbara George, the wife of Ronald George, the Chief Justice of California, who was the President of the Council, inducted me into the organization, and at the same time, she was inducted into my heart. I fell in love with Barbara five minutes after meeting her, as did anyone who ever met her. She and her husband became great pals of Hal's and mine, and we treasured that friendship.

Hal was invited to perform at a PRS (Performing Rights Society) gala in London. He was going to sing a duet with Petula Clark, and was really looking forward to it. But I'd fallen (again) and was in a hugely uncomfortable cast from my foot to my knee. I knew that if I told Hal I could not make the trip, he would cancel going - and I didn't want him to do that.

So, with a lot of help from Hal and Air New Zealand personnel, I was able to manage the flight.

The night of the show, Hal spoke about how much he'd loved working in London in the early years of his career, and how many hits he'd written there. He sang "Close to You" and "I'll Never Fall in Love Again." Petula Clark dedicated "Raindrops" to the wonderful French singer Sasha Distel, who had recently passed away, and then she sang, "Don't Make me Over" and "A House is Not a Home." The audience, most of them British songwriters, were yelling and screaming as though they were at a rock concert.

Then Hal and Freda Payne performed "One Less Bell to Answer," and Petula joined forces with them to sing "What the World Needs Now" - with the audience singing along with them.

ASCAP executives John Lo Frumento, Karen Sherry, and Roger Greenaway all called the next morning to tell us that they'd been coming to these events for years, and there had been some fabulous entertainers who performed at them, but they'd never seen any of them get a standing ovation from the staid Brits - as Hal had received last night. We were delighted with that high praise.

A review in Dooley's Diary in London said of the evening, "A top-notch line- up brought some sparkle to the stage for a set of Bacharach and David classics. It was a pretty remarkable performance given their combined ages of two hundred fourteen years...."

Before the year was out, Hal had another "gig" - another pro bono! He'd been asked to appear in the Los Angeles High School for the Arts student production of Die Fledermaus, an operetta by Johann Strauss II. The opera has a show within the show, and Hal was asked to be the performer for "the show within." That was certainly a first for Hal, and he said he'd had great fun experiencing something new.

Later in the year, Walter Mirisch was asked to produce a show in honor of Gordon Davidson, the founding artistic director of the Center Theatre

To My Love

This Valentine is one day late
But one day more in loving you
And one day more in losing you
Is something nothing can undo
And there is one more holiday
More wonderful than Valentine
That very very special day
You promised me that you be mine

Happy Valentine Day
I'll love you always
H. D. That is me
2/15/05

Group. Walter was not only a major player in the movie world, he was also interested in theater, and had sat on the board of the Center Theatre Group at the Music Center for many years. He asked Hal to write some special material about Gordon, to be sung at the opening of the show. Here are some snippets of what Hal wrote, to the tune of "Close to You."

> On the day that he was born
> The angels all decided someday there would be
> A Music Center stage
> And they waited to deliver it to Gordon
> Until Gordon came of age.

> In the hands of Davidson
> The Taper and the Ahmanson
> Are magical for everyone to share
> There are comedies and musicals and dramas
> Always staged with loving care.

We ended the year with our usual Christmas/New Year's cruise, this time to Mexico, but, found the area not as exciting as it had been in years past, and we decided it would probably be our last visit to that country.

In 2005 we teamed up with the friends for an odyssey through Turkey on the Goldstein's Blue Belle, with the land portion planned for us by our close friend and famed hotelier Ali Kasikci. That became another thrilling trip which we were able to cross off our bucket list. It started with a dinner hosted by the warm and lively Leyla Umar, who is known as the "Barbara Walters of Turkey." She gathered a group from all walks of life, to match the interests of the friends we were traveling with. As we ate dinner on the roof-top of Leyla's art-filled home, lined with pictures of many of the famous people she'd interviewed - including Fidel Castro - we periodically heard the call to prayer from the electronically-wired minarets surrounding the building. However, the group we were with just continued what they were doing and saying, paying little heed to the call.

Just a few days after we returned home, we learned that a minibus had been blown up in Kusadasi (which had been one of the stops on our trip) and had killed three foreign tourists. Kurdish rebels bragged that it was their doing. We were lucky with the timing of our visit.

I had my right hip replaced in July. My doctor, Brad Penenberg, the Co-Director of the Cedars-Sinai Institute for Joint Replacement, had devised a new, minimally invasive procedure called the MIS-2 Incision Hip Replacement, allowing an incision of only two and a half to three inches long, which helps a patient to recover quickly. It certainly worked for me, because I was walking without a cane and without a limp in just a couple of weeks, and the excruciating pain I had leading up to the surgery was completely gone.

I had recently joined a group called Women of Los Angeles, and in September, when they held their 2005 Highlight Awards: "Recognizing Men Who Make a Difference," they honored Hal, along with The Honorable Armand Arabian, an Associate Justice of the California Supreme Court and Steven Lavine, President of the California Institute of the Arts. I was asked to introduce Hal.

Naturally I told about how we met, and how I'd known he was for me when he said he was used to living in hotels and eating in restaurants. That story always resonated with women. Then I took a page out of Dorothy Hammerstein's book when she said that her husband wrote "Old Man River" while Jerome Kern only wrote "dum, dum, dum, dum," by saying "While Burt Bacharach wrote dum, dum, dum, dum, de dum dum, dum, here is the man who wrote "Raindrops Keep Fallin' on My Head," my husband, Hal David." That was a crowd pleaser.

For the past eight years or so, Hal had been having an MRI every six months so that his cardiologist, Dr. P.K. Shah, could monitor his aorta, which was gradually expanding. Finally, in December, after an MRI had been taken, P.K. decided it was time to take action. The surgery that Hal needed was called a Bentall procedure: Hal's Mitral valve had to be replaced, and he was going to have several bypasses.

Hal took the news very calmly, but not me: I was a total wreck, with Hal trying to console me, rather than the other way around.

We had planned a much-looked-forward to Christmas cruise to New Zealand and Australia with Bonnie and Bernie Hodes, but naturally that had to be cancelled. We were staying close to home prior to the surgery. Hal even stopped playing tennis, for fear of falling. Dr. Alfredo Trento, the Director of the Division of Cardiothoracic Surgery at Cedars scheduled the procedure for January 4th, and it was a total success.

Before the year was out, Hal, thanks to our great friend Ali Kasikci who was the general manager of the Peninsula Hotel in Beverly Hills, was interviewed for the Peninsula Magazine which was distributed to Peninsula Hotels world-wide, as well as to about fifty thousand patrons who had formerly stayed at the hotels. Michelle Hodan, the Director of Public Relations for the hotel came over with a young woman from Hong Kong, who was the editor of the magazine, and a photographer. The interview went beautifully, and the resulting article was terrific. We were amazed at how many people told us they had read and enjoyed the article.

That year we spent a very quiet Christmas and New Year's Eve, in anticipation of Hal's surgery.

Hal had been writing wonderful Valentine's Day love letters to me. Now it was my turn to write a love letter to him, and I wrote him the following letter on the eve of his surgery.

January 3, 2006

My Darling:
I don't think I have ever written you a letter before, but I can't think of a more appropriate time to do so. With our hectic schedules and busy lives, we seem to use "sound bites" when we want to express our feelings toward each other. But at this important junction in our lives, I want you to know just how deeply in love with you I am.

You are my life, and have been from the moment I first met you- some 18 years ago.

I just know in my heart of hearts that all will go well with your surgery, and that you will recover in your usual brave and heroic way. I'm looking forward to at least another 18 years - or even more - wonderful, exciting, stimulating years by your side.

You have all of my love.

I signed the letter "Jose," which was one of the terms of endearment Hal used for me, in reference to his song "Do You Know the way to San Jose."

On the morning that the surgery was scheduled, some of Hal's family members gathered around, and many friends came to keep me company and to hold my hand while Hal was in surgery. The regular waiting room at Cedars became so crowded that the volunteer on duty that morning came over to tell me that she had received permission for us to gather in the private Founder's Room of the hospital, so that we could be by ourselves (what she really meant was so that we would not disturb the others waiting to hear about their loved ones). I was very grateful for the privacy, and the twenty-five or so friends who were gathered there with me were much more comfortable in the lovely Founder's Room.

Every hour or so a young man who had been stationed inside the operating room came into the Founders Room to give me a report on how Hal was doing. It was a very long day, but eventually, I was informed that Hal was in recovery. After visiting him there periodically, I went up one last time to say goodnight before heading home. When I peeked into Hal's room, I counted at least six people gathered around Hal's bed, so naturally my reaction was to panic!

It turned out that Hal had been cooled down to such a degree for surgery that his blood was not coagulating, so they had to put him under again, and open up his chest a second time to find out where the excess bleeding was coming from, even after he'd received seven transfusions. So he had to undergo two major surgeries in the one day!

Eventually, I was "ordered" to go home. Around 2:30 in the morning I called ICU to see how Hal was and the charge nurse told me he was doing well. She said that she would promise to tell him I'd called if I would promise her that I'd go back to sleep. That seemed like a good deal to me.

After a week in the hospital, Hal was sent home, and aside from a few bouts with atrial fibrillation, after a period of rest, he was good to go. He had a very positive attitude and I believe that was one of the reasons he healed so well.

Paul Williams, a wonderful actor, comedian and great songwriter, whom Hal had mentored over the years, sent this message to Hal. It not only showed what a good writer he was, but what a good friend he was, and continues to be.

Welcome home, Hal
Your pump has been mended

A sweet new beginning
With spanking new parts

It's the least God could do
He owes that much to you
For the years of sweet tears
Born of joy in our hearts

Yes, joy that you put there, my Mentor and friend
With passion and purpose and without end

It's what you deserve Hal
What courage you've shown
How we line up to love you
Perhaps more than you've known

Heal quickly
Love life
And LISTEN TO EUNICE!
When you're feeling real feisty
You can show us your scar
We ask only one thing
For God's sake don't Moon us!

Mariana and I send our love and Thank God for answering
our prayers. You're two tree top angels and we're blessed to
know you.

Love for sure,
Paul

Long before Hal's open heart surgery, we had planned a trip to South Africa for mid-April, just four short months after the surgery, so we didn't know if the doctor would release Hal to travel.

The day before we were supposed to leave, with our friends already in Cape Town awaiting our arrival, Hal received the go-ahead from Dr. P.K. Shah, who asked him "Do you really want to go on this trip?" When Hal eagerly

On a scale of 1 to 10
10 the most + 1 the least
I'd have to say I love you twenty
In case you think that isn't plenty
I'd have to say I love you thirty
In case you think that's down + dirty
I'd have to say I love you forty
In case you think that's kind of shorty
I'd have to say I love you fifty
In case you think that isn't nifty
I'd have to jump up to a million
On second thought I'd say a billion
Just to be safe I'll say a trillion
And that's as high as I can count
So put this in your love account
Where it will keep accumulating
As long as we keep demonstrating
            L O V E

            Happy Valentines Day
                    2/15/06

shook his head in the affirmative, Shah laughed, and said, "Well, I'm not going to be a party pooper. You can go." With that, we were on our way.

We toured Cape Town and drove to the Cape of Good Hope, the most southwestern point of the African continent, stopping in Stellenbosch to taste some of the excellent wine produced in the area.

One of our traveling companions was Fred Hayman, who was known as "Mr. Beverly Hills" and was credited with almost singlehandedly creating the mystique about Rodeo Drive, with his Giorgio Boutique anchoring the street at the corner of Rodeo Drive and Dayton Way. He traded stories with Hal throughout the trip, since they knew many people in common and every time someone's name was mentioned, Fred's pen and paper would come out, and he would make a note to be used in his upcoming autobiography.

We learned a great deal about pre and post-apartheid life in South Africa, especially when we drove through the township of Khayelitsha and saw life in the raw there, and when we took the ferry to Robben Island, where Nelson Mandela was imprisoned for almost twenty-seven years of his life.

We ended our trip with several remarkable game-viewing stays at private nature reserves. The first reserve was at Singita Ebony. It was built in the shade of large Jackleberry trees, and each of the nine luxurious double suites was completely private, cool, and spacious with their own plunge pools and outdoor decking for game viewing.

By the time we settled in, it was time for our game run. With our great white hunter and our eagle-eyed spotter, off we went in a Range Rover, over rutted dirt roads, through mud holes, and across the grasslands, spotting exciting views of game along the way, including a pride of lions eagerly chewing on some zebra bones.

Pretty soon it was time for a "sundowner," which our guides laid out on the hood of the Range Rover. We ate the delicious, and by then very welcome hors 'oeuvres, and enjoyed the South African wine, while watching the incredible sunset, one of the most thrilling sights in the world.

Next day the knock for our game run came on our door at 5:30 am. It was freezing outside, but our guides provided us all with hot water bottles and warm wraps, and off we went. It was as thrilling to see the sunrise as it had been to see the sunset last night. On that run, we saw many more animals: giraffes, rhinos, zebras, and a leopard, definitely on the hunt. We followed him in our Range Rover as he waded across a swiftly flowing river, and stalked his prey, a young, lone water buck that never had a chance. We saw a huge herd of elephants with their babies; wart hogs so ugly that they were beautiful; and graceful antelopes called Nylas; and scary-looking Cape buffalos. We came across another pride of lions, leisurely sunning on the dirt runway we'd landed on the day before.

We knew that a group of lions was called a pride. We also learned that a group of giraffes is called a "journey" and a group of zebras is called a "dazzle," just in case you wanted to know.

On one of our runs we saw a herd of hippos (also called "pod," "dale," or "bloat"), luxuriating in their natural habitat: the water. One hippo with several babies put on quite a show for us, splashing around, and yawning with her huge, gaping mouth.

One night, as we were driving along in total darkness, we suddenly took a turn and were startled to see a huge bonfire burning brightly in the dark night, sending sparks high into the air. The bonfire was ringed by candles, with gaslights lighting up the area. We soon realized that we were right in the middle of the runway of the Singita airstrip, which is where the lions had been sunning themselves earlier in the day.

We were served champagne, and sat around the fire in awe of our surroundings. Donanne and Ali had dreamed up this evening as a total surprise to us, with the personnel at Singita making it happen. Tonight turned out to be our "I" themed evening. We had Italian, Indian, and Icelandic food: incredibly delicious pasta, Brioni rice, and baked chocolate mascarpone tart with cream. Imagine all that food, served to us out in the middle of nowhere! And who knew what was lurking in the bush surrounding the landing strip?

The evening ended with Fred enjoying his evening cigar and a snifter of Brandy in front of the roaring fire, as we received a lesson in astrology from our guide.

After a stay at another Singita camp, we overnighted at the Westcliff Hotel, located on a hilltop with spectacular vistas of Johannesburg. It was built like a Tuscan village, with terracotta buildings set around swimming pools and beautiful terraced gardens.

The list of safety tips in the room told us that Johannesburg was obviously not the safest city in the world. It read:

Avoid obvious displays of expensive jewelry, cameras, and other valuables.
Do not carry large sums of cash on you
In the evening, keep clear of dark, isolated areas

Let the hotel recommend a reliable taxi service
If in a car, keep doors locked at all times
Lock valuables in the trunk of your car
At night, park in well-lit areas
Do not pick up strangers

I guess those suggestions could really apply to any big, cosmopolitan city, although Joburg is known to have a big crime rate.

We knew many of Ali's friends were traveling to Joburg to join us for a dinner party he'd organized this evening, but we had no idea of a surprise which he'd had his friends pull together for us while we were in the bush.

Suddenly two young singers and a pianist pushed an electric Yamaha keyboard into the room, and we were treated to fifteen songs from the Hal David Songbook, including my favorite, "To All the Girls I've Loved Before."

Hal couldn't stop beaming, and Ali had the biggest smile on his face that I'd ever seen, knowing that he'd pulled off a great coup to end our trip.

Ali had planned our adventure exquisitely, with great attention to every detail: we got to meet some extremely interesting people - real movers and shakers in South Africa; we saw some gorgeous scenery; sipped some magnificent wine; and had a fantastic experience in the bush. We all came away with some unforgettable memories.

With Hal still doing very well - in fact, getting stronger every day, we stuck with our plans to stop in Atlanta on our way home to visit our friends Ann and Bob Holder. The Holders are exceptional hosts wherever they are, but Atlanta is their main home, and they excelled there.

But at one point, Hal, feeling a bit tired out by all the activities, suggested that we skip going to New York afterward, as planned, and just return to Los Angeles. I didn't know what to do because the Songwriters Hall of Fame was planning a huge, surprise birthday party for Hal there, and I'd been keeping that secret for months, hoping that Hal would be well enough to make the trip.

As a ruse, I convinced him that the CEO of ASCAP needed his advice on something that could not be discussed over the phone. Hal bought that, and so we proceeded to New York, as planned.

We'd timed our arrival at the Marriott Marquis Hotel so that we would arrive after the hundred or so guests had arrived. Someone who had been stationed in the lobby called up to alert people in the room that we were on our way up, so they all crowded into the entrance of the private dining room and screamed "Happy Birthday" as Hal and I walked in. Even though Hal did by then have an inkling that something was going on, he was still totally surprised to see so many people in the industry, and so many personal friends gathered there.

People had flown in from D.C., San Francisco and Los Angeles, proclamations were presented; there were singers, including B. J. Thomas, Freda Payne, Chuck Jackson, Archie Jordan, Charles Strouse singing "Too Young to be Old," and even Dionne Warwick, as well as speakers, including Francis Preston, the President of BMI, the rival organization to ASCAP, who was very gracious in her remarks, saying that in the five short years that he'd been Chairman of the SHOF, Hal had completely changed the organization around, and brought it into the prominence that it now enjoyed. That was high praise, coming from a competitor.

In May Burt Bacharach called Hal to tell him that about twenty of their songs were going to be featured on the popular TV show *American Idol* during its final show of the season. Burt played the piano on the show, and many of the former contestants who had been on *American Idol* performed Bacharach/David songs, as did Dionne Warwick. The winner that year show, Taylor Hicks, received more votes than the President of the United States had ever received! It was a wonderful legacy for both Burt and Hal that their songs were still popular, even though some of them had been written over fifty years ago.

Our trusty producers worked another miracle at Hillcrest in August. Ron Rosen, Hal, Walter Grauman, and I - naturally with the help and support of Berry Gordy, one of our esteemed Hillcrest members - put on a show called *Motown at Hillcrest* which turned out to be a real winner. Two of the major performers were Smokey Robinson and Stevie Wonder. Those two alone would have been fantastic, but they were backed by wonderful singers and dancers, and the show was deemed a success by the eight hundred or so club members who attended.

As we grow older, our friends start disappearing from our lives. We lost Howard Koch back in 2001, and continued to miss him. Our pal Red Buttons passed away in July of 2006. We'd had a lot of fun with him over the years when he'd been married, when he'd been dating, or when he'd been alone.

Our friend Marshall Wais passed in November. His wife, Lonna asked Hal if he would perform at the memorial, which was held in the beautiful garden of the De Young Museum in San Francisco. Several of the Wais's friends spoke, reflecting on their friendship with Marshall, and then Hal sang, "What the World Needs Now is Love," one of Marshall's favorite songs.

On a happier note, our friend Walter Grauman was being honored by the Board of Governors of Cedars Sinai Hospital, and Hal was asked to be the featured performer for the evening. Hal suspected that they'd probably gone through a list of "real" performers, and were reaching out to him because they couldn't get anyone else. But Walter was such a close friend that he agreed to do it anyway. So, with Chris Caswell accompanying him, he sang eight of his standards, to an enthusiastic audience. People seem to love to hear a less than perfect performance. In any case, the hospital raised over one million dollars on that one night alone, so the evening was definitely a success.

The Hodeses were unable to join us this year for our annual cruise, but we decided to go anyway, traveling on the Silver Shadow from Ft. Lauderdale to St. Lucia in the Caribbean. One of the highlights of this trip was a tour of Firefly, a retreat that Noel Coward built in Jamaica in 1955. Hal was especially interested in the Bechstein piano, badly deteriorated, but still on display.

The year 2007 started out well, in that when we arrived in Los Angeles after our Christmas cruise, there was a call waiting for me from my oldest son, K.C. Forester. His first grandchild - meaning my first great-grandchild - had been born on December 29th. Nora was a beautiful little redhead - the color of her hair inherited from her proud father, Nick Potter.

We welcomed one new person to this earth, but had to say goodbye to another one, albeit one in the public eye: President Gerald Ford passed away in January. Also, Burt Bacharach and Angie Dickinson's daughter Nikki left this earth, after battling Asperger's disorder for many years. Then, right on top of that, Steve Krantz, with whom Hal had been in the army and who was the producer husband of the novelist Judith Krantz, passed away on January 4th. We thought, enough, already!

In our apartment in the Museum Tower in New York, I had always loved looking out of the windows of our forty-first floor and wondering who lived in all the surrounding buildings. I wanted to know who built them and what their histories were. So I hooked up with my friend Denise LeFrak Calicchio,

For Jose better known as Eunice

Falling in love is easy
Staying in love is hard
But staying in love with you
Is easy for me to do
Because you're beautiful
You're smart
You're talented
And most of all you love me too ——

From your Valentine

Falling in love is easy
Staying in love is hard
But staying in love with you
Is easy for me to do
Because you're beautiful
You're talented & smart
And you have a warm
& caring heart

Valentine 2/14/07

Fred and Betty Hayman with Eunice and Hal
Permission for use granted by Betty Hayman

who became as enthusiastic as I was about writing a book about the subject. Denise and I picked out about thirty A-list co-ops that we wanted to write about and hired Kathryn Livingston to do the research and finalize the book. Hal came up with the title, which aptly described exactly what the book was about: *High Rise Low Down: Who's Who and What's What in New York's Most Coveted Apartment Houses.*

It was pretty exciting to get my hands on that very first book, hot off the presses. Soon we began a round of book-signing parties and events, the first for the Costume Council of the Los Angeles County Museum of Art, and then at a big party at the Peninsula Hotel, and at a gathering Betty and Fred Hayman hosted at their lovely home in Beverly Hills, to which Fred invited his own list of Beverly Hills officials and celebrities. There we were greeted by a lively mariachi band (one of Fred's signature touches), Fred's antique yellow Rolls Royce sitting at the curb, and a wonderful buffet, sent over from the Peninsula.

I was already feeling pretty elated about everything, but to top things off, the author Judith Krantz sent me a note in which she said that she thought the book was "unputdownable!" How was that for an endorsement?

It wasn't long before Hal and I were in New York, where my co-author Denise and her husband and John Calicchio hosted a book-signing party in Denise's beautiful apartment on Park Avenue, which just happened to be one of the buildings we'd written about.

Later John Calicchio hosted a book-signing party for Denise and me at Club Colette, an exquisite private club in the heart of Palm Beach, Florida. But we almost didn't make it to our own party. It snowed the morning of our flight and the plane had to be de-iced twice before we were finally able to take off - two anxious hours late. We were told that after our flight left, no other Jet Blue flights were able to take off. However, once at Club Colette we sold a lot of books, and our book hit the number one spot of all books sold in Florida that week.

In March, Denise, Kathryn, and I had another book-signing event at the Guggenheim Museum. There were over three hundred people gathered in the beautiful atrium, where our event was held. It was a winner, but unfortunately the museum completely sold out early in the evening, and had to take orders from people who were unable to buy a copy that night.

Later, Barbara George, whom I'd met when we were both on the California Arts Council, organized a book-signing event for me in San Francisco at the glorious Nob Hill apartment of Carole and Robert McNeil, which had formerly been owned by William Randolph Hearst. The guest list was a combination of my friends, Barbara's friends, and Carole's friends, and made up a wonderfully eclectic group of San Franciscans. I was reminded of the cocktail party scene in the movie *Breakfast at Tiffany*, as I looked around the room at the sophisticated, glamorous group, sipping drinks, eating the delicious hors d'oeuvres, and waiting for the "author" to tell them about her book. Was I - the author, nervous? You bet!

Ron Rosen, Hal, Walter Grauman, and I again put our heads together and came up with another great idea for a show for Hillcrest Country Club members. Hal asked Christine Andreas and Michael Feinstein to team up, and the show opened with Christine's not-to-be matched rendition of "Alfie." It turned out to be another sold-out, wonderful event at the Club and another fulfillment of Hal's promise when we became members to help the club in any way he could.

Ever since Ann and Bob Holder had blown into town from Atlanta, and taken Los Angeles by storm (they knew more people than I did, and I was born here), we'd been fast friends. We knew we'd like to travel with them some day, and that day came with a quick trip to Cabo San Lucas in March, where we stayed at Las Ventanas, a beautiful hotel about midway between San Jose del Cabo and Cabo San Lucas.

On our way from the airport to the hotel, we cruised through a barren, but starkly beautiful, landscape: dry desert dotted with dramatic Saguaro cactus and bordered by the jagged cliffs of the Sierra de La Laguna range. When we finally arrived at Las Ventanas, we were struck by the sight of the hundreds of stark cactus plants dramatically arranged in the sand, with colorful flowers circling the borders. Each bed of sand was meticulously raked to form intricate patterns.

It didn't take us long to start our sight-seeing, with a visit to the Cabo landmark, El Arco, a natural rock arch, and on the last night of our short visit, we were led to a secluded area of the beach, which was ringed with candles brightly glowing in glass containers. Again, the entire area had the most wonderful, intricate designs inscribed on the sand, plus, in big bold lettering the words: **WELCOME TO YOUR DINNER.**

Another night to remember.

Toward the end of May, Fred Hayman was honored on his eightieth birthday with a big blowout, during which Dayton Way (right in front of the Grill on the Alley) was closed. The Grill had a narrow dirt alley-way behind it, separating the restaurant from what had been Giorgio's when Fred owned the store (where Louis Vuitton is now located). During the party, several Beverly Hills City Council members came to the stage to unveil a new street sign that would forever after read "Fred Hayman Place."

Hal was asked to write some special material for Fred, and here are some of his lines.

Nothing so glamorous
As walking into Giorgio's
And walking out with something very chic
Mr. Hayman had a way of making
Every single woman feel unique
That is why everyone in town
Follows him all around
Just like me, they long to say thank you Fred

The Waldorf back in old New York
Soon led him to the Hilton here
And here he made a thousand L.A. friends
And his contribution to our town
Is like a gift that never ends
That is why everyone in town
Follows him all around
Just like me, they long to say, thank you Fred
Mr. Beverly Hills * Mr. Beverly Hills* Mr. Beverly Hills

Producer George Schlatter did a wonderful job as Master of Ceremonies, and even Placido Domingo got into the act, singing "Happy Birthday" to Fred.

Hal and I, in keeping with our desire to see more of the United States, took a trip to Santa Fe, New Mexico in May to go to the opera and visit some friends. As we were leaving the plane in Albuquerque, I noticed that the woman in the seat in front of us was carrying my book, *High Rise Low Down*. I tapped her on the shoulder and asked if she was enjoying the book. She said she just loved it, so I told her I was the author. With that, she whipped out a pen and asked me to sign it for her. That was a great way to start our trip.

We made a dinner date with friends of ours who had a home in Santa Fe, and they asked if they could bring another couple. The diners at the Compound Restaurant were treated to more than what was on the menu, as Vic Damone, who joined us with his wife Rena, stood up at our table and sang "The Four Winds and the Seven Seas," remembering the lyrics perfectly, even though he had recorded that song in 1949. Frank Sinatra once said that Vic Damone had the best set of pipes in the business: Vic proved him right this night.

This year when the Los Angeles County Library prepared to host their dine-around dinners, where each host or hostess has an author present in their home, I was invited to be one of the authors on the strength of my book *High Rise Low Down*. I was assigned to the home of Jane and Stephen Ackerman, who thought it would be fun if Hal would perform as part of the evening's entertainment. It was another case of diners getting more than they paid for.

After Hal reached the pinnacle in the pop music field, he'd had considerable success writing with John Cacavas for the Library Music field. Now, Adam Taylor, the President of APM Music, paired Hal to write what was termed "a genre-busting collection of new songs" with a group of independent L.A.-based rock artists: Robert Navarro, Bret Levick, John Andrew Schreiner, and Sven Spieker. The songs were recorded at the Total Access Studios in Redondo Beach, California where the CD titled *Pop, Rock & Alternative* fused brand-new catchy lyrics by Hal with the edgy riffs and modern beats of today's pop, rock, and alternative music scene.

APM Music threw a release party at Hollywood's Roosevelt Hotel, which drew people from every spectrum of the music industry, anxious to hear Hal's "new sound." The songs didn't become "standards," but did quite well on the charts.

In December, Mark Edelman produced a show titled *Love, Sweet Love,* which was performed at the Thousand Oaks Civic Arts Plaza. The critic Steven D. Harris, reminded readers that 2007 marked the fiftieth anniversary of the collaboration of Burt Bacharach and Hal David. The show, featuring thirty-one Bacharach/David songs, told the story of four contemporary Los Angeles women looking for love during the week leading up to Valentine's Day. Happily, both F. Kathleen Foley of the *Los Angeles Times* and Mr. Harris gave the show good reviews.

We took our usual Christmas/New Year's cruise this year, which brought us to Key West, Florida, where we toured Harry Truman's Little White House in Mallory Square in the heart of Old Town Key West, it wasn't exactly a presidential library, which Hal and I had on our bucket lists, but it did have displays of many highlights of the Truman presidency.

Our friend from Oregon, Gordon Sondland, owns a chain of boutique hotels in Oregon and Washington, and in March, he opened a new hotel in Tacoma, WA. The Hotel Murano featured a-world-class collection of glass art which was displayed in its lobby and by the elevators on each floor.

Gordon organized a fundraiser for the opening night party, the proceeds of which were going to the Tacoma Art Museum and the nearby Glass Art Museum. He hired Burt to be the featured entertainer for the guests, with one caveat: that his friend Hal David perform one song during Burt's show, to which Burt agreed.

Once Burt's show was over, he called Hal up to the stage where, with Burt accompanying him, Hal sang, "I'll Never Fall in Love Again," and told the story about how he had written the lyrics while Burt had been in the hospital with pneumonia. Someone held up their iPhone, and the next thing we knew Hal was on You Tube, and still is. Just type in *"You Tube, Hal David:"* it is still there, after all these years.

In April, Hal and I drove to Hyde Park to fulfill our hopes of visiting all of the presidential libraries.

First we toured every nook and cranny of the Roosevelt home and grounds, before being invited into the hallowed library, where scholars who come to write about President Roosevelt usually have to wait downstairs while they request a certain document, and then and only then do they get to read it. But Bob Clark, the curator of the more than seventeen million pages of documents housed there, took us upstairs into the private stacks, usually only accessed by eight people on the staff of the Library. I felt as though I should be whispering, surrounded by all of the remarkable, historical works stored there.

I actually held in my hands the original first draft of the speech that President Roosevelt made on December 7, 1941, after the bombing of Pearl Harbor by the Japanese, which included his hand-written corrections and additions on the margins of the typewritten note. I remembered very well

For my little girl Eunice

Waking up on Valentine's Day
After sleeping all night with you
That's my favorite thing to do
I could do it my whole life thru
If I could have just one wish
One wish I could make come true
Every day would be Valentine's Day for me
If I could spend every day with you

with love, love, love + more love

Val
2/14/08

where I was that infamous day, when as a teenager, I heard the news of the bombing of Pearl Harbor. Holding that document in my hands vividly brought the events of that long-ago day back to me.

We traveled again in May. This time Vicki and Murray Pepper and Betty and Fred Hayman joined us on a river boat trip, which started in Dresden, where we saw pictures of the devastation that our bombers had done to the city during WWII. It was remarkable to see how the city had been rebuilt, with all the buildings purposely made to look just as old and weather-beaten as they had been before the war.

We followed the Elbe River into Bad Schandau, Switzerland and then into Czechoslovakia and the city of Decin, photographing everything as we cruised.

We happily celebrated Hal's eighty-seventh birthday on board the MV Dresden, where our waiter asked the pianist to play "Raindrops," and then proudly announced to the other diners that he was serving the man who had written that song.

When we were on shore, trying out the various local restaurants along the way, we hardly ever looked at a menu. We knew what we wanted: bratwurst, sauerkraut, and beer. What a diet!

The Haymans had to leave us once we arrived in London, but we and the Peppers stayed for a wonderful visit with Ambassador to St. James's and Mrs. Robert Tuttle at the U.S. Ambassador's residence in Regency Park. Maria Tuttle created a stunning book about the residence, which we took home with us as a treasured reminder of our visit.

While we were in London, the BBC filmed Hal for a documentary they were making on the relevance of songs in love stories and movies. To the question they posed "Can a song really tell a love story?" the answer was decidedly "yes," especially if Hal David had written the lyric!

We didn't get to see the documentary, but received a notice from Clare Beavan, who produced and directed it, that it had been very well received.

The four of us then flew to Moscow, where we couldn't get over how much more modern everything was since the last time we'd been there. But we were pleased to see that even though Moscow was very much a city on the move, it had maintained its heritage, even in the design of its brand new skyscrapers, shopping malls, and churches. One thing that was also modernized, but in a negative way, was the traffic: it was horrible, and made getting around the city very difficult and very time-consuming.

While we were in Moscow, Vicki, Murray, and I, went with Hal to the office of Ekaterina Ananieva, the Deputy Director General of RAO, the Russian Performing Rights Society. She and their director of international relations put Hal on the hot seat, complaining they were not getting the proper royalties for Russian songs performed in the States. (How many Russian songs have you heard sung in the States?) But Hal was not intimidated, and promised to look into the situation for them as soon as he returned home, which seemed to mollify them.

When I mentioned to Ekaterina that Vicki had been the Mayor of Beverly Hills, she opened her eyes wide, very impressed that a woman had held such a prestigious position. She wanted to know more about what Vicki had to deal with in a man's world. That broke the ice, and soon we were invited to lunch.

We ended our trip to Moscow with the saying "do syidaniyal" (duh syee dah nee ye), which roughly means "'till next time" in Russian.

Hal and I went on without the Peppers to meet the ASCAP group in Rome, where we attended a CISAC meeting, after which we stopped in New York before heading back to Los Angeles.

While we were in New York, Hal had an episode during which his legs felt rubbery, and would not hold him up. Paramedics immediately got us to New York Cornell hospital. Nine very long and agonizing hours later, during which Hal was hardly even looked at, we both got so angry, that, with approval of Hal's cardiologist in Los Angeles, but without an approval of the hospital's ER doctor, we checked him out of the hospital. The ER doctor on duty (the second shift without any attention to Hal), was a young woman who seemed to dart hither and yon as fast as her short legs would carry her, without lighting anywhere, certainly not in Hal's cubicle. When I tried to say something to her, she snarled at me and said that she was too busy to talk to me. It was a very bad experience, so bad that I almost went to the New York Times with our story, but doing so would have meant we would have had to stay in New York longer than we had planned and we were anxious to return to Los Angeles. Thankfully, Hal was feeling fine by the time we returned to our apartment, exhausted, and realized that it had been Father's Day. What a way to spend it!

We were still in New York in June when Charlie Fox and his wife Joan organized a benefit show called *The Songs of Our Lives,* and Hal was invited to be one of the songwriters showcasing their songs on the show. He sang

"This Guy's in Love with You," and a medley of six songs after that, and was given a standing ovation. I always thought he got so many standing ovations because the audience didn't expect him to be as good as he was, and then when he was good, he just bowled them over.

Our friends Ann and Bob Holder from Atlanta shared our interest in Presidential Libraries so when they were in Los Angeles in August, we headed south to the Richard Nixon Library, in nearby Yorba Linda, California. This was before the library was transitioned into the Federal Presidential Library System, so some of the Watergate material was not exhibited as fully as eventually mandated.

When the National Archives took over in 2007, they had removed the Watergate exhibit that had been in place for seventeen years. After three years of empty exhibit space they planned to reopen it to their own specifications, without consulting the Nixon Foundation, which added fuel to an already volatile situation that existed between the federal government and the Nixon family, who would have preferred to not have material on the whole Watergate scandal on display.

A docent took us through the one thousand square foot two-story prefab home that Nixon's father bought from a Sears Roebuck catalog in 1910 and erected himself. Nixon's mother, father, and three brothers lived in that tiny space, with the four boys sharing two beds in the miniscule upstairs bedroom. Usually visitors are not allowed upstairs, but since friends of ours had arranged this VIP tour for us, the docent was allowed to take us up there. She told us that in her 12 years at the Library, this was only her second time upstairs.

We planned a twentieth anniversary party, and one day toward the end of August, I happened to look across our partner's desk at Hal and saw that he was busy writing something that I assumed was a new song. But it turned out to be a love letter to me, which he insisted on showing to me the minute he finished it, rather than waiting to read it to me at our party. That prompted me to show him a letter I'd composed just the day before, which I planned to surprise him with on our anniversary.

Twenty years of married life hadn't dimmed our love affair one iota. At our anniversary party there were tributes from friends and family, but the one I treasured the most was this one written by Hal, who read to me that night.

My darling, My Sweetheart
my Eunice
I still can't believe how lucky I was
to meet you
How wonderful it was
to fall in love with you
How great it has been
To share these last 20 years with you
I don't know
How many years I have left
But I can't imagine living them
with anyone else than you
Just in case you haven't guessed

I love You

8/25/08

August 28, 2008

Dear Hal:

Twenty years! Twenty glorious years! Boy, that's pretty good for two old fogies like us. The beauty of those twenty years is that, thanks to you and your wonderful outlook on life, I don't feel like an old fogie. In fact, because of my abiding love for you, I feel like a teenager with her first crush.

I do love you, Hal, with all of my heart. You brought light into my life, helped me grow, and showed me how to enjoy every single day that we are blessed to have together.

We've had a wonderful, fun-filled, adventurous life: it has been packed with exciting and unusual experiences. But one of the best parts of our relationship has been our ability to sit perfectly still in the same room with each other, without uttering a single word, yet being able to absorb the love, respect, and admiration that we feel for each other. That to me is a sign of true love: our true love.

Darling, 20 is only the beginning. Let's try for at least another 20!

All my love,

It seems to me as if it was only yesterday that Eunice and I were married in New York, and here we are, twenty precious years later, in Los Angeles.

In these twenty precious years, we've traveled the world over together, had wonderful times together, supported each other's dreams and endeavors together - always together.

As I look back, I don't think we've been apart more than four or five days in all that time, and as you can see, we're still having fun together.

We've absorbed two families into one, two sets of friends into one, two ways of life into one, and I can't imagine having a more loving and better partner to share my life with than Eunice.

That guy definitely had a way with words, didn't he?

To top things off, Nancy Kanter and Hal sang "Too Young to be Old," which had become our theme song.

My eighty-first birthday was on September 16th, just as the financial world was reeling. Lehman Brothers, the venerable hundred fifty-year old invest-ment banking firm, filed for bankruptcy, and Bank of America bought Merrill Lynch, which was about to go under. By the end of the month, the Dow had plunged almost a hundred and seventy-eight points, the largest point drop in its hundred twelve year history. But that trauma was put aside for the moment, when we attended the marriage of my son Donald Forester and Judy McIsaac in Gloucester, a city on Cape Ann in Essex County, Massachusetts. It was a glorious New England setting for a very happy occasion. Donald had reserved B&B's all over the little town for his friends, who were flying in from far and wide. During the ceremony, they combined sand from the beach in Balboa on the west coast, with sand from a beach on the east coast, signifying the combining of their two lives, as a loving gesture of their new lives together.

Dan Foliart, then President of the Society of Composers & Lyricists, called with the announcement that Hal was going to be named an "Ambassador" by the Society. Their Ambassador program recognizes a select group of com-posers and lyricists whom the Society considers has made valuable contribu-tions to the artistic community.

After Dan's glowing introduction of Hal at the award dinner, Sally Keller-man sang, in her inimitable sultry way, "This Girl's in Love with You," and then, protesting that it was hard to follow Sally, Hal did just that by singing "I'll Never Fall in Love Again" and" Raindrops."

We had to leave right from the Riviera Country Club, where the event was being held, to take the red-eye to New York, where Hal was scheduled to sing at a Grammy event the next day. However, the Grammy event had been cancelled at the last minute, but the organizers had not been able to notify us before we left. Fortunately, we were able to sleep in once we arrived at our apartment in New York, which is where we finally got the word.

Rather than taking our usual cruise this December, we jumped at a window of opportunity to go to Egypt, where things seemed calm at the moment in that area of the world.

There was a terrifying terrorist attack in Mumbai shortly before we were to leave on our trip and our friends in Los Angeles tried to talk us into cancelling, even though they knew we were going to Egypt, not India. But there were no travel advisories for Egypt from the State Department, so we continued with our plans. We'd tried three previous times to travel to Egypt, but something always dissuaded us from going, things like young men shooting at passengers on ships travelling on the Nile and political and ethnic protests. But as it turned out, we timed our trip perfectly. But, just seven days after our return, fighting erupted on the Gaza strip, right on the border of Egypt, when Israeli troops and tanks massed along that border, claiming that their attacks were in retaliation for sustained rocket fire from Gaza into Israeli's territory.

We took in all the requisite sights, including seeing the pyramids from the vantage point of the back of a camel. After climbing up monuments and scrambling down into tombs, we flew about four hundred fifty miles south of Cairo, to Luxor, known as the city of the Gods and once one of the greatest capitals of the Ancient world.

We spent four glorious days on the Nile and fortunately there were no incidents or problems, although I did get a picture of some young boys pointing their hands, made to look like they were holding guns, at our boat.

The Aswan High Dam was, of course, very impressive. The lake created by the building of the dam was five hundred miles long, and at the time it was built, was the world's largest artificial lake. Both American and French engineers came up with viable plans for the proposed dam, but due to Nasser's involvement with the Russian government and his mistrust of American politicians, the contract to build the dam was given to the French, and was financed by Russia.

From Aswan we flew to Abu Simbel. The scope of it was monumental especially considering that the temples had been moved from their previous location, piece by piece (with some pieces weighing as much as thirty tons), because they were in danger of being submerged by the waters of Lake Nasser. It took four years, but the temples were preserved.

The previous August, I had to talk Hal into producing another *The Writer, The Singer, The Song*, show. I was always ready to do so, but Hal needed a little encouragement. He wanted to make sure that the Blue Ribbon members were not tiring of our shows. Nothing could have been further from the truth. Our show was always voted the most popular activity of the organization, so, Hal agreed to put on another one. Of course, we always had to first get Karen Sherry of ASCAP, who was really and truly the producer, on board, as well as Paul Williams, who always graciously agreed to be our M.C.

The 2009 lineup for the show The Writer, The Singer, The Song was:

Ashford & Simpson	Marilyn McCoo & Billy Davis, Jr.
Jeff Barry	Darlene Love
Alan Bergman	Siedah Garrett
Felix Cavaliere	Kenny Rankin
Hal David	Steve Tyrell
Paul Williams	Dave Goelz & Gonzo the Great

It was once again a great group of talented, generous artists, and we were happy that we'd been able to bring another unique experience to the Blue Ribbon members.

One evening, as Hal and I were sitting in a restaurant having dinner, a fellow came over to tell Hal what a great fan he was, and that he had enjoyed Hal's lyrics for years. When we finished our meal and asked for our check, the waiter said that the man who had been talking to us had taken care of it. Fortunately, he and his daughter were still in the restaurant, so we went over to thank them. The daughter said that they loved Hal's songs so much that they even named their dog Alfie. We learned the dog's name, but never did get the name of our benefactor.

This year when Karen Sherry produced the ASCAP show to which legislators were invited, she came up with a new twist. She got legislators from the states of the songwriters to introduce them before their performances,

Dear Jose

I love you one day more
Than I did the day before
Every day since the day
I fell in love with you
With 20 years of happiness
And all the love that I possess
In this year 2009
I promise you
My whole life through
You'll always be my Valentine

Farewi's
2/14/09
N.y.C.

thereby including them in the festivities, and making them feel that they were a part of the program. That really went over well, and helped to keep the legislators invested in what we were in D.C. for: to promote better copyright laws.

August brought the sad news that our dear friend Senator Edward Kennedy had passed at seventy-seven. Hal had written some special material for Ted over the years. These are a few of the bridges that Hal wrote to the melody of Close to You:

> On the day that he was born
> The Angels got together and created someone with a helping hand
> So they gave him lots of courage
> And they made him unafraid to take a stand.
> Hal ended that ditty with:
> Standing on the Senate floor
> And fighting for our civil rights
> Well he became a giant for all time
> When our country is in trouble
> There's no mountain that's too high for him to climb

Fortunately, Ted was still alive when Hal wrote that, so he heard Hal sing the song to him.

For our twenty-first anniversary I asked Hal what he would like as a gift. He usually asked for a new jacket, or something mundane like that. But this year he surprised me by asking me to buy him a wedding band after all these years. So off we went to XIV Karats in Beverly Hills, where we found a beautiful, plain wide gold band which looked just perfect on Hal's finger. They sized it while we waited, and we walked out with it glittering in the sunshine.

When Hal was in the hospital just before he passed away, I asked the nurse to remove that band from his finger and not having a pocket in the jacket I was wearing, I slipped it onto my own finger, and put my wedding band in front of it so that it wouldn't slip off. Those two bands are still on my finger, and help keep Hal close to me. I think of him every time I fiddle with those rings, and it comforts me.

We were in New York in December, not only for an ASCAP Board meeting but so that Hal could have his picture taken with Rosanne Cash, Johnny Cash's daughter, and with Paul Hampton, a BMI songwriter, who wrote the melody to "Sea of Heartbreak" to Hal's lyric. The back story is that before he died, Johnny Cash gave his daughter Rosanne a list of 100 songs that he thought she should learn and record. The List, the first album she made from that list of songs, included "Sea of Heartbreak," which Rosanne recorded as a duet with Bruce Springsteen. "Heartbreak" was the number one song on the album, which had just been nominated for a Grammy.

In deference to Johnny Cash's iconic way of dressing in all black clothing, Hal wore a black shirt, black pants, and a black blazer, and Rosanne was also dressed in black. The photographer took a great series of photos of Rosanne, Paul, and Hal, and we all had a great time at the offices of BMI, where the photo session had been held.

"Sea of Heartbreak" was originally recorded by Don Gibson in 1961. It was the last top-forty crossover from Don Gibson's extensive country career, and was also the only early Gibson hit he didn't write himself. Gibson's cover of the song was so successful that it was remade by Kenny Price in 1972 and later by Poco, climbing to #2 on the country charts.

Rosanne said during a radio interview in October that "the song is a rare successful example of a tricky songwriting device: the extended metaphor. It uses a metaphor, and it keeps that metaphor all the way through, and many songs that try to do that kind of fall over into kitsch." She went on to say, "This song starts with that metaphor of sailing on the sea of heartbreak, and it uses it to absolute perfect effect - 'the lights in the harbor don't shine for me.' Oh! It just breaks your heart." Her quote shows that she really understood the meaning of the lyrics: she really got it. Actually the "sea of heartbreak" line had been suggested to Hal by Paul Hampton based on his own experience: he was going through a contentious divorce, and felt he was drowning in that sea.

While still in New York, Hal again joined the cast of *The Songs of our Lives,* which our friends Joan and Charlie Fox produced annually to benefit the Fulfillment Fund. The show is usually held in Los Angeles, but in 2009 it was held at the Fiorello H. LaGuardia High School of Music & Art and Performing Arts, which is where Charlie had studied.

The other performers that year were Alan Bergman, Charles Strouse, Charles Fox, Paul Williams, Alan Menken, and David Zippel. Steve Tyrell made a guest appearance. It was another great show, for a good cause.

That December we sailed on the Silver Shadow with Bonnie and Bernie Hodes, our friends from New York, and friends from London. The Caribbean was getting a little old-hat for us by now, but it was still one of the few places to travel to at this time of year because of the great weather. In spite of the lack of exciting ports of call, we all had a grand time, and, after sailing for three thousand, two hundred and fifty-one nautical miles, we found it a wonderful way to start the New Year!

2010

Eunice
If there is one thing
I would miss
If I didn't have you
It would be you I would miss
Walking hand + hand with you I would miss
Climbing into bed with you I would miss
Going to a show with you I would miss
Flying to New York with you I would miss
Going on a cruise with you I would miss
Going to Hillcrest for lunch with you I would miss
Giving dinner parties with you I would miss
Making love to you I would miss
and so much more
and so much more
And so much more

with all my love and that's
a whole whole lot
Hal
2/14/10

We were in New York in February to attend a reading of *Promises, Promises,* prior to it appearing on Broadway after an absence of forty-two years. *Will and Grace*'s Sean Hayes, along with Kristin Chenoweth were the stars. Katie Finneran appeared in the role of a hilariously funny drunken pickup in act two, a role which won her a coveted Tony Award.

I found it enormously interesting and exciting to sit on the sidelines as the actors went through the whole show while seated around a big table, reading their lines. When a song was called for, it was sung, but other than that, it was just the "reading." It was clear to see how the actors were already starting to get into their roles - and feeling out their characters. Hal was as excited as I was at being there, along with Neil Simon, his wife Elaine Joyce; Rob Ashford, the director; and several of the producers.

I always banked at the Wells Fargo office in Beverly Hills, and as I was coming out of the elevator there one day, a friend called out to me. It happened to be Dick Rosenzweig, who had been the Executive Vice President of Playboy Enterprises since 1988. He also sat on the Annenberg Cultural Center Board with me. He told me that the then-Mayor of Beverly Hills, Jimmy Delshad, wanted to have a stirring song written as a theme song for the City of Beverly Hills. After all, Chicago had a theme song, San Francisco had one, and of course, so did New York. Dick asked me to ask Hal if he would write the song. Hal was very enthusiastic about the project, and immediately called Charlie Fox to see if Charlie would write the music to Hal's lyric.

It wasn't long before I organized a cocktail party in our apartment to preview the song "90210 Beverly Hills" for some people closely associated with the city, including the Mayor and a number of other city officials.

With Charlie enthusiastically playing our Yamaha piano, and Hal and Charlie belting out the lyrics, "90210 Beverly Hills" was officially launched.

One of the reasons Jimmy Delshad was anxious to have a song written for Beverly Hills at this particular time was because September 2, 2010, was coming up soon, and Jimmy was planning a big celebration to promote the city, its restaurants, its products, and its way of life. 90210 was a zip code, known around the world as belonging to Beverly Hills.

The end of the year brought a flurry of fundraising and preparations for the building of the first Beverly Hills Rose Parade float in 23 years. The city's entry, titled "City of Dreams Come True," appropriately fit the theme of the parade, which was "Building Dreams, Friendships and Memories."

The hard work and dedication that the committee and volunteers put into the beautiful float, built by Fiesta Parade Floats, paid off when the float won the Mayor's trophy for most outstanding city entry - national or international. Hal and Charlie's song "90210 Beverly Hills" was played all along the parade route.

"90210 Beverly Hills"
I long to be where the sun is shining
In 90210 Beverly Hills
For every cloud there's a silver lining
In 90210 Beverly Hills
Movie stars walk down the street
The same as you and I
And every night it's fun to eat
Beneath a starry sky

I hate to brag but the grass is greener
In 90210 Beverly Hills
And you can breathe 'cause the air is cleaner
In 90210 Beverly Hills
Window shop Rodeo Drive
Makes you glad you're alive
In 90120 Beverly Hills

It's California with a smile
No matter what you wear you're right in style
It's golf and tennis, swimming pools
And don't forget we've got the greatest little schools
I long to be where the sun is shining
In 90210 Beverly Hills
For every cloud there's a silver lining
In 90210 Beverly Hills
Big hotels and small cafés
It's wonderful to spend my days
In 90210 Beverly Hills.

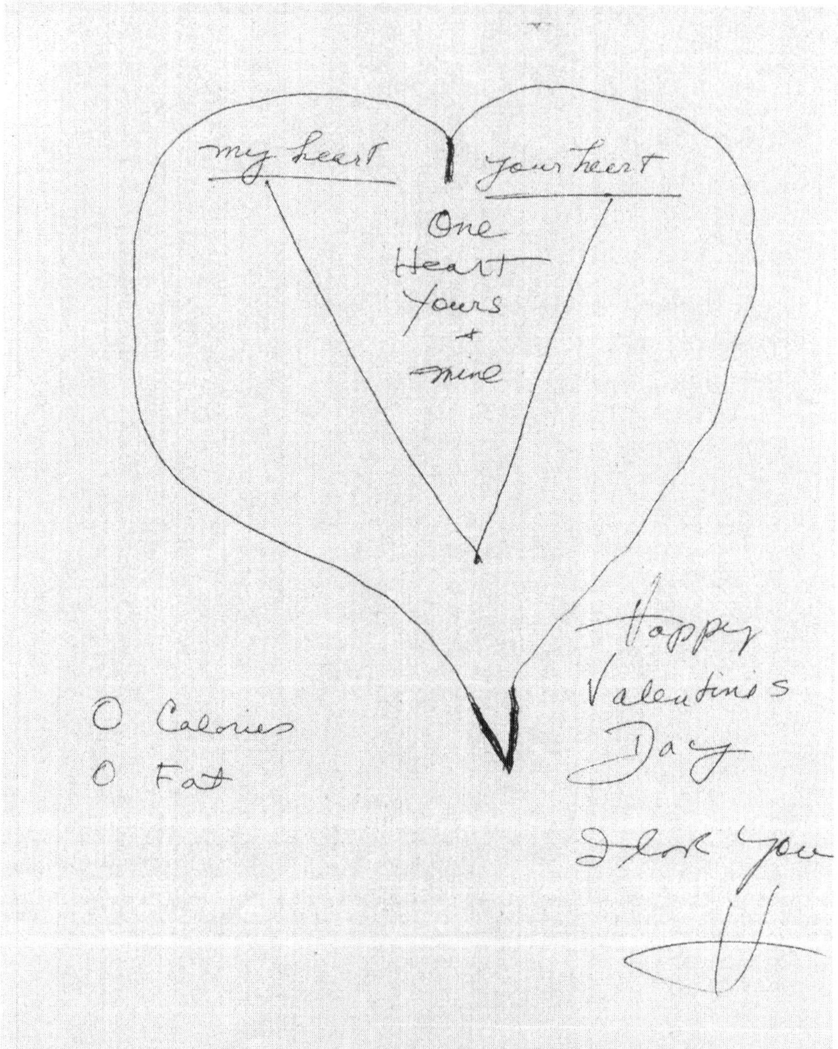
my heart
your heart
One Heart Yours + mine
Happy Valentine's Day
I love you
0 Calories
0 Fat

After celebrating Beverly Hills, we were back in New York in April, during one of the preview nights of *Promises*, for which ASCAP had purchased a large block of tickets for a PAC fundraiser. This was the first time we'd seen the show other than at rehearsals, so we were pretty excited. Hal felt that Rob Ashford, the talented director/choreographer had turned the show into a real "musical," as opposed to the original show, which Hal described as a "play with songs." There were many more dance numbers in this production, which he felt really fleshed out the show.

At the after-party at the Novotel, just around the corner from The Broadway Theater, a huge group was waiting for us. There was the traditional round of applause as we walked in, and I must admit that it was pretty heady stuff.

John LoFrumento, the CEO of ASCAP, gave a lovely speech, reminding everyone that it was Hal who had hired him in the first place, when Hal was President of ASCAP. He said, "It's been a wonderful ride for me." Hal suddenly got so emotional that I felt he was close to tears. It was a very touching moment.

Then: Opening night: April 25, 2010! The red carpet was very glamorous. I didn't even recognize all the celebrities who were piling into the theater, although there was a great flurry of excitement when Burt, Hal, and Neil Simon were all together, with flashbulbs popping like crazy.

Once the lights dimmed, I could feel a great sense of anticipation in the theater. The audience was filled with invited guests, and many Broadway greats, who all came to support their fellow actors and performers. Naturally they were enthusiastic and laughed throughout the show, applauding loudly after each number. It was all very exhilarating for both Hal and me - and our friends who were with us.

There was another long line of photographers and reporters waiting at the Plaza Hotel, where the after-party was being held. After running the gauntlet of reporters and after the photographers had their fill of taking pictures, we wound our way inside to try the table that had been reserved for us. In years past, we would have stayed up all night, waiting for the early morning newspapers for reviews of a show. Not so nowadays, with the Internet. So, even as we were served drinks at our table, people were already reading early reviews of the show on their ever-present iPhones. In spite of our buoyancy and high hopes, the reviews were only mixed. Many reviewers felt that there wasn't any real chemistry between the two principal actors, Sean and Kristen. So our spirits were dimmed a little, but we still maintained the heady feeling we'd arrived with.

Apparently the audiences were not quite in agreement with the naysayers, because the show had to be extended by several months until January 2, 2011. It was consistently one of the five top-grossing shows on Broadway, even with seventeen hundred seats to fill.

Years earlier we had met Catherine and Wayne Reynolds, who head up the Academy of Achievement in Washington, D.C., which recognizes outstanding achievement in a variety of fields, including the arts, business, science, politics, and the humanities. This year the Reynolds notified Hal that he was going to be the recipient of their Golden Plate Award at a ceremony in the gorgeous Academy of Achievement headquarters building on Sixteenth Street NW, and, he was going to be inducted into the Academy's Achievement Museum.

On May 15, the day of the event, we were at the Academy's building with senators and congressmen, prominent writers, newspeople, Ambassadors, protocol people, presidential advisors, society matrons, and many others; the men looking elegant in their tuxedos and the women done up in their best finery, with jewels glittering.

The evening started with a sing-along led by Nina Totenberg, NPR's award-winning legal correspondent, and General James Jones, USMC (Ret), who was then National Security Advisor for the Obama administration. Nina led the group in singing "Close to You," and James sang a rousing rendition of "What's New Pussycat," which just broke up the audience, given that he was such a stern and proper-looking gentleman.

After an elegant dinner, General Jones, in his role as M.C., introduced B. J. Thomas, who sang "To All the Girls I've Loved Before," quipping that Hal should have given the song to him instead of Julio Iglesias and Willie Nelson. Then, of course, he sang "Raindrops Keep Fallin' on My Head," the song which propelled him to the top of the charts.

Dionne Warwick had also been brought to Washington for this event, and after her medley, Hal was asked to sing "What the World Needs Now" as a duet with her, which they both managed beautifully, even though there had been no chance for a rehearsal. Next, Sam Donaldson, the long-serving ABC news anchor, gave Hal a rousing introduction in his usual boisterous style, and David Rubinstein, the recently appointed Chairman of the Kennedy Center, placed a beautiful medallion around Hal's neck.

The entire event, from start to finish, was done with the epitome of charm, grace, and exquisite taste.

We flew from D.C. to Atlanta, to visit Ann and Bob Holder, who were taking us to see both the Jimmy Carter Library, right there in Atlanta, and the William Jefferson Clinton Presidential Library in Little Rock, Arkansas. Bob had a schedule of our activities during our stay all mapped out for us, which was a great help and kept us on our toes - and looking at our watches periodically to make sure we weren't off-schedule.

At the Jimmy Carter Library, which had a staff of 160 people, we marveled at the high-tech capabilities of numerous exhibits, and enjoyed the temporary exhibit of photographs taken by Howard Baker, who had been Chief of Staff of President Gerald Ford, as well as a former Senate Majority Leader and a Republican U.S. Senator from Tennessee.

The Holders had a special surprise in store for us after our tour of the Carter Library. We were driven through downtown Atlanta to the renowned Paschal's Restaurant, one of the best soul food restaurants in the city. We were welcomed by their long-time hostess Miss Pat, and before long were joined by Herman Russell, the owner of Paschal. Herman and Bob had partnered in a number of major building projects in Atlanta, which is how they met and became fast friends. Mr. Russell believes that "by being your best and never accepting mediocrity, you will be paid back tenfold." That motto has held him in good stead throughout his life.

With Herman suggesting what Hal and I should eat, we had one of the best meals, albeit most of it fried, that we'd ever had.

The next morning, we boarded Bob's corporate jet, for the one hour fifteen minute flight from Atlanta to Little Rock. The Clinton Library is situated on a thirty-acre park on the banks of the Arkansas River. It was very contemporary in design, and we found it to be most impressive.

A knowledgeable docent showed us around the Library, including the special exhibit of Madeleine Albright's collection of pins and broaches, which she wore to depict her various moods when she was dealing with foreign dignitaries in her capacity as Secretary of State.

Back home in Los Angeles, we didn't stay long because we had to fly to London so that Hal could record another CD with John Cacavas. From there we flew to Bilbao, where we attended a CISAC meeting, and then on to New

York, for the 2010 Songwriters Hall of Fame Induction Gala. In 2004, the Board, unbeknownst to Hal, had created the Hal David Starlight Award, to honor gifted songwriters who are at an apex in their careers and are making a significant impact in the music industry via their original songs. This year, 2010, Taylor Swift was the recipient of the Hal David Starlight Award. Still only twenty- one, she told a charming story about how when she first started recording, her mother had to pick her up at school and drive her to the sessions because she was too young to get her driver's license.

Instead of returning to Los Angeles as soon as the SHOF Awards gala was over, we drove to the Berkshires with fellow ASCAP board member Irwin Z. Robinson and his wife Joan. We stayed at the Inn at Stockbridge, and drove all over from there. One of our most memorable stops was at Chesterwood, the home of Daniel Chester French, the creator of the sculpture of Abraham Lincoln, seated in the Lincoln Memorial in D.C., and of course, we toured the Norman Rockwell museum while we were there, which we'd seen many times in the past, but never tired of.

One of the highlights of the trip was when we saw the newly-written play, *Freud's Last Session*, by Mark St. Germain, which the producers were hoping would find a home in New York. It not only did find the home they'd wished for, but went on to great success across the U.S and into Los Angeles. We knew that night when we saw it that it had legs.

We were in Nashville in September for the annual ASCAP Board meeting there, and to attend the ASCAP Country Music Awards event. The usual awards were handed out; best group, best individual, best song, etc. But for me, the highlight of the show came when Connie Bradley, who was retiring, was called to the stage. Connie had been head of the Nashville ASCAP office for the past thirty years, and was highly respected in the music business: she gave a heartfelt speech, during which she related the story of how, thirty-one years earlier, Hal David, when he was President of ASCAP, appointed her head of the Nashville office, against her better judgment, since she didn't feel qualified for the job. But Hal prevailed, and Connie did a magnificent job of helping put ASCAP on the map. Hal also gave Karen Sherry (now an Executive Vice President of ASCAP and the ASCAP Foundation Executive Director) her start, as well as John Lo Frumento (who was the CEO of ASCAP) and he also talked Paul Williams into running for the ASCAP Board. In 2009, when Marilyn Bergman stepped down as president, after fifteen years, Williams was elected to that position. Hal had an uncanny ability to judge how well people could do - and he had the same ability to judge the opposite.

Hal, over the years, has had a very positive influence on the ASCAP organization as well as his dealings with legislators in Washington, D.C., and elsewhere. He always had the interests of songwriters as a whole in mind: he was never self-centered. I think that was one of his most endearing traits.

Back in L.A., we attended a performance of Christine Andreas at the Segerstrom Center for the Arts, and, as usual, she mentioned that Hal David was in the audience. Someone slipped Hal a note written on the program booklet, which read:

> *Dear Mr. David:*
>
> *I sang "What's it All About Alfie" to my infant son every time he went to sleep. Thank you so much for such a meaningful reminder of what it is all about, in the most beautiful set of sounds. It's still one of my favorite songs, and a lovely memory of my life.*

That, not unsurprisingly, made Hal's night.

In October, the Songwriters Hall of Fame opened a gallery at the Grammy Museum in downtown Los Angeles. It wasn't quite the Hall of Fame that was the ultimate goal of the SHOF, but it was a big step, and there was great excitement about it.

The show that was presented that night was called *Legends in the Round*, and featured Hal, Paul Williams, Lamont Dozier of Motown fame, Mac Davis (who wrote one of my favorite songs "In the Ghetto"), and Ashford and Simpson (great rock and roll singer/writers). Each writer told touching and funny stories about how they came to write certain of their hit songs.

Another opportunity came up for Hal and me to go on safari, and we eagerly counted the days until it was time to leave. We traveled with Donanne and Ali Kasikci, and had some wonderful experiences with friends of theirs along the way, many of whom we had met on our previous trip to South Africa.

We had a wonderful visit, arranged by Ali Kasikci, with Luke Bailes, the owner of the Singita properties in Kruger National Park, where we'd stayed the last time we were in South Africa. While at Luke's spectacular mountain-top home in Cape Town, overlooking Clifton Beach, a neighbor of the Bailes joined us. Mike Rutherford, who was originally the guitarist with the Genesis group headed by Phil Collins, heard that Hal was going to be visiting next door to his home, and he told Luke that he'd like to come for a short visit. Mike encouraged Hal to tell stories about his songs and his career, which he loved listening to.

We flew first to Gaborone in the Republic of Botswana. This was only a stopping-off place: our real destination was Maun where, once we landed and our luggage was off-loaded, the four of us squeezed into a single engine plane and, flying low over the edges of the Okavango Delta, landed on the bumpy, dirt landing strip at the Jao Camp airport. With our driver waiting for us in a Land Rover, off we went, following a well-worn sandy path with deep ruts, through the Kalahari Desert toward Jao Camp, situated on a private concession bordering the Moremi Game Reserve right in the heart of the Okavango Delta. We were quickly assigned to our own canvas and thatch rooms, which were elevated on high wooden platforms overlooking vast flood plains. Since the Wilderness Safaris group, under whose auspices we were traveling, commits resources and time to the Jao Lion Monitoring Project, they encourage photographic safaris because they are "non-consumptive", adhering to the practice of leaving nothing but your footprints,and taking nothing but memories.

In the bush and on the Delta, we saw our share of "the big five" as well as every other form of wildlife that the area had to offer.

Leaving Jao for Mombo meant another short flight in another tiny plane, but this one only took a few minutes. When we asked our guide why we needed to fly to a camp that was so close, he explained that it would take about two days to drive to Mombo from Jao on the sandy, rutted roads, as opposed to this five-minute flight: on hearing that, we definitely opted for the flight.

In the heart of the Okavango Delta is the Moremi Game Reserve, an area of land that is mostly dry throughout the year. On its circumference, however, are hundreds of palm-fringed islands, untouched and deserted, offering some of Africa's last pristine game-viewing opportunities. Mombo was built on one of those islands.

Right from the porch of our very comfortable, even elegant room, we could see families of baboons scrambling around with their newborn babies, the mothers, being overly protective of their little ones.

In this area we saw giraffes (my favorites), elephant herds, zebras, hyenas, and the one and only wild dog in the area. Of course, we were constantly on the lookout for lions, and were not disappointed. Everywhere we turned there were babies just learning to walk on their wobbly legs, and staying close to their protective mothers.

As we were about to leave Mombo Camp, a slight glitch developed. A huge elephant had decided he didn't want to go around the elevated walkway we used to get to our cabins, so he did what any self-righteous elephant would do: he went right through it. But that meant that we couldn't get to our cabins to pack to leave. Finally, with the use of a shaky ladder and some pushing and tugging, we climbed up to an area of the walkway that had not been destroyed and packed, while a crew hastily rebuilt the path to our rooms so that we could leave in a more dignified manner.

After clearing customs at the Kasane International Airport in Botswana, we took off in a little single-engine six-seater for Zambia. Our pilot pointed out a spot on the Zambezi River below where all four bordering countries came together: Zambia, Namibia, Botswana, and Zimbabwe.

As I've mentioned, I'm fond of waterfalls, and we were on our way to one of the most spectacular waterfalls in the world. After the Zambezi River travels about a thousand miles from the north, it reaches the edge of one world and plummets three hundred fifty feet into another. Victoria Falls, between the borders of Zambia and Zimbabwe, is more than a mile wide, a boast that no other waterfall in the world can match. During peak season, more than three hundred thousand gallons of water cascade over the falls every second. We weren't there at peak season, but the noise created by the rush of water was still deafening, and the spray was spectacular. I loved every soggy moment of it, which we got to view from both the Zambian side and the Zimbabwean sides.

Constance Towers Gavin, the Blue Ribbon President who is married to former movie star/Ambassador to Mexico John Gavin, met me for lunch to ask if Hal and I would produce another *The Writer, The Singer, The Song* show for the Blue Ribbon. Karen Sherry of ASCAP had suggested something different for a change, which I presented to Connie, and there and then, in December of 2010, one of the greatest shows ever presented at the Music Center was created.

My dearest darling Eunice

I love you 24 hours a day, everyday
If there more than 24 hours in a day
I would love you more than 24 hours a day

If this isn't love
I don't know what love's all about
Cause you are the one thing in my life
I just can't live without

From Hal with love
2/14/11

At the beginning of 2011 I started working on *Love, Sweet Love*, Hal's ninetieth birthday celebration that I was organizing as a fundraiser for the Children's Festival of the Blue Ribbon of the Los Angeles Music Center. One of the really smart things I did was to ask Ricki Ring, a Blue Ribbon member, to chair the event for me. We had not met before, but word of her expertise preceded her, and I thought she would be perfect for the job. She accepted on the spot, and it was due to Ricki and the team she assembled that the final result, in October of 2011, was such a huge financial success, and it was thanks to Karen Sherry that it was so successful theatrically.

For the next nine months I worked on getting forms designed, tribute pages collected, and a program book organized. It took that full nine months to get the show produced - in almost every respect, just like having a baby. But, just like having a baby, it was well worth the effort.

In March, when we flew into New York for an ASCAP Board meeting, Hal and I plunged into readying our apartment so the movers could clear it out for us. Hal had decided to sell our Museum Tower apartment, after owning it for more than thirty years (he'd been an original tenant.) ASCAP was only planning to have two meetings a year in New York, as opposed to the six or seven it had previously held there, so it didn't seem practical to keep the place. Hal had gifted the apartment to his two sons several years previously, so they were going to receive the proceeds from the sale, but Hal and I had the job of closing it up. The apartment had not taken long to sell and the buyer, a single woman executive from Angola, purchased quite a few of the furnishings, including the upright Yamaha piano which, as part of the purchase package, she asked Hal to sign. It took Hal most of one day to search for just the right pen that would show up on the shiny black-lacquered piano. But sign it he did, in handwriting that was somewhat shaky from the tremor he had recently developed.

We packed up personal belongings and gave away or donated many items. We were so concentrated on stripping the apartment that we almost missed the news of the huge earthquake that hit Japan, with a resulting tsunami which literally wiped out whole cities and killed many thousands of people.

Pieces of buildings, piers and other structures were still washing up on the shores of the United States three years after the event. Hal and I often ate sushi for dinner on Sunday nights. The tsunami put an end to that for quite a while because radio-active leakage from their nuclear plants, which were damaged in the earthquake and resulting tsunami, polluted the water, and we didn't want to take any chances by eating raw fish that came from Japan.

Finally, on March 17th, the day of the annual St. Patrick's Day Parade on Fifth Avenue in New York, Hal and I packed up a couple of pieces of luggage, and headed to the nearby Plaza Athenée which was going to be our home away from home from that day forward. Hal and I had been perfectly fine with the idea of moving out of our New York apartment, but as we walked through the lobby for the last time and the concierge came over to shake our hands and tell us how much he was going to miss us, I must admit that we both got quite choked up.

At our ages, it was only expected that our friends would be leaving us. In March, the same month that movie star Elizabeth Taylor died at seventy-nine, Bernie Roth passed at ninety-five. Bernie, the founder of World Oil Corporation and an early promoter of self-service gas stations, and his wife Flo had been a part of the group of seven couples with whom Hal and I shared birthday dinners. They had been married for seventy-four years, and although Flo survived Bernie, she wasn't well, so we were expecting the other shoe to drop before too long. We'd had a busy day the day that Bernie passed: we'd celebrated our grandson Adam's fourteenth birthday, celebrated Bernie's life, and attended the fiftieth anniversary party of Carolbeth and Ambassador Lester Korn. Those events pretty much encompassed the cycle of life.

Jackie Cooper, the child movie star who went on to become an adult star and a producer, died in May. He'd lived in the same building as we did in Los Angeles and, sadly, after his wife died, the manager of our building frequently had to accompany him back to his apartment when he was found wandering around our lobby in his tattered bathrobe and floppy slippers. Arthur Laurents also passed away in May. Hal and Charlie Fox had finally, after a good twenty years of haggling, gotten Laurents to sign over the rights to the show they'd written based on the movie *The Turning Point*, just two weeks before Laurents' death.

At last there was some happy news. Prince William, second in line to the British throne, married Catherine Middleton, his college sweetheart in a ceremony with all the pomp and circumstance that anyone could have wished for. Both bride and groom were gorgeous, and the wedding could not have been more glamorous or beautiful.

On the heels of that unforgettable marriage, news came to us that Osama bin Laden, the hated and feared Al Qaeda leader, had been tracked down and killed at his compound inside of Pakistan, leading President Obama to declare that "justice has been done."

This year, when Hal finished singing "I'll Never Fall in Love Again" and "Raindrops Keep Fallin' on My Head," at ASCAP's annual show for legislators, he started to walk off the stage, but was called back by Paul Williams, who was the M.C. Paul mentioned that Hal was going to turn ninety in a few days, and then Jackie DeShannon came out and sang her signature song, "What the World Needs Now," as a tribute to Hal. Although the song was written in the sixties, the lyrics were relevant then and are still relevant today; maybe even more so than when they were originally written.

The next day the Washington Post appeared with an article by Roxanne Roberts and Amy Argelsinger, which read, "…But the scene stealer was, like most of the performers, a behind-the-scenes guy: Hal David of "Alfie" and "Raindrops Keep Fallin' on My Head" fame, who sang his own "I'll never Fall in Love Again" in a surprisingly strong voice, just weeks from turning ninety."

Hal had never been called a "scene stealer" before, and he got quite a kick out of his new title.

While we were in New York in June, we went to the Broadhurst Theater to see the show *Baby It's You!* It told the story of Florence Greenberg, the thirties-something stay-at-home mom and wife who parlayed "Tonight's the Night," an unlikely hit record by a teenage group she named "The Shirelles," into a career as the head of Scepter Records, and became a major player in the independent record label field in the 1960's. The show goes on to tell the story of how when the Shirelles were no longer recording hit songs, two young fellows came to Florence in 1962, with a girl singer they wanted her to record. You guessed it, the two young guys were Burt Bacharach and Hal David, and the terrific girl singer they had with them was Dionne Warwick. What fun it was to see that story told on a Broadway stage!

Hal and Burt had three songs in *Baby It's You!* And they had the opening song in *Priscilla, Queen of the Desert,* making four songs of theirs being performed on Broadway at one time. Hal was pretty jazzed about that.

Earlier in 2011, Hal had resigned as Chairman of the Board and CEO of The Songwriters Hall of Fame. It was getting to be too much for him, and he felt it would be fair to give someone else a shot at that top spot. That someone else turned out to be Jimmy Webb. Since Hal had resigned, he was not involved the year's Annual Induction Gala, at least not in the way he had been when he was the Chairman of the Board. However, the members of the Board, as a surprise, created a special honor, the Visionary Leadership Award, which they presented to Hal during the Induction ceremonies. Trisha Yearwood sang a medley of six of Hal's songs, and there was a rousing ovation from over one thousand people in the audience as Hal went to the stage to accept the award. It was bittersweet for Hal. He'd loved his leadership role, and felt that he had left his mark on the organization. He knew that he would miss the excitement of being involved, even though he knew in his heart of hearts that it was the right time for him to step down.

Some months ago, in my capacity as the President of the Wilshire Corridor Board President's Group, a group formed to discuss common problems of high-rise condominiums along "the Corridor", the area of luxury high rise apartments on Wilshire Boulevard between Beverly Hills and Westwood, I invited our Councilman Paul Koretz to be our guest speaker. When I mentioned to him that my husband was going to be ninety years old, he insisted on honoring him at a Los Angeles Council meeting at City Hall in downtown Los Angeles. During their session, Councilman Koretz read the proclamation that had been prepared, and then introduced Hal, who said a few words of thanks. Then a policewoman by the name of Roz Curry beautifully sang a medley of Hal's songs a-cappella. She told me that she is usually asked to sing at the funerals of fallen police officers, so this was a pleasant change for her!

In August, just as Hal was preparing to leave the apartment to join a friend for lunch, the phone rang. I was almost always the one to answer the phone in our home, because Hal liked me to screen his calls. When the phone rang this time, Hal hesitated at the front door to see if call was for him. It was. The call was from Dr. James Billington, the thirteenth Librarian of the United States Congress, was calling to ask Hal if he would be willing to accept The Library of Congress Gershwin Prize for Popular Song the following May. Hal's face lit up as he said he would be delighted to accept the award!

Hal and I were sworn to secrecy until the news was officially announced that both he and Burt Bacharach were going to receive the Gershwin Prize.

After the phone call, Hal left for his luncheon date with Murray Pepper, but he told me when he returned that he'd had a hard time eating his lunch, and an even harder time having a "normal" conversation with Murray. But he hadn't given the secret away. I couldn't get anything done at my desk after I heard about the honor, so I tried to read. But I had to read each sentence at least twice to figure out what I had just read: nothing seemed to penetrate my mind besides news of the great honor that was going to be bestowed on Hal. The Gershwin Prize for Popular Song, bestowed by the Library of Congress, was the highest honor the United States could confer on a songwriter, so both Hal and I were naturally very excited about this news.

We were on the go again in late August, on a river boat trip, again with Joan and Irwin Z. Robinson, from Prague to Strasbourg. We enjoyed visiting many cities on this trip, but the most chilling stop was the stadium in Nuremberg where Hitler used to hold rallies, with a good hundred thousand people in the stands and another hundred thousand standing in the big open space in front of the stadium seats.

The Documentation Center, adjacent to the stadium, featured pictures of the Nazi era, and atrocities inflicted by that regime. The German government felt that it was important for people to be faced with what actually happened during World War II so that hopefully by showing the atrocities, they will never be repeated.

Our cruise ended on September 6th, and we returned to Los Angeles to news that Hurricane Irene had smashed into the East Coast of the United States while we'd been gone.

Hal, Walter Grauman, Bob Holder, and an interesting, eclectic group of men belonged to what Walter dubbed "the old guys." They periodically had lunch together with one of the fellows hosting the group at his country club or some other venue. Hal was originally reluctant to join the group because of its name; he didn't want to be considered an "old guy." But he liked the men and found their conversations stimulating so he reluctantly agreed to become a member. He certainly qualified!

One day the lunch was being held at Hillcrest Country Club. I'd been there for a meeting of one of my organizations, and when we finished, I went over to the table where the Old Guys were sitting to ask Hal if he wanted a ride home. He wasn't there, and the men had not heard from him. Naturally my first reaction was to panic, and I couldn't wait to go home to see if there was a message from a hospital, or the police.

As I was waiting at the front of the club for my car, I noticed a very bedraggled-looking man slowly trudging up the driveway, jacket haphazardly thrown over his shoulder because of the extreme heat. As he came closer, I could see it was Hal, huffing and puffing and sweating - but gamely moving forward.

He'd had his driver drop him off at the Los Angeles Country Club, thinking that was where the lunch was being held. By the time he found out he was in the wrong club, the driver had left and instead of calling a taxi, he hoofed it from Wilshire Boulevard to Pico Boulevard, some two miles away. Hal became the hero of the group for making that trek, but I, on the other hand, chided him for not calling a cab!

Before leaving on our cruise, I'd been extremely busy organizing a tribute book for Hal's upcoming ninetieth birthday celebration at the Music Center, and working with Karen Sherry on the production of the show, along with Walter Grauman and Ron Rosen. Now that I was back, I got busy again. We were getting so many tributes that the book was expanding daily. And we were getting so many reservations for people wanting to attend the show that we had a waiting list of over one hundred fifty people (all of whom were going to be angry with us if we couldn't get them seated). The fire marshal had already allowed us to squeeze in more seats than the Mark Taper Forum would ordinarily hold, doing everything legally within his power to accommodate us, but we still could not accommodate everyone who wanted to attend.

The weekend from October 14th to the 17th, during which we celebrated Hal's ninetieth birthday turned out to be magical for both Hal and me. It started when we were informed that Hal had been selected to receive a star on the Hollywood Walk of Fame on Friday, October 14th. There were many friends who had come in from out of town to attend the *Love, Sweet Love* show, which was going to be at the Music Center just a few days later, so they were here to watch as the big star was placed into the sidewalk, and to hear both Steve Tyrell and Paul Williams sing Hal's praises.

In his speech, Paul Williams called Hal "a warrior for his efforts on behalf of songwriters," and Steve Tyrell said, "I have been asked many times, where did you go to college? I always answer with the same response: I'm a graduate of the Bacharach/David University!"

Hal David, Eunice David, Paul Williams
Photo by Ron Rosen
Permission for use granted by Steve Tyrell and Paul Williams
Permission for use granted by Hollywood Chamber of Commerce

The President of the Hollywood Chamber of Commerce commented that Hal was the oldest person on record to have a star placed on the Hollywood Walk of Fame. It was the two thousand, four hundred fifty-first star, appropriately placed in front of The Musicians Institute on Hollywood Boulevard. Hal was so overcome that he was only able to give a very short acceptance speech: but I think it expressed everything he wanted to say, even if he did paraphrase George M. Cohan. He said:

From time to time, I found myself star-gazing on the famous Hollywood Walk of Fame—never dreaming that one day I would have my own star. My lovely wife Eunice is excited, my grandchildren Adam and Sara are excited, my family and friends are excited—and what do you know—I am even more excited than they are! I'd like to thank you all—each and every one of you— for being here to share this experience with me.

A delighted Hal receiving his star on the Hollywood Walk of Fame
Los Angeles, October 14, 2011, Reuters/Gus Ruelas

The Birthday Boy.
Photo by Eunice David.

The seventy or so people who attended "the unveiling" were invited to join us for lunch at the Hillcrest Country Club, where there were many toasts to the man of the hour.

Friends, and even people whom we only knew slightly, started sending us pictures they'd taken from their iPhones as they drove by the Pink's hot dog stand on La Brea Avenue near the corner of Melrose. There was a huge sign spread across the front of the famous hot dog stand that read: "Happy 90th Hal David!"

When Gloria Pink called to tell me they were putting up the banner, I said, "Great, we'll come to Pink's for lunch on Sunday with our family, instead of taking them to Hillcrest, as planned." She couldn't believe we wanted to go to Pink's rather than Hillcrest. But we certainly did! In fact, we packed as many family members who were in town into four different cars, and headed off to La Brea and Melrose.

There was a "pink" room all set up for us, with pink tablecloth, pink napkins, pink plates and utensils, pink roses - the whole nine yards.

259

I had been asked to bring a picture of Hal, and it was quickly framed and placed on their celebrity wall, as Hal, adorned with a Pink's cap, enjoyed not one, not two, but three helpings of hot dogs with chili!

The day wasn't over for us yet. Our friends from Oregon hosted a dinner party at Spago's, to which many of our friends were invited, along with many of their friends whom we had not previously met; it was a wonderful mix, which also included Mariana and Paul Williams and Jane and Burt Bacharach. At one point in the evening the Maitre'd brought someone into the room who started talking to both Burt and Hal. It turned out to be Sergio Mendes, who led the great Brazil '66 band. He'd been having dinner in the main dining room, and heard that both Hal and Burt were "in the house." Lani Hall, Herb Alpert's wife, who was scheduled to perform in *Love, Sweet Love* on Monday, had been Sergio's featured singer. It was a nice moment when the three fellows got together to exchange hugs and good wishes.

Monday, October 17th arrived, after those busy few days. We had told Hal that he was not to come to the Mark Taper Forum during rehearsals; we wanted him to be surprised at what was in store for him.

Here is the line-up of the once-in-a-lifetime show that we produced at the Music Center: Herb Alpert, Burt Bacharach, Jackie DeShannon, Lani Hall, Albert Hammond, Michele Lee, Smokey Robinson, Valerie Simpson, B. J. Thomas, Steve Tyrell, Dionne Warwick, Stevie Wonder, and Dwight Yoakam. The Los Angeles Jazz Ensemble from the Los Angeles County High School for the Arts also performed. Chris Caswell was the Musical Director for the show and he gathered a stellar group of musicians to make up the band. It clearly showed the power of love and the amount of respect those remarkable performers had for Hal, that they were all willing to give of their time and incredible talent, to celebrate Hal David on his ninetieth birthday.

There were many surprises for Hal as well as the audience that night. Smokey Robinson, also a brilliant songwriter, played the piano as he sang (a first for him). Stevie Wonder flew in from Washington D.C. at the last minute to perform. Burt was very touching in his remarks to and about his long-time collaborator, and when Dionne Warwick took the stage, she remarked that many of the other performers had already sung "her" songs, but that didn't stop her for a moment, she just sang them over again, in her own very special style.

Dinner for the over eight hundred people who had attended the event was held in the Dorothy Chandler Pavilion. Hal and I tried our best to make the rounds of guests seated on both the first and second floor of the building, but it was hard to do, we had so much to say to each of our friends who were there that night. In his thank-you speech, Hal said that of the ninety birthdays he'd had so far, this was by far the greatest of them all. He thanked all the appropriate people, and then added,

My lovely wife, Eunice, is on the board of the Blue Ribbon, and I am on the Board of the ASCAP Foundation, the two organizations that the proceeds of this concert will benefit. It turned out to be a win-win situation, inasmuch as we sold out almost from the beginning, with Eunice at the helm and Ricki Ring as the chairman of the event committee - what else would you expect?

And so, I would like to propose a toast to Eunice, who keeps me healthy and happy and forever young, and to everyone else who worked so tirelessly to make this concert a big success.

The e-mails for the next week or so never stopped flowing in. The staff of our building all signed a note of congratulations to Hal. Columnist George Christy wrote about it in the *Beverly Hills Courier,* and news of the concert was all over the Internet. It was a very heady time for us - and as it turned out - very good timing, as Hal's health began to fail soon after.

Needless to say, I spent days writing thank you notes, all lovingly sent to those who had helped make *Love, Sweet Love* such a humungous success.

After a trip to London in November, where Hal received an award at the ASCAP dinner where members of the British PRS organization are honored for best song, best writer, best publisher, etc., we went to Palm Desert, where Hal, Michael Feinstein, and Jack Jones, all backed by the Les Brown Band of Renown, were going to perform at a benefit for the Barbara Sinatra Children's Center twenty-fifth Anniversary Gala. Hal had been asked to write special lyrics for the three women who were going to be honored at the Gala: Philanthropists Barbara Sinatra, Nelda Linsk, and Helene Galen.

The gala was held on November 14th, and the special material that Hal wrote and sang that night was vintage Hal David.

On this anniversary
The angels keep blessing every child
Who's at the center Barbara built
Never more to be the victim of abuse
No more to cry the tears of guilt

That is why everyone in town
Follows them all around
Just like me, they long to be
Close to Barbara, and Nelda - and Helene.

We left the desert at 7 A.M. the next morning so that I could attend a Blue Ribbon Board meeting back in Los Angeles. I was excited to announce how well Hal's ninetieth birthday concert had done financially – well enough for the Blue Ribbon Children's Festival to proceed unencumbered for the next three years, as well as helping the ASCAP Foundation produce their successful musical programs in schools.

When we were in New York in December, Hal was interviewed at the Lombardy Hotel by people who were making a documentary on Jewish songwriters. Hal had turned down the interview some time ago, because he wanted to be known as a "songwriter," not categorized as a "Jewish songwriter." But a friend of a friend prevailed upon him, so he went ahead with it, as a favor to her.

On the day of the taping, Hal was unable to remember the details of some of the stories he told most frequently and unfortunately, he even forgot the plot line of *Promises, Promises*. That was a sure sign that it was time for me to screen Hal's public appearances more carefully. In a small social event, he was just fine; in fact he was more than fine. There he eagerly engaged in conversations, telling jokes and totally relating to everyone. But we both realized that interviews such as this one were going to have to end. Hal knew he had not done his best, and it really bothered him.

We finished the year 2011 with our usual cruise, which started at Amelia Island, Florida and, traveled along the Intercostal Waterway south to Charleston. Hal, always interested in southern history, was delighted with the trip. It was an easy trip for him, and our fifty-three stateroom ship was very comfortable.

Ever since I started writing this memoir, I've been thinking about how to write this next chapter - the last chapter of my life with Hal. But then I realized that it really is not the last chapter because, as the title of this book says, there is always something there to remind me. And there will always be something there to remind generations to come about Hal David because of the lasting legacy of the songs he wrote - and yes, because of the legislation he helped fashion for which songwriters and their heirs will thank him for, years into the future.

We were invited to Mac Davis' seventieth birthday party in January, which had been planned to the nth degree by Lisë, Mac's beautiful, talented, and loving wife. It was almost impossible to recognize the Bel Air Country Club as we drove up because huge piles of hay were all over the entrance-way, the theme for the evening definitely being "country." Mac's original band and backup singers were at the party, and they all performed, along with Mac. Dolly Parton was even there, to sing "Happy Birthday" to Mac as only she could!

There was southern fried chicken served, along with Pink's hot dogs. We sat at a table right at the edge of the dance floor and it was clear from some pictures that were taken that night that Hal was looking frail, but he had a great time as did the three hundred or so other guests, and we were among the last ones to leave the party.

A loop of pictures was shown all night long of Mac, his family, and important moments in his life. That gave me the idea to have something similar made for Hal and me, which would include our family, friends, and lots of pictures of our travels. I set about getting that done immediately, and Hal even got involved by helping me to pick out the pictures he wanted, and deciding what music he wanted played throughout the tape.

Hal's old friend Bob Silverstein passed on January 29th. That was a real blow to Hal because the two of them were very close, and it made Hal feel even more vulnerable about his own health. Anita, Bob's wife, asked Hal to be one of the pallbearers, but realizing how frail he had become, she suggested that he serve as an Honorary Pallbearer, so he would not have to be one of the men lifting the heavy casket. Hal had been concerned about that, but hadn't wanted to turn Anita down.

We attended the annual Music Cares event in February, sitting at the ASCAP table, as always. This year Paul McCartney was the honoree. After walking around the auction area in the vast L.A. Convention Center for quite a while, we finally wound our way to our table, right up front, as usual. It wasn't long

To Eunice My love

I love you
and if you love me
I love you 2
and if you love me
I love you 3
and if you love me
I love you 4
and if you love me
I love you more
     and more
     and more
     and more
     and more

From the one you love I hope
Happy Valentines Day

2/14/2012

after we were seated before Hal leaned over to me and told me that his shoulder hurt him. In fact, he was lifting his jacket off his shoulder because it hurt so badly that even the weight of the fabric of his jacket was causing him pain.

We both realized it was imperative that we leave immediately, even before the concert started, not knowing exactly what was happening to Hal. So I helped him take the long walk to the lobby of the building, where I quickly produced two aspirin tablets, which I always carried in my purse - just in case. I immediately called our driver, and between the time that I gave Hal the aspirins and the time our driver arrived, he was already feeling a little better.

In the meantime, still during Grammy Week, the world received the shocking news that Whitney Houston had been found unconscious, submerged in the bathtub of her hotel room at the Beverly Hilton Hotel in Beverly Hills. There were no signs of criminal intent, and the Coroner's office reported the cause of Houston's death as drowning and the "effects of atherosclerotic heart disease and cocaine use." That news struck a sad note with everyone who loved Whitney and her incredible voice.

Hal's "incident" occurred on a weekend, so the first thing Monday morning I drove him to Dr. P.K. Shah's office at Cedars Sinai Hospital, where Hal had a CAT scan and some other diagnostic tests to try to determine what had happened to him at the Grammy event. We had an uncomfortable couple of days while we waited for the results of the tests. Finally the word came down. Hal had a blockage in an area of his heart that was going to be difficult to get to, but that would eventually require surgery. But on top of that, the CAT scan showed a dark spot on Hal's lung, that scared us more than anything else.

When Hal went to see Dr. Bob Wolfe, his pulmonary doctor, Wolfe didn't pull any punches, and told us that he was quite sure that the spot on Hal's lung was most likely Cancer (with a capital "C").

Between P.K. and Dr. Wolfe, it was decided to tackle the cancer situation before attending to the heart problem.

With all of Hal's charts, procedures, and medical information available on Cedar's computers, Hal and I met with Dr. Robert McKenna, widely respected in the medical community as one of the most knowledgeable and experienced thoracic surgeons in the field. He agreed to perform the necessary surgery on Hal, jokingly telling Hal that when he went to D.C. to receive his Gershwin Prize, he should insist on staying in the Lincoln Bedroom at the

White House, rather than at a mere hotel. But, more importantly, Dr. McKenna was quite sure that Hal would be well enough to go to D.C. to receive his prize in May.

I promise I'm not going to lead the reader through a step-by-step of what happened. But the short version is this.

After being approved with a clean bill of health for surgery by every doctor Hal could think of to go to, the surgery was scheduled for Wednesday, March 14th. When we arrived at Cedars at six fifteen in the morning, he was immediately whisked off to the pre-op room. I gave Hal a big kiss as he was placed on a gurney, and off he went through those ominous double doors. In the Founder's Room of the hospital, where catering had set a beautiful table overflowing with bagels, sweet rolls, juice and coffee, it wasn't long before friends started to arrive, along with Hal's two sons and Craig's wife Annette. Jim's wife was coming down with a cold, so she didn't feel that she should come to the hospital. It was wonderful for me to have all those people surrounding me; I felt wrapped in a special, loving cocoon.

It seemed like no time at all before Dr. McKenna appeared to tell us that the surgery was over, and that it had gone very well. Hal was in recovery. By the time he was assigned to a regular room in the hospital, it was close to 9 P.M. Since I'd been there since six in the morning, I figured I'd better get home or I'd be a danger on the road if I stayed much longer.

When I arrived at the hospital the next day, I was shocked to see Hal's condition, and immediately started checking with his attending doctors. Indeed, I learned Hal had suffered a stroke while on the table; something that none of the doctors could have predicted. The Cancer had been completely removed, so from that point of view the surgery was a total success - but Hal's problems were just beginning, due to his stroke.

As the time drew near to the date in May when Hal was supposed to receive the Library of Congress Gershwin Prize, the doctors and I clearly realized that there was no way that he could make the trip; because of his tracheotomy, he wasn't even able to talk, and because of his stroke, he was just learning to walk again, and he was extremely weak. He was in the rehab unit of the hospital, where he was getting better day by day, but the progress was slow. I was reluctant to leave Hal to go to D.C. to receive the award in his stead. The doctors all assured me that Hal was in capable hands, and that it would be all right for me to leave him for a few days, in fact, they encouraged me to go. Hal, when he was able, also indicated that he wanted me to go. But it wasn't an easy decision. Hal was terribly disappointed that he was not up to making the trip, or up to facing the public. Who could blame him? The Gershwin Prize was the highest honor, of the many honors that he'd ever received and he could not be there in person to accept it.

I was having terrible guilt feelings about leaving Hal while he was in the hospital, but our doctor, Paul Rudnick, told me that I was "nuts" to feel that way, and he offered to help me talk to Hal about Hal not being able to go. We made arrangements for Hal to make a video acceptance speech, but when we watched it, we saw that he really wasn't speaking clearly, and we knew he wouldn't want people to see him in that condition. One afternoon, after Paul Rudnick had a very frank talk about him not being able to accept the Gershwin Prize in person, Hal told us that he was "disappointed," but he was not "depressed." Hal came up with that nuanced wording by himself, which both the doctor and I thought was a good sign that his thought process was working well. Later in the day Dr. Shah came over to back up what Dr. Rudnick had said, and Hal told him he was okay with it. In fact, he insisted that I, as his wife, go to accept the Prize in his stead.

The rehab people had a wonderful tool to help Hal integrate back into everyday life. They brought him down to the gift shop at the hospital, and asked him to find three different items: a baby gift, M&M's and a gift card. The therapist was disappointed when Hal went directly to the woman behind the register to ask her where the items were, rather than searching for them himself. But I laughingly explained to her that Hal was just doing what he always does: he always asks for directions, when he doesn't know where something or some place is. It would have been totally unlike Hal had he gone from aisle to aisle to look for the items himself. I thought that therapy session went a long way toward helping Hal feel that he would do just fine once he returned home.

I left Los Angeles on May 6th, having drawn a calendar with smiley faces on it, showing Hal when I would return and bring him home. Hal put on his own smiley face as we said goodbye, and promised to work hard during his therapy sessions so that he would be ready to come home when I returned to Los Angeles. Mentally, he was already more than ready to come home.

Once again my friends rallied around, and a whole contingent from Los Angeles, Beverly Hills, San Francisco, New York, Portland, and Atlanta called to say that they would meet me in Washington, D.C. so I wouldn't have to be there alone. Hal's sons and daughters-in-law and two of his grandchildren, my two sons, and their wives, who came in from Oregon and Massachusetts were also in D.C. It was difficult being there without Hal, but my friends and family really helped pull me through the tense days while I was in Washington.

The people at the Library of Congress made sure that my family and friends had a wonderful experience while in D.C., and they were especially solicitous of me, knowing how difficult it was for me to be there while Hal was stuck in Cedars.

They even prepared a "call sheet" for me, with my day planned hourly, to help me keep all my meetings straight.

The morning of May 8th, my family members and I were scheduled to see a display of some of the musical treasures housed in the Library, which included some three hundred-year-old music books and some equally old musical scores. The curator made sure to have some current Bacharach/David sheet music also on hand.

Every room in the Library of Congress is beautiful, so it was hard to decide which was my favorite but the Member's Room, where lunch was served, was right up there at the top of my list. Buffy Cafritz, a Washington D.C. philanthropist, generously underwrote the luncheon, which made it possible for my group of twenty-four family and friends to attend. My friends and my side of the family also got to attend the show that evening in the Coolidge Auditorium, but only Hal's two sons, two daughters-in-law, and two grandchildren were invited to the show at the White House the next day, which had very limited seating.

When I was escorted into the luncheon, I was immediately shown a wonderful display of several certificates that had been prepared for Hal and Burt, an American flag for each, beautifully enclosed in a wooden container, and the prestigious Gershwin Prize itself – a gorgeous medallion with likenesses of Ira and George Gershwin engraved on it. The flags had been flown over the capital in honor of Burt and Hal; a first ever and a very meaningful touch.

There was an eclectic group in attendance at the luncheon, which included Gershwin cousins, Congressman John Dingell (the longest serving member of the United States House of Representatives in history) and his wife, and there were a number of other legislators, most notably Nancy Pelosi, who spoke warmly about Hal and about how much he was missed.

When lunch was over, several of us, including Burt, his wife Jane, Vicki Reynolds Pepper, and I, along with Dr. Billington were driven to the Capitol for a "meet and greet" with Speaker of the House John Boehner. Vicki brought up some pertinent questions pertaining to Beverly Hills, which Boehner asked his chief of staff to check on, and then were driven back to the Library, where another car was waiting to drive us back to the Four Seasons Hotel in heavy D.C. rush-hour traffic. (Apparently official cars have varying approvals for driving to different spots around town, hence the "musical cars.")

The evening's activities started with a small reception in the elegant private Librarian's office, I was escorted to my seat in the Coolidge Auditorium, and the show began. The performers were Sheryl Crow, Michael Feinstein, Diana Krall, Lyle Lovett, Mike Myers, Rumer, Sheléa, Arturo Sandoval and, of course, Dionne Warwick. Dionne told about visiting Hal in the hospital just before she left Los Angeles to come to D.C. Unstable as he was, he insisted on walking her to the elevator because it was the gentlemanly thing to do! That brought on a few tears. The performers all had heart-warming things to say about both Burt and Hal, and the show was predictably a big hit.

All during dinner, in the vast main hall people table-hopped and took pictures. There were celebrities, legislators, family and friends – and I tried not to miss anyone as I made my way from table to table to say hello. Stevie Wonder gave me an especially big hug and whispered that I could call on him for anything, that I was "family." He is such a sincere person that I knew he meant it.

On the 9th, I hosted a luncheon, which Hal had helped me plan, for twenty eight people; family, friends from out of town, ASCAP "family," Katherine and Wayne Reynolds, who had presented Hal with the Academy of Achievement Award a couple of years ago, and Madge and Ben Palumbo, the former lobbyist for ASCAP. Many of the guests didn't know each other, so I decided to make a few remarks about each person present. I surprised myself by remembering everyone's name, but the tears flowed liberally as I was speaking. At one point I heard myself say, "Oh, shit, I thought this was going to be easy." With that, the maître d' rushed over with a big box of tissue which helped to dry my tears, but it was too late to clean up my language.

When I returned to my hotel room to relax and get ready for the evening concert at the White House, I received a call from the producer of the show who told me that, while they had not asked me to come up to the stage at the Library of Congress performance to receive the Gershwin Prize for Hal when Burt received his last night, at the televised White House show this evening they were going to call me to the stage so that President Obama could present the award to me in person.

One of the producers of the show escorted me to the White House and helped me navigate the basement hallway with the phalanx of service men and women in full dress uniform lining the long walk to the stairs, greeting us and pointing the way. I was comfortably ensconced in the Green Room, in the capable hands of a handsome young Marine, who knew exactly where I should be, and when. One of the production people "borrowed" me for a few minutes for a rehearsal. I was shown where my seat was, and practiced walking onto the stage, with a stand-in for Burt, who was going to escort me onstage. Then I was shown the Gershwin Prize, and instructed how to hold it, how to use the hand-held mike, and I learned that the President would be escorting me off the stage and back to my seat. With that, I was taken back to my waiting Marine.

At the door to the Blue Room, where the family and I were going to have our picture taken with the President and First Lady, another serviceman with lots of braid and many medals on his chest, explained that we would be escorted in, and told where to stand. I was instructed to stand next to President Obama.

As we were being photographed, President Obama was very gracious and expressed his regret that Hal wasn't with me. Then "snap," the picture was taken, and we were escorted out of the Blue Room and right into the Red Room, where the show was going to be performed.

The show at the White House was almost a repeat of the one at the Library of Congress the previous night, except that Dionne Warwick was unfortunately unable to appear, due to a little tax problem, which precluded her from appearing at the White House. Stevie Wonder concluded the show with a wonderful rendition of "Alfie," and then President Obama took the stage. He made a short, heartfelt speech about the Gershwin Prize for Popular Song being the highest honor that our country can bestow on a songwriter, and then he added,

I want to say a word about someone who is missing tonight. Even though Hal cannot be here with us, this celebration is for him. And we're happy that his lovely wife Eunice David is here to receive his award – this award on his behalf.

With that, Burt and I made our way to the stage, where we were each presented with the beautiful Gershwin Prize medallions.

I had been cautioned to keep my acceptance speech short because the event was being taped for PBS and time was limited. So I barely said thank you, and with that the President leaned down, gave me a big kiss, and escorted me off the stage and back to my seat. It was an awesome experience, and my heart ached because Hal wasn't there in person to experience the moment with me.

By the time I was ready to leave the White House, it was pouring. My escort grabbed a tiny umbrella out of the cloak room, which could hardly protect a quarter of me, but I was more concerned with protecting the Prize than I was in protecting myself. When we got to the turnstile area, which we had to go through to leave the White House grounds, we realized that my car was a good fifty feet away from it. My escort appealed to the guard, who was originally not going to let him go through the turnstile with me to get me to the waiting car and then return to the White House. But the guard finally "got it" and realized that there was no way I could get to my car without being soaked (my silk shoes were already ruined), so he told my new best friend that he would ignore protocol just this once, and let him accompany me with the umbrella, and then get back into the White House grounds.

I called Hal the minute I returned to my room to tell him about the show. A friend, Dan Foliart, had gone to a tremendous amount of trouble to organize getting a special TV brought into Hal's room so that they could watch the show streaming on the Internet, but for some reason, PBS would not allow it to be piped into the hospital room. Hal was very disappointed, but I assured him that we would be sent a tape of the show as soon as possible.

I'd arranged to take the earliest possible flight I could get back to Los Angeles because I was going right from the airport to Cedars-Sinai Hospital to get Hal released and bring him home. When I arrived, he was waiting in his room, all dressed up, with a huge smile on his face, more than ready to leave. Of course, as usually happens, there were a few delays, and Hal got quite anxious, until everything was eventually resolved. As we were waiting, Hal first edged his wheelchair into a little lobby area near his room. As time passed, he edged the chair into the hallway, and eventually it ended up half way down the hall closer to the elevators. Was he anxious to be out of there? You bet! In fact, once in the car, and convinced that he was really on the way home, he said that he felt as though he had just been released from jail!

I had caregivers waiting to receive him at home, and I had set him up with all the medical supplies and accoutrements that he would need in our den, which was on the first floor of our duplex apartment, but one day a couple of weeks after that, we looked all over the first floor of our apartment for Hal worried that maybe he had gone out the front door without telling us. But when we went upstairs, there he was in our bedroom, happily ensconced in in our king-sized bed on his usual side. He said that was where he belonged, and that was where he was going to stay!

Hal recovered much faster – and more happily – once he was home, in his own environment. He had some issues, but basically he was doing beautifully, ready for the social scene once again and to go to his office twice weekly, as he had always had. Even if he wasn't one hundred percent, going there made him feel that he had hit his full stride – or nearly so.

One Saturday, when he had been home from the hospital for just nine days, he insisted on going to Hillcrest Country Club for lunch with Peggy and Walter Grauman as usual; walking in without a cane or walker, standing tall, and happy to be back in the swing of things. Once friends realized that he was home, e-mail messages started to pour, in as well as flowers and plants. It was heartwarming to see how touched he was, as he dictated thank you notes for me to send to everyone.

Along with Hal's caregiver we attended one of Charlie Fox's shows for the Fulfillment Fund. Burt was one of the stars in this one, and Hal was anxious to hear him perform. Burt made some lovely remarks about Hal, as a partner and a lyricist, giving him equal credit for the success of their songs. As a surprise to us, Charlie dedicated the entire show to Hal, which encouraged the other performers to include some touching comments about Hal, and how he had affected their own careers. The others in the show that evening, besides Burt and Charlie, were Babyface Edmonds, Arthur Hamilton, Sergio Mendes, J.D. Souther, and Billy Steinberg. All wonderful songwriters and wonderful performers.

Hal insisted that he wanted to attend the ASCAP Board meeting scheduled to be held in New York in June. So, with approval from all of Hal's doctors, and with a caregiver in tow, we flew to New York. After the meeting, I was told that, though Hal had a little difficulty getting his words out quickly the Board members were happy to have him back to offer his usual sage advice. I felt that he had turned a corner while we were in New York. He was more alert than he had been, and he definitely joined in on conversations more than he had done when we were out with friends before we'd left Los Angeles. So in spite of my reservations, the trip to New York had clearly done Hal a world of good, and I was very glad we'd made the effort to go.

While there we also attended the annual Songwriters Hall of Fame Gala. Bette Midler had been awarded the SHOF Lifetime Achievement Award and it was Hal who had made the phone call to her, encouraging her to accept the award. So he was especially anxious to be at the event to greet Bette.

Hal seemed to be recovering beautifully, to the point where we planned a short cruise. But Hal woke up one morning with excruciating pain and shooting pains in the back of his head, and he was running a high temperature. Naturally I called 911 immediately, and we were at Cedars by 5 A.M. All sorts of tests were taken immediately, but none of them showed anything alarming. At one point it was thought that perhaps Hal had meningitis, which really scared me, until that was ruled out. But there was an infection, and the headaches continued, no matter what medications were prescribed, which meant that Hal had to remain in the hospital for a week, and also meant that we had to cancel our plans to go on the cruise. That was not only a disappointment to us and our travelling companions but also to B.J. Thomas, who was performing on the cruise, and who had been expecting Hal to be a passenger.

Once back at home, Hal started to feel more like his old self, we realized that he needed some activities to keep him occupied and involved. So I signed him up for a series of singing lessons and a series of Pilate's sessions, both of which he really enjoyed. They kept him involved, and his voice got stronger because of the singing lessons.

In August, three friends passed. Flo Roth, who had already lost her husband Bernie, slipped away from us. Martin E. Segal, one of New York's most powerful and influential cultural figures, passed at ninety-six. Like the Roths, Martin and his late wife Edith were close friends, and he and Hal had great mutual admiration for each other. Then the news came that Marvin Hamlisch had passed at 68. He was a major composer and a great influence in the music world. We knew that all three would be sadly missed, not just by us, but by many people – worldwide.

Hal seemed to be getting better and stronger day by day. We no longer needed a caregiver at night or on the weekends. We just kept Denis, whom both Hal and I liked a lot, during the week, because he not only helped Hal when needed, but he was Hal's driver as well.

Hal had gained all the weight he'd lost when he'd been in the hospital, he was taking long walks around Holmby Park, near our apartment, and was exercising regularly. We were pretty complacent, and feeling sure of Hal's complete recovery.

BUT one morning – August 28th to be exact – when Denis came in at seven thirty to get Hal up and dressed, he called me into the bedroom where I found that Hal was completely unresponsive. He was breathing, but he would not respond to anything we did to try to rouse him. An emergency crew of five strapping young men almost immediately showed up at our apartment, but they, using all the methods they knew, could not rouse Hal either.

The paramedics quickly got Hal into the back of their ambulance and, with me riding in the front seat and with siren screeching, we raced to Cedars. I called Dr. Rudnick to alert him that we were on the way, and I also called Hal's son, Jim, to ask him to meet us in the emergency room.

Hal was soon made as comfortable as possible and, according to his specific wishes, no heroics were performed. He always said that he didn't want any heroics to keep him going, but he did tell me to make certain that the doctors were damn sure there was no chance of survival before the plug was pulled. This time the doctors agreed that Hal should just be made comfortable. There was nothing more they could possibly do. It really was the end.

Once again my multitude of friends gathered around me – just being there if I needed a shoulder to cry on and helping to distract me from what was obviously going to happen soon. Flowers arrived, food arrived, friends arrived: it was wonderful and very helpful to me.

I slept on a cot in Hal's room for the next four nights, listening to any little change in his breathing pattern. When two friends saw the rumpled hospital garb that I was wearing at night, they immediately went down to the gift shop and bought me a beautiful gown and slippers. Even if Hal could not see me in my new finery, it made me feel good.

On the morning of Saturday, September 1st, Dr. Patrick Lyden, Hal's neurologist came in to check on Hal, and we talked about how to make Hal more comfortable. Shortly after that, Dr. Michael Bush, who was covering for Dr. Rudnick came in and tried to ease my sorrow. I must admit that I wasn't paying close attention because I was so fixated on watching Hal, and I suddenly noticed that his chest was not heaving up and down, as it had been since Tuesday. So that was it: 9 A.M. on Saturday, September 1, 2012, one day before our twenty-fifth anniversary! How abruptly, how quickly, it all ended.

Sunday, September 2nd would have marked twenty-six years since I'd first met Hal. Where had the time gone? We'd had a wonderful life together – just wonderful. We traveled the world, met interesting people from all stages of life, and led a life full of love and happiness, and yes, full of luxury. What was going to happen now? I had no idea: I was lost, beyond thinking past the next moment.

Hal's son Jim wanted his funeral to be private, family only, so in deference to his wishes, that's the way it was.

But, given whom Hal was and his status in the entertainment world and given the number of friends he and I had, it would have been impossible for me not to send him off in style. So Karen Sherry from ASCAP and I planned a memorial in his honor, to be held at Hillcrest Country Club.

Hal's youngest son, Craig David, welcomed our friends, while a collection of photos of Hal and me and our family and friends that we'd recently had compiled, played on a big screen. We had planned to give this compilation to our children as a Christmas gift, and fortunately it had been finished early enough so that we could show it at Hal's memorial.

Walter Mirisch and Vicki Reynolds gave heart-warming remembrances of Hal, as did Paul Williams, John LoFrumento, Ali Kasikci, Irwin Z. Robinson, and Jimmy Webb. Congressman Howard Berman was also one of the inspiring speakers. It was an eclectic group representing Hal's personal and professional life, and clearly reminded us of the many facets of Hal's wonderful, loving, long life.

The performers whom Karen assembled loved both Hal and me, and they gave their all the night of September 21st. Archie Jordan, the Nashville writer with whom Hal had written some wonderful songs, was scheduled to attend, but at the last minute was unable to fly in. So Mac Davis was asked to learn "If I Could Love you More" overnight, so that he could sing it at the memorial. The song meant so much to me that I wanted to be sure it was performed at the memorial, and Mac was a very good sport to agree learn it on such short notice. He performed it brilliantly. The others who performed that night were Steve Tyrell, who sang "This Guy's in Love with You;" Sheléa, "Anyone Who Had a Heart;" Nancy Reed Kanter, "We're too Young to be Old;" Marilyn McCoo, "One Less Bell to Answer;" Elvis Costello, "I Just Don't Know What to Do With Myself;" Valerie Simpson, "I Say A Little Prayer;" Burt Bacharach, "Windows of the World" (brilliantly); Jackie DeShannon, "What the World Needs Now is Love;" and Stevie Wonder, who sang "Alfie." Dionne Warwick sent a note, which was read that evening, saying that the only reason she wasn't there was because she was performing for the Pope in the Vatican. She wrote, *"My spirit and heart are there."*

I, with the help of a Valium and a glass of wine, was able to tell my favorite Hal David story – the one about how we met, and how I knew Hal was the guy for me.

The hundreds of cards, letters, e-mail, and condolence cards that I received warmed my heart, but nothing could fill that empty space in my heart – or in the bed next to me at night.

This may seem like an abrupt ending to this story about Hal and me, but it was an abrupt ending to my life with Hal. I'm certain that he died peacefully, and I know for sure that he is in a good place now. I wish I could say the same for me.

ACKNOWLEDGMENTS

This book was written during the nights after Hal's passing when I couldn't sleep: it helped keep Hal close to me. As a result, I poured everything I had into it. Fortunately, I had two wonderful editors who helped clarify my message and steered me onto the right track.

So a great big shout out to Maureen O'Brien and Nancy Hardin for all the help and insight they provided.

About the Author

Eunice David devotes her time to philanthropic work, serving on numerous boards including the board of governors of Cedars-Sinai Hospital and the Annenberg Center for the Performing Arts. As a founding member of the Los Angeles Music Center, Eunice serves on the board of the prestigious Blue Ribbon Organization, associated with the center. Both she and her late husband, Hal David, produced the successful shows titled *The Writer, The Singer, The Song*, which generously benefitted the Blue Ribbon's Children's Festival and the ASCAP Foundation.

Her previously published book *High Rise, Low Down* is the ultimate insider's tour of New York City's most sought-after addresses. She has also written numerous travel journals, which incorporate her passion for writing, urban planning, travel, and photography.

Eunice is the widow of Hal David, the Oscar and Grammy-winning lyricist who, with composer Burt Bacharach, wrote "Raindrops Keep Fallin' on My Head," "What the World Needs Now," "Alfie," and "The Look of Love," to name just a few.

INDEX

CREDITS FOR LYRICS